William Charles Kitchin

Paoli: The last of the missionaries

A picture of the overthrow of the Christians in Japan in the seventeenth century

William Charles Kitchin

Paoli: The last of the missionaries
A picture of the overthrow of the Christians in Japan in the seventeenth century

ISBN/EAN: 9783337175696

Printed in Europe, USA, Canada, Australia, Japan

Cover: Foto ©Lupo / pixelio.de

More available books at **www.hansebooks.com**

THE ENGLISHMAN'S RAPIER PIERCED HIS ADVERSARY'S WRIST. *Frontispiece.*

PAOLI:

THE

Last of the Missionaries.

A PICTURE OF THE OVERTHROW OF THE
CHRISTIANS IN JAPAN IN THE
SEVENTEENTH CENTURY.

BY

W. C. KITCHIN,

WITH ILLUSTRATIONS BY G. A. TRAVER AND HENRY BOUCHE.

NEW YORK:
ROBERT BONNER'S SONS, PUBLISHERS,
1890.

COPYRIGHT, 1890,
BY ROBERT BONNER'S SONS

(All rights reserved.)

PRESS OF
THE NEW YORK LEDGER
NEW YORK.

AMONG THE CHRISTIAN MISSIONARIES IN JAPAN, A FEW EARNEST SPIRITS, BELIEVING THE WORLD TO HAVE OUTGROWN THE RELIGIOUS BIGOTRY AND INTOLERANCE OF THE PAST, HAVE DARED TO DREAM, THAT IN THE "LAND OF THE MORNING," THE SCHISMS WHICH SO LONG HAVE DISFIGURED CHRISTENDOM MIGHT BE HEALED IN THE UNION OF ALL SECTS IN ONE INDEPENDENT CHURCH OF CHRIST FOR JAPAN. TO THESE THIS VOLUME IS INSCRIBED.

"If we see that the minds of the Japanese are fit and prepared for evangelical cultivation, we shall not hesitate to inform the Holy Father himself concerning the matter, since those who are prepared to come to the bosom of the Church and the obedience of the Supreme Pontiff, must be a part of the charge of him who is the Vicar of Christ, the Father of all nations, and the Pastor of all Christians."

FROM FRANCIS XAVIER'S FIRST LETTER FROM JAPAN; DATED KAGOSHIMA, NOVEMBER 11, 1549.

"The Christians have come to Japan to disseminate an evil law, to overthrow right doctrine, so that they may change the government of the country and obtain possession of the land. If they are not prohibited the safety of the state will assuredly be imperilled; and if those charged with the government of the nation do not extirpate the evil, they will expose themselves to Heaven's rebuke."

FROM THE EDICT OF THE SHOGUN IYEYASU AGAINST CHRISTIANITY; ISSUED JANUARY 27, 1614.

PREFACE.

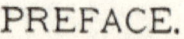

THE title-page sets forth the character of this book. It is an historical picture, in which truth outweighs fiction. Nirado Shiro, Ashizuka, Chijiwa and Oyano; their foes, Nabeshima, Itakura and Yamada,—all were actual personages, prominent in the stirring events that attended the overthrow of Christianity, and the achievements ascribed to them in the following pages are substantially those which manuscript-chronicle and tradition have connected with their names. Francesco Paoli and Lord Mori are types: the former of that courageous but intolerant zeal which, in the name of religion, strove to establish, during the sixteenth and seventeenth centuries, an European sovereignty over Japan; the latter of that spirit of protest against priestly intrigue and corruption, which, in the persons of a few independent thinkers among the native converts, lifted up its voice in denunciation of the claims of an imperious church and in behalf of a purer faith.

From October, 1882, until August, 1885, the author's home was in the picturesque city of Nagasaki, on the crest of Higashi-yama, the hill so frequently mentioned in the earlier part of the narrative; and it was while he was standing, one of the summer evenings of 1883, upon the summit of the rocky islet Takaboka, with its awful memories vividly before him, that the idea of telling the story of the fall of the Christians, in the form of an historical novel, first took shape in his mind. Henceforward, his leisure time was spent in visiting the various places associated with the last desperate struggle of the doomed church; in the study of what had already been written upon the subject; and in gathering from the lips of the people legendary accounts of "the great rebellion of the *jashiu-mon*,"* which have been handed down from father to son for more than two and a half centuries. During the course of his investigation, two hitherto unknown manuscripts, written by eye-witnesses of the war concerning which they gave a minutely detailed account, were brought to light. Upon these the present volume is mainly based, and where the author has deviated from them, it has been to follow what he is convinced is a more truthful account; or, where unessential particulars are concerned, to give the novelist an opportunity for reproducing, by the creation of imaginary incidents and characters, the social physiognomy of the age in which the historical personages lived and moved.

BOSTON, *August*, 1890.

* Corrupt-sect.

CONTENTS.

	Page
PREFACE	9
INTRODUCTION	17

BOOK FIRST.—TWO MEN OF DESTINY.

    I. Captain Van Neist's Passengers . . 25
    II. Nirado Shiro makes a Startling Declaration 30
    III. Further disclosures 38
    IV Anjiro, *alias* Paoli 43
    V. The Bishop of Japan 46
    VI. A Vision of War 57

BOOK SECOND.—TAKABOKA.

    I. Captain Van Neist receives a Letter . . 58
    II. The Governor's Deputy loses his sword . 62
    III. The First Officer makes an Explanation. 69
    IV. A Conference 72
    V. The Battle 77
    VI. Ine Tanaka 83

BOOK THIRD.—BISHOP PAOLI AND NIRADO SHIRO BEGIN THEIR LABORS.

    I. In the Storm among the Dead . . 88
    II. The Story of a Church Militant . . 93
    III. "Takaboka and Vengeance, in the Name of the Lord" 100
    IV. Among Friends 104
    V. The Cave-Chapel of Kayaki . . . 108

	Page
BOOK FOURTH.—THE STRANGE ADVENTURES OF MARMION BEAUMONT.	
I. Mynheer Van Sylt has something to say	117
II. The Plot of Kanshin, the Deputy	121
III. Ten Thousand Ryo Reward, Dead or Alive	132
IV. An English Rapier encounters a Japanese Sword	135
V. The Story of a Martyrdom	142
VI. The Bishop of Japan appears in a New Rôle	147
VII. Marmion Beaumont Falls into another Adventure	153
VIII. The Ordeal of the Cross	159
BOOK FIFTH.—THE HOUR OF THE CHRISTIANS' WOE.	
I. Ine Tanaka's Strange Lover	168
II. Lord Oda's Place of Entertainment	180
III. Ando the Hunchback	184
IV. The Warrior-Pilgrim Recounts a Family History	189
V. A Climax of Perils	193
BOOK SIXTH.—THE HOUSEHOLD OF MORI.	
I. Una the Eurasian	200
II. The Protestant of Unzen	204
III. The Story of the Rescue	212
IV. Hopes and Fears	218
V. The Hermitage	221
VI. A Dream and a Portrait	224
VII. The Host of the Kwassui-ya has a Tale to Tell	229
VIII. Old Foes in New Surroundings	233
BOOK SEVENTH.—FRIENDS AND FOES STRANGELY MET.	
I. An Incident by the Way	240

		Page
II.	Fortune favors Yamada the Ronin	246
III.	Back to Life.	248
IV.	Una meets her Hero	252
V.	Exultation	255
VI.	Him whom we would Shun we Meet.	260
VII.	Nabeshimi meets a Fair Foe and is Conquered	262
VIII.	Enemies and Rivals	266
IX.	The very Wonderful Exploit of Bishop Paoli	269
X.	Her Foe and Lover	276

BOOK EIGHTH.—HOW THEY KEPT CHRISTMAS AT ARIMA.

		Page
I.	A Surprise that was no Surprise	283
II.	Takaboka is Revenged	289
III.	The Rivals meet.	293
IV.	Yamada the Ronin again	300

BOOK NINTH.—HOW NIRADO SHIRO KEPT HIS VOW.

		Page
I.	Gathering Shadows	307
II.	A Woman's Battle and Victory	310
III.	At the Hermitage	317
IV.	The Komamonoya's Wooing meets with an Interruption	324
V.	A Discovery that came none too soon	329
VI.	The Return of the Chief	331

BOOK TENTH—FRIENDS BECOME FOES.

		Page
I.	Another Midnight Conflict.	335
II.	Death before Disgrace	341
III.	Bearding the Foe	344
IV.	Sword or Famine, Which?	347
V.	An Awakening	352
VI.	The Eve of Battle	355
VII.	Nirado Shiro makes his Fate	360

		Page
VIII. The Servant becomes the Master	.	364
IX. A remarkable re-conquest .	.	373

BOOK ELEVENTH.—DEATH HATH MANY DOORS TO LET OUT LIFE.

I. In the Camp of Kai	.	379
II. The Coming of the Christians .	.	382
III. Prince Nabeshima's turn comes .	.	387
IV. Devotion, Destiny, Deliverance .	.	394
V. The Beginning of the End .	.	399
VI. Saved !	.	405
VII. The Messenger of Heavy Tidings	.	409
VIII. Faithful to the Last .	.	412
IX. Alas, too Late ! .	.	421
X. An Unexpected Meeting	.	423
XI. Retribution .	.	429
XII. "Paoli to the Rescue !"	.	431
XIII. At Last	.	437
XIV. Joyful Tidings .	.	440

BOOK TWELFTH.—THE LIGHT GOES OUT IN DARKNESS.

I. A Victory that was almost Defeat	.	445
II. The Prince of Kai astonishes Marmion Beaumont	.	447
III. The Day Decreed by Destiny	.	451
IV. The Prince of Kai becomes a Prophet	.	457
V. The Church of Christ in Japan	.	462

LIST OF ILLUSTRATIONS.

		Page
1.	The Englishman's rapier pierced his adversary's wrist	Frontispiece
2.	Head-piece to Preface	9
3.	Head-piece to Introduction	17
4.	The Spuyten Duyvil	25
5.	Shiro makes a startling declaration	33
6.	The islands in Nagasaki Bay	49
7.	Captain Van Neist watching the approach of the factory boat	58
8.	The boat bringing the Governor's deputy	65
9.	They were on the extreme edge of a ledge of rock	81
10.	The boat of the three Christians	88
11.	A confused clamor of voices arose in the government boat	97
12.	Shiro was now standing by the side of Paoli	113
13.	Nagasaki	117
14.	The three men were seated on the mats	129
15.	The old man bent his head over the Englishman's shoulder	145
16.	She knelt reverently beside the cross	161
17.	Page putting on a warrior's armor	168
18.	Higashi-vama	177

		Page
19.	Mt. Unzen	200
20.	"I beheld the Jesuit's terrible form towering over Lord Nebeshima"	209
21.	Sanji before the Lord of Kai	240
22.	The girl stood regarding the outlaws with a terrified look	241
23.	The Ronin dashed himself against the Englishman	257
24.	Straight to the place where Shiro was sitting he strode	273
25.	Paoli on the wall	283
26.	Full on the forehead of the Prince of Kai fell the bolt	305
27.	Ine Tanaka	307
28.	"In Heaven's name, what means this? Nirado Shiro!"	321
29.	Ready for the foe	335
30.	The stranger turned and disappeared within the gate	337
31.	He looked down into the eyes of Ine Tanaka	369
32.	Discharging fire-arrows upon the camp of Nabeshima	379
33.	"Ho, men of Kai, we are saved!"	401
34.	She swung the lantern above her head	417
35.	Paoli, reeling in his saddle, fell heavily to the earth	433
36.	After the last conflict	445
37.	"Who are you?" he calls out wildly	465

INTRODUCTION.

SIXTEEN years from the time that Ignatius Loyola and his associates founded the Society of Jesus, Francis Xavier, one of the most illustrious members of the new brotherhood, organized the first Christian church in Japan. During the next twenty years, the number of converts to the foreign faith, through special circumstances furthering the work of propagandism, increased to upwards of thirty thousand; and, at the close of the sixteenth century, according to the official reports of the missionaries, there were six hundred thousand Japanese Christians. Another score of years, and this number had dwindled down to less than half, and in 1637, the year that witnessed the beginning of that unhappy struggle, the story of which is to be told in these pages, there could not have been more than sixty thousand both secret and openly avowed believers. What were the causes of the marvellous success which

attended the labors of the Jesuit missionaries in Japan? What were the causes of the astonishingly rapid decline and the final extirpation of the native church?

When Xavier landed in Japan, the time was ripe for a religious revolution. For centuries civil war, anarchy and misrule had oppressed the country, and the people groaned beneath a burden of ever increasing misery. In their utter wretchedness, they looked to Buddhism for consolation, but an ignorant and morally depraved priesthood had neither ear to listen to nor heart to pity the cry of distress that rose to them throughout the length and breadth of the land. The Jesuit missionary came; and his holy earnestness, his thrilling story of the sacrifice of the cross, and his doctrine of patient endurance in this life and immediate entrance after death into the joys of an eternal paradise, melted the hearts of thousands and won them to his faith. Nor did the convert, in his change of religion, find the transition a difficult one. The church of the Christians, he discovered, was but little different from the temple of the Buddhists, and, with proper sprinkling and blessing, the images, pictures, bells, beads, incense, candles and vestments of his old faith could serve the purposes of the new.

Another powerful motive for the friendly reception of the foreigner's religion—a motive operating mainly among the ruling class—is to be found in the material interests which were thus promoted. The Japanese princes were quick to perceive the intimate relation that existed between commerce and Christianity, and that to welcome the missionary was to attract the merchant. It was this, which, more than anything else, brought about the wonderful success that attended the labors of the Jesuits. The native princes, vying with one another for the emoluments of the Portuguese trade, became Christians themselves and compelled their subjects to follow their example. Christianity became popular and was eagerly embraced by thousands ignorant of its doctrines and indifferent to the purity of life it enjoins. Thousands, too, forced to submit to its baptism, at heart hated it, and were little less than an army of spies and conspirators in the secret service of the heathen party.

Thus it happened that one of the principal causes contributing to the spread of Christianity in Japan, was, at the same time, a cause of its approaching decline and ultimate overthrow. The church became powerful; and with power came pride and arrogance. The humble missionary grew into the haughty prelate, assuming for himself the authority and *regalia* of a nobleman. Expediency, conciliation, respect for rulers not Christian, and tenderness toward harmless manners and customs dear to the hearts of the Japanese people, were forgotten when once the triumph of the church seemed to be assured. A strict ecclesiastical espionage was established over the native converts, and the supremacy of the church over the government and the duty of the Christians to acknowledge an unquestioning allegiance to the Pope were clearly taught. A persecution of the Buddhists, as cruel and unprovoked as it was impolitic, was begun and carried on for the space of twenty years. The priests were either banished or put to death, the idols and temples were destroyed, and the believers were compelled to choose between exile and submission to Christian baptism. The Jesuit historian, Charlevoix, extols the zeal of the Christian princes, who, in obedience to the solicitations of Spanish and Portuguese priests, conducted this crusade against the ancient religion. "In the year 1577," he says, "the lord of Amakusa issued a proclamation, by which his subjects were required either to turn

Christians or to leave the country the very next day. They almost all submitted and received baptism, so that in a short time there were more than twenty churches in his domain." Again, in speaking of the Prince of Takatsuki, the same writer tells us how he "labored with a zeal truly apostolic to extirpate the idolators out of his state." Thus were sown by the missionaries and their followers the seeds of bitterness, jealousy and revenge that were to grow up and to ripen into a harvest of ferocious hatred and merciless persecution against themselves.

In 1587 Hideyoshi, successor in the Shogunate to Nobunaga the enemy of the Buddhists and the patron of Christianity, issued an edict commanding all foreign priests to leave Japan within twenty days. The Jesuit missionaries, to the number of sixty-five, assembled at Hirado, but after a consultation together, they decided to remain in the country, and, at the invitation of the Christian princes, they distributed themselves throughout their dominions. Even then, had the missionaries been conciliatory and careful not to give further offense, the storm of persecution, the first warning blast of which had already fallen upon the church, might have been averted. But their zeal for what they, doubtless, conscientiously conceived to be their duty, outweighed their discretion; and, though they were permitted for a time to go unmolested save by repeated injunctions to quit the country, they at last paid the price of their temerity. February 5, 1597, just ten years after the promulgation of Hideyoshi's edict of expulsion, three Portuguese Jesuits, six Spanish Franciscans, and seventeen native Christians were crucified at Nagasaki. The martyrs met their fate steadfastly and joyfully. In 1862 they were canonized by Pope Pius IX.

The government now became alarmed for the nation's safety. The story is told how a Spanish sea-captain was showing some Japanese officials a map of the Spanish dominions, and being asked by what method his king had acquired such enormous possessions, answered that the usual way was first to send out missionaries to convert the people to Christianity, then to send soldiers to protect the priests and their converts, and with these to subdue the country. The heathen princes, remembering the sort of instruction in statecraft, which their Christian countrymen were receiving from their foreign teachers, and hearing the inflammatory denunciations of the government, with which the Jesuit missionaries spiced their spiritual ministrations to their converts, had sufficient cause for apprehensions without the revelations which the Spanish captain made ; and it is to be borne in mind that it was not opposition to Christianity as a religion but as a cloak for political conquest which led Hideyoshi and his successors first to check and then to extirpate it.

It was not, however, until 1614 that the threatened storm broke with all its long pent up fury upon the heads of the devoted adherents of the new religion. In that year Iyeyasu Tokugawa, first Shogun of his family, issued his famous edict which declared Christianity to be an evil calling for extirpation from the soil of Japan.*

The persecution that followed was appalling. The government, through its fear for the independence of the country, was maddened into wanton cruelty ; the Buddhists were eager to revenge the persecution the Christians had inflicted upon them ; and the lawless portion of society hailed with savage delight this opportunity to

---

* For quotation from this celebrated proclamation, see page facing preface.

revel in outrage and slaughter. The large number of persons who had become Christians, either from policy or by compulsion, had already abandoned the church; and, of those that remained, few renounced their faith. Thousands fled to Formosa, China, and the Philippines; thousands more died upon the cross, were burned at the stake, beheaded, or buried alive. Never in the history of Christian martyrdom have greater constancy, more unflinching courage, and more joyful and triumphant faith been displayed than that witnesssed during the first half of the seventeenth century upon the execution grounds of Japan.

Nor had the missionaries taught their converts a doctrine, from an application of the consequences of which to their own lives, they themselves shrank. As they had instructed the native believers to live a life of obedience to the church, so, in the hour of trial and suffering, they taught them by example how to endure and how to die for her glory. In various disguises and at the peril of their lives, they lived among their suffering Japanese brethren, exhorting them to endure with uncomplaining patience and gladness the persecution of their foes. He most gravely errs who permits his prejudice to withhold the tribute of praise and admiration which the Jesuit missionaries, laboring in the Japan of the seventeenth century, so richly deserve. Despite their bigotry, their intolerance, their political scheming and intriguing, the deathless devotion, which they manifested toward their church and their converts, may well claim our profoundest reverence.

The persecution, which Iyeyasu's edict had begun, was continued by his son and by his grandson, Hidetada and Iyemitsu. In 1621 Japanese subjects were forbidden to leave the country, and three years later Japan was closed against all foreigners, with the exception of the Chinese and the Dutch. Iyemitsu, furthermore, ordered the destruction of all Japanese ships, and thereafter only small junks were allowed to be built. Having thus taken every precaution that his countrymen should no longer come in contact with the forbidden nations, the young Shogun turned his attention to the extermination of the native Christian church; and it was in the fourteenth year of his rule that the events narrated in the following pages took place.

PAOLI;

THE LAST OF THE MISSIONARIES.

BOOK FIRST.

TWO MEN OF DESTINY.

I.

CAPTAIN VAN NEIST'S PASSENGERS.

OWARD the close of a warm September day in the year 1637, a large Dutch merchantman, the *Spuyten Duyvil*, Jansen Van Neist, master, shook out her sails to the wind, and gliding slowly out of the harbor of Manila, turned her prow northward toward the island-empire of Japan. Nearly a year had passed by since the good ship had sailed from Amsterdam laden with a cargo of merchandise for the factory of the Dutch East India Company at Hirado and a private trading station at Nagasaki ; but storms and calms had conspired together, it had seemed, to oppose her progress, until her hot-tempered captain had sworn that of the many voyages of his twenty-five years of seafaring life, this one had been the most unsatisfactory and annoying. As the voyage dragged its wearisome course along, this observation of Captain Van Neist's, uttered with daily increasing vehemence, gradually took the place of his ordinary morning greeting to the sole European passenger aboard the *Spuyten Duyvil*. This passenger, Marmion Beaumont, a young Englishman, had come aboard at Amsterdam as the representative of a company of London merchants who, from 1614 to 1624, had conducted a factory at Hirado on the west coast of the island of Kiushiu, and who now was sending an agent to collect, if possible, some outstanding debts from the Japanese traders.

In addition to Beaumont there were two other passengers aboard, bound for Japan. While the *Spuyten Duyvil* lay in the harbor of Manila, where she had put in for repairs, Van Neist and the Englishman, whom the associations of the long voyage had made fast friends, formed the acquaintance of a young Japanese named Nirado Shiro, who had come to the Philippines from his native land, in the company of a missionary some ten years before. He had spent these years in study at the Jesuit college in Manila, and spoke Spanish very fluently. Shiro asked passage to Nagasaki for himself and a friend who was wishing to return to Japan. Van Neist cheerfully consented to take them, and the following evening the young Japanese and his friend, who gave his name as Anjiro, came aboard, both dressed in the fashion peculiar to their country.

At first but little attention was paid to Anjiro, who

seemed to be a silent and reserved sort of a person, never speaking except to answer some question addressed to him, and then always, if possible, in monosyllables and with a decided Japanese accent. Whenever any communication of difficult meaning or of great length was made, Anjiro would call upon his friend to interpret for him, his knowledge of Spanish extending, it seemed, no further than the understanding of easy sentences and common-place remarks. He was tall and well built; Van Neist on one occasion remarking to Shiro, who was extremely slight of figure, that his friend Anjiro was the largest and strongest looking Japanese he had ever seen; but Shiro assured him that much heavier built and taller men were quite common in the extreme south of his country.

Among the crew of the *Spuyten Duyvil*, Anjiro soon came to be regarded with feelings of mingled respect and fear. One sailor declared that he believed that the big Japanese, as Anjiro was called by the seamen, was either a snake-charmer or a sorcerer. Another affirmed that he had seen him one night standing in the bow of the ship swinging his arms and uttering strange ejaculations, and that, in less than an hour afterwards the wind was blowing a heavy gale. He was convinced that he was a magician. A third believed that he had dealings with the devil, and would not be surprised to find that some misfortune befell everything on which his evil eye had looked.

One evening, about a week after the *Spuyten Duyvil* had left the Philippines, Anjiro was standing alone in the bow of the vessel, above where the rushing prow furrowed the calm surface of the sea into two diverging lines of foam. There was, indeed, something about this strangely silent man that could not fail to arrest the attention of the beholder. Apparently about forty-five years of age, his well-knit frame and vigorous constitution betokened perfect health. His noble and commanding figure, military bearing, and thoroughly intellectual countenance would have made him conspicuous anywhere. But more remarkable than all else were his eyes. The square chin and firmly set mouth might betoken a strong will; the finely-chiseled features and high, full forehead, intellectual power; but no one could catch a glance from those wonderful eyes, that shone forth from his swarthy countenance like wells of living fire, without feeling conscious that he stood in the presence of a man possessing qualities that raised him above even the more gifted of his fellow-men. On the evening we have just spoken of, as he stood in his chosen place for solitary meditation, his gaze was fixed straight forward on the distant horizon as if he would call up a vision of the shores that lay still far away beyond. He had cast off his hat, and with his head thrown slightly back, he stood as motionless as a statue, only the lines of his face revealing that he was thrilled by some transporting joy or terrible grief. Then, as he stood thus, apparently oblivious to all his surroundings, his frame seemed to tremble with the deep emotions that surged through his soul, his features grew rigid, his eyes slowly closed, his hands stole quietly to his breast and were clasped together as if in prayer, the lips moved and then closed tightly, his face grew ashy pale, and for a moment the strange being seemed to have fallen into a trance. But it was only for a moment. The color rushed back to his face, the lips parted, and a fluttering sigh broke from them, the hands unclasped and dropped again to his side, his features relaxed, and his chin sank upon his breast, his eyes remaining closed.

The sound of footsteps behind him roused Anjiro from

the reverie into which he had fallen He raised his head, and with a mighty yet imperceptible struggle crushed down all evidences of his recent display of emotion. It was Shiro who was approaching, and behind him, at some distance, Anjiro saw Beaumont and Van Neist. The strangely luminous eyes of the elder man met those of Shiro, and with a voice steady enough, but still evincing the difficulty with which its owner kept it under control, he said :

"I have seen it again, Shiro. The days of visions are still upon the earth. I saw again the red horse of war, his mane clotted with gouts of carnage ; I heard the roar of battle, the hoarse shout of the warrior, the shriek of the dying. I beheld the midnight skies flame red with the burning temples of the accursed Buddha ; I looked, and before me armed bands of men contended for the mastery ; I saw them locked together in the death grapple ; my heart stood still as they reeled to and fro in the mad fury of the fight, covering the green earth beneath them with their slain. At last one army broke and fled away into the darkness ; I saw the victors as they followed after in swift pursuit, and as their conquering banners swept past me, lo ! I beheld emblazoned thereon the figure of our Christ and his cross, and sweeter than angels' song, was borne to my ears the '*Yaso-Maria*,'* the battle cry of the Christians—the pæan of triumph. But hush ! they who have no part with us are at hand !"

* Jesus and Mary.

II.

NIRADO SHIRO MAKES A STARTLING DECLARATION.

It was Van Neist and the young Englishman who were now coming up to the place where the two friends were standing. Turning around, Shiro joined in conversation with them, but Anjiro relapsed into his accustomed silence, replying only in monosyllables to the remarks that Beaumont addressed to him.

The conversation turned finally upon religious subjects and particularly the persecution which the Japanese Christians were then suffering. Beaumont was outspoken in his denunciation of the barbaric character of a government that was visiting its unoffending subjects with such wanton destruction for their religious belief.

"Mynheer Beaumont," interposed the captain, "you are not to forget that if religious persecution be taken as a mark of barbarism, our Western civilization would scarcely be worthy of American savages. Had the missionaries who went to Japan been more the peace-bringing servants of Christ and less the intriguing emissaries of a foreign power, the result, I doubt not, would have been different."

"True, perhaps," responded Beaumont, who understood what Van Neist's allusion to a foreign power meant, "yet despite their bondage to an ecclesiastical system, the devotion of these men to their converts that has led them to remain with them at the peril of their lives, or, having left the country, secretly to return, and with their native brethren to suffer untold persecutions and death, is to me one of the most touching pictures of Christian loyalty that the history of the church affords ; and were it in my power to aid such zeal and constancy I should consider myself thrice happy in the opportunity."

Beaumont spoke with impassioned earnestness, his fine eyes glowing with fervid enthusiasm. Van Neist scanned his face closely and then said : " I caution you, Mynheer, that you be more reserved in expressing your views after we reach Japan. I am only a plain, unlearned man, but twenty-five years of voyaging through all seas, and to almost every land, has taught me some things; and especially have I learned the imprudence of uttering one's thoughts too freely ; and should the opportunity to help a Catholic missionary, which you seem to crave, come to you, I trust you will not attempt to do it aboard the *Spuyten Duyvil*, seeing that we are bound by the most solemn promises to the Japanese government to grant passage or to render assistance to no foreign priest. I would not interfere with your liberty, nor do even a Jesuit wrong, yet on behalf of my employers and their interests in Japan I must make this request."

Beaumont was rebuked by the words of the captain and he felt that he had allowed his enthusiasm to carry him beyond the bounds of prudence.

" Believe me, Captain Van Neist," he said, humbly, "my zeal outran my discretion, as you have said ; but I assure you I shall do nothing that will compromise my friends."

"I shall accept your word for it."

"You may with safety. I shall endeavor to follow your advice, and be more cautious hereafter."

"There is need of it, I do assure you, my young friend. You will find the Japanese officials jealous of all foreigners ; a word will arouse their most bitter prejudices, and that would be fatal to the interests which has brought you to the East."

The captain of the *Spuyten Duyvil* now left the little group to give some instructions to his officers; and Beaumont, as he watched the retreating figure of the kind-hearted fellow, felt that he had offended him. Shiro spoke, and the young Englishman could not fail to note the sarcasm in his voice:

"Our worthy captain, I would judge, then, is not a friend to the suffering church of my country."

"You misunderstand him, I think," answered Beaumont, quick to take up the championship of his friend. "Van Neist is an honest, well-meaning man; he has just said that he would not interfere with any one's liberty, or wrong even a Jesuit."

"I heard him. If he spoke the truth he is one among a thousand of his countrymen."

"Why," asked Beaumont, in surprise—"why do you say that? What have the Dutch done that you should speak thus? Have they wronged your people?"

The other laughed bitterly.

"Ask any Japanese Christian what they have not done to ruin the cause of Christianity in Japan. Sordidly selfish themselves, they looked with jealous hatred upon the favor formerly shown by the Japanese princes to the Portuguese. Like vipers, they wormed themselves into favor with a few disaffected nobles. Into the ears of these they poured their libelous poison about the Portuguese traders, and the religion of the Portuguese priests. When the Japanese government assumed a hostile attitude toward Christianity, they became the spies of the persecuting power, and during all these years of trial and bloodshed they have ever arrayed themselves against the Christians."

"Your words are a revelation to me, but I am certain that whatever kind of men his countrymen in Japan may be, you will find no enemy in Jansen Van Neist, so long as you do not undertake to deceive him."

"It would be a redeeming feature in the conduct of the Dutch in Japan," pursued Shiro, as if unconscious of Beaumont's interruption, "did they oppose us on religious grounds, were they teaching the Protestant faith of their own land and fighting us as a corrupt form of Christianity, there might be a show of reason for their hostility. But so far from this has been their attitude toward Christianity that they emphatically deny any connection with it. Ask one of them in Hirado or Nagasaki if he is a Christian and he will answer, 'No, I am a Dutchman.'"

"What is their object in all this?"

"Merely to gain the paltry foreign trade of the country. And they are succeeding. The intercourse of Japan with Europe is fast falling into their hands. All other nations are finding it too insignificant or loaded with too many humiliating conditions to care to maintain it. They will not stoop to petty truckling, or prostitute their honor to play the hireling spy against fellow-Christians. The Dutch, on the other hand, are content to submit to the most unjust exactions of the Japanese princes; the scanty profits of the trade seem to satisfy them, and I feel assured that before long they will be the only Europeans allowed to come to Japan."

"But our friend, Señor Beaumont, is not one of them," said Anjiro, speaking now for the first time, and with much greater fluency than he had ever hitherto displayed in the presence of strangers; "we have his word that he bears no ill will to either the Catholic missionary or his suffering converts. Is it not so, Señor Beaumont?'

"Assuredly," replied the young Englishman, concealing, as best he could, his astonishment at the readiness with which Anjiro was able to speak Spanish.

"And did not Señor say that if it was ever his opportunity to render assistance it would be gladly done?"

Beaumont remembered the caution of Van Neist and resolved to be discreet. Anjiro preceived his hesitation, and with a smile continued :

"Señor need not compromise himself. We heard the warning he received a short time ago. We believe we can trust you. And since, for the sake of others, you have promised to be careful hereafter not to allow yourself to speak too freely what you feel, we are confident that you will also be careful, for our sakes, not to implicate us, as it might hereafter be possible for you to do."

"You may depend that I shall do nothing that will either injure you or bring harm to your cause."

"I felt from the first time I met you in Manila," broke in Shiro, "that I could trust you ; yet I somehow feel that hereafter you will be on the side of my foes. I have had dreams of the struggle to come, and in the ranks of the enemy I have seen your face looking out upon me, but it was not full of savage hatred like those of the others about you, and I fancied that at heart you were not my enemy."

"Your words are lost upon me," replied Beaumont, "for I do not understand them. That I wish to be your friend you may be assured ; but how I can ever be found in the ranks of your enemies I cannot conceive."

"Nor I either. But mark me, it shall be so."

"Impossible! But your enemies—who are they?"

Shiro was silent for a moment. Beaumont fancied

that he had caught a glimpse of an interchange of glances between his two companions and a nod of approval from the elder man. Then Shiro spoke :

"Señor Beaumont, there is a limit, is there not, beyond which passive submission to wrong becomes a sin ? The most timid beast of the forest can by wanton cruelty be goaded to such desperation that it will at length turn with savage fury, and, if possible, destroy its tormentors. We believe that the hour has come when the long-suffering church of Christ in Japan should take up arms in self-defence. It is now more than fifty years since the government began to issue its edicts against our religion. From that hour until now the soil of nearly every province in central and southern Japan has been reddened with the blood of Christian martyrs."

"The history is indeed a terrible one. But will not a declaration of war bring on still more fearful calamities ?"

"It cannot; it cannot. The heathen princes are determined to stamp out Christianity in Japan. It is either a question of renouncing our faith or of being exterminated. The former none of us will do, and we may as well die in honorable battle as be destroyed by persecution. But such shall not be our fate. We shall be successful. We are still powerful throughout Kiushiu. In my province an army of ten thousand men can be raised in a day. With a victory or two on our side, many thousands more throughout the nation, who are Christans at heart, but fear the consequences of an open profession, would join us, and the government would be compelled to yield us freedom of worship."

Here the speaker paused and looked at the young Englishman as if he wished him to express his opinion on what had just been said. Beaumont, still remembering Van Neist's warning, was resolved to be as non-committal as possible.

"Unless you are mistaken," he said, "in the number of your adherents and their readiness to join promptly in the revolt, something might be done—"

Shiro interrupted him, speaking rapidly, though quietly:

"Something has been done, Señor Beaumont. A week ago the uprising took place; last night and early this morning a sanguinary battle was fought; even at this moment the broken ranks of the government troops are in flight before the banner of the cross."

III.

FURTHER DISCLOSURES.

Beaumont heard with wonder enough this strange declaration. He looked keenly at Shiro, but the calm, composed countenance of the Japanese youth gave no evidence of excitement. He stood firmly erect, his slight figure raised to its full height, his expressive and finely molded features wreathed with the faintest smile, as he continued:

"You are surprised, but it is the truth I am speaking to you. I tell you this now that, when in a few days we reach Nagasaki and you hear it from the lips of others, you may remember this, and believe me when I say that this is but the beginning of a struggle that will end in making Japan a Christian nation."

Beaumont's voice betrayed the incredulity he felt, as he responded:

"If what you say has already taken place proves to be the truth, I shall feel inclined to believe anything else you may affirm. But dreams, remember, are often misleading—"

"It was no dream," broke in Shiro, still speaking rapidly and in a low, even voice. He did not seem to notice Beaumont's incredulous smile. "It was no dream, Señor," he repeated; "all that I have told you of was seen in an hour of wakefulness, in broad day, and aboard this ship. How or by whom is not mine to say."

"You certainly astonish me; this insurrection—this war—who is to be your leader in so hazardous an undertaking?"

"I am commander-in-chief of the insurgents and it is the will of Heaven to make me the first Christian ruler of our Japan." Shiro spoke with the quietness of assured confidence, no trace of boastful exultation in his voice. The Englishman's astonishment found expression in an exclamation of surprise. "You are amazed at what you hear, Señor Beaumont," the Japanese youth went on, speaking even more softly and deliberately than before; "and you no doubt think me a madman, or, at best, a most hopelessly visionary fanatic, and it may do no good to assure you that I am neither. Why should it be thought incredible that God in these latter days should raise up a deliverer for His people? Did He not do so of old? and is the arm of the Lord shortened now in this, the hour of the affliction of His people? In ancient times the chosen vessel of the Most High was conscious of his call to become the liberator of the down-trodden and suffering children of God. He announced himself as such, both to those he was to save and to those he was to destroy. Cannot he who is the instrument of salvation now be as conscious of the fact as was the Lord's messenger in former times? And has he not as much authority as they to declare his mission?"

He paused; but Beaumont still made no reply. Anjiro, a little removed from them, was intently watching the young Englishman's face. Shiro continued:

"You perceive that I am trusting you completely, Señor Beaumont. I am sure I can do this with perfect safety."

Again he paused; this time his eyes met the listener's and Beaumont read in them a mute appeal for sympathy. Interested and fascinated by the words of the youth, the Englishman could still make no answer to Shiro's simple avowal of trust in him further than a bow.

"Listen, Señor. I have said that I am the leader of the insurgents. It is even so. I have been raised up of Heaven for that very purpose. Before I was born was my mission announced. On the face of a rock jutting out from the bald, precipitous side of a lofty mountain overhanging my native village happened a miracle. High up the steep cliff, and at a point apparently inaccessible to human hands, the villagers saw one morning, as the rising sun flashed his first beams upon the smooth surface of the rock, the promise which some other hand than man's had written there to comfort the suffering people of God with the assurance of coming deliverance. 'After a score of years from now,' ran the inscription on the rock, 'a great man shall arise among the Christians. He shall deliver his brethren and shall rule the people of his nation. Then shall many stand up with the cross on their helmets, giving praises to God for the glory of Heaven that shall in that day fill sea and river, the mountains and the desert.'

"A few months afterwards I was born in that village. During the interval that prophecy on the mountain side had remained, despite the most strenuous attempts of the government officials to have it removed. Liberal rewards were offered to any one who would scale the cliff and erase the writing. In vain. Many ventured, but no one succeeded. It was inaccessible from below, nor could it be reached from the top of the cliff. What the finger of fate had traced upon the mountain side was beyond the reach of those whose discomfiture it foretold, and became to the persecuted Christians God's testament in stone that the hour of their deliverance was at hand.

"The night in which I was born Heaven again spoke in miracles declaring me to be the foretold deliverer. A mighty earthquake shook the village and surrounding country. The great rock upon which the prophecy was inscribed was torn loose from the mountain side, and, crashing to the earth, rolled downward through the valley. In its mad course it struck a Buddhist temple and also the office of the government tax-gatherer, and both buildings were crushed level with the earth. No other damage was done, and the fallen rock came to rest before the door of my father's house. Thus it was foretokened that it was I who was to deliver the church from the hand of her oppressor, overthrowing heathenism and destroying a government that has leagued with Satan in the work of persecution."

He ceased speaking, and again turned a questioning glance toward the young Englishman. Anjiro had been closely watching the effect of his friend's words. It was evident that the two had some object in view in thus taking a third person into their confidence. Beaumont felt assured of this, and hesitated to say anything that might seem to encourage further disclosures. If they revealed their plans to him, he was determined they should do so on their own responsibility. He turned his eyes seaward, and appeared to be watching the flight of a flock of gulls that were hovering about the ship. His thoughts, however, were busy pondering the words of

Shiro. He had met men before who were enthusiasts and almost fanatics whenever the subject upon which their hopes were set, and around which their thoughts and labors gathered, was touched upon. But here was a man whose mind was filled with projects the most visionary, and the sole object of whose life seemed to be the realization of a plan that, to any disinterested person, must needs appear in the highest degree impracticable.

Yet Shiro displayed none of the fervor, the excitement, the rashness and intemperance of language that characterize the fanatic. He was profoundly earnest; he was, likewise, simple as a child, and transparently sincere. Evidently he conscientiously believed himself to be a man of destiny, the instrument of God in working out the divine will in the history of his people.

He waited for Beaumont to speak, but observing his silence, he inquired:

"What does Señor think? But why need I ask? Señor has had the goodness and patience to listen to the tale of one he would call a visionary fanatic."

Beaumont felt compelled to say something.

"You have applied that epithet to yourself," he said, "I have not."

"I have; and you have also, in your heart! Be frank with me! Have you not?"

The Englishman was on the point of speaking, when the cabin boy, approaching him, said:

"Mynheer Beaumont, the captain wishes to see you at once in the cabin."

"Tell him I shall be there presently," responded the Englishman, and then, turning to Shiro, he said in parting:

"Believe me, I have been much interested in what you have told me. I may not be as hopeful of the result as you are; yet, since you say the struggle is already begun, it would seem that the die has been irretrievably cast, and it now remains to be seen whether the desperate valor of the Christians can prevail against the overwhelming number of their foes."

IV.

ANJIRO, ALIAS PAOLI.

On his way to the cabin Beaumont decided to acquaint Van Neist with the conversation he had just had with Shiro. He determined to take this course for two reasons. In the first place, he thought he knew the captain well enough to be certain that it would be, so far as Shiro and his friend were concerned, both safe and advisable to do so; and he also considered it his duty to inform Van Neist of the character of his passengers. Beaumont was aware that stringent regulations had been imposed by the Japanese government upon the Dutch merchants. One of the most rigidly enforced of these rules was the prohibition against giving any Catholic priest passage to Japan or aid or comfort in the empire itself. In the present strained condition of affairs, if it were known that the *Spuyten Duyvil* had brought home the avowed leader of an insurrection, the consequences might be serious enough.

Beaumont found the captain pacing the floor of the little cabin in a high state of excitement. Never before had he seen him so thoroughly aroused. No sooner had Beaumont entered than Van Neist faced the young Englishman, and, looking him keenly in the eye, said, in a voice that trembled with excitement:

"I sent for you, Mynheer Beaumont, because I need your counsel. But first, you have been talking with the Japanese passengers. Did you learn anything from them that I ought to know?"

Beaumont was startled by the suddenness of the question. Evidently, whatever it was that was disturbing the captain's mind had some connection with what he had just decided to tell him; and he at once proceeded to repeat in substance the conversation which he had had with Shiro, Van Neist listening intently to all he said. This information seemed to increase the captain's uneasiness. For a time after Beaumont had finished his story he continued to pace the floor in great agitation. Then he said:

"What you tell me, Mynheer, confirms what my second officer told me a few minutes ago, and makes our position all the more alarming. Something must be done, and that at once. Those two fellows must go in irons, and upon our arrival in Japan they must be handed over to the authorities, to be dealt with as their own rulers may see fit."

Beaumont could not repress a shudder. Once in the hands of the government, it was easy to surmise their fate. But what was the information that Van Neist had received? The young Englishman almost regretted that he had acquainted him with Shiro's story. Had he been mistaken in his estimation of the captain's character? Were the Dutch all that Shiro had painted them, and was Van Neist no better than his countrymen in Japan? Such were the thoughts that coursed through his mind as he watched his companion's excited movements. At length the captain broke the silence:

"Mynheer Beaumont, have you ever heard of Francesco Paoli, the Jesuit missionary to Japan?"

"I have not."

"Then you have not heard of one whose name is hated above every other name by the Japanese government. Large rewards have been offered for his capture, dead or alive, but thus far he seems to have led a charmed life. The Christians, too, did they know it, ought to hate him as cordially as do their enemies. He has been responsible for all the persecutions that they have suffered during the past twenty years. He headed a great conspiracy to call in the assistance of Spain and Portugal to establish the supremacy of the Pope in Japan. He was detected in the midst of his plot, and was banished from the country. He returned in disguise. The Japanese authorities, hearing of this, set a price upon his head, and for years he was hunted like a wild beast. Twice was it thought that he had been killed, and once was a foreign priest crucified in Nagasaki, the officials believing him to be Paoli. Two years ago he went to Rome, where he was appointed Bishop of Japan. Less than half an hour ago I learned that the self-same Paoli is now returning to Nagasaki aboard the *Spuyten Duyvil*."

"Impossible!" cried Beaumont, astonished beyond measure. "There must be some mistake. A stowaway could not have kept himself concealed so long as this, and, besides myself, the only passengers aboard are Shiro and his friend Anjiro."

"Anjiro!" cried Van Neist. "A thousand curses upon him. A thousand curses on the day I consented to take him aboard! Anjiro, Mynheer, is none other than the Jesuit, Francesco Paoli, in disguise!"

It was indeed so. Anjiro was the Jesuit missionary, Francesco Paoli, returning to his field of labor disguised as a Japanese.

V.

THE BISHOP OF JAPAN.

For the space of twenty-five years previous to the time of the opening of our history, this same Francesco Paoli had been the most widely known missionary laboring in Japan. An Italian by birth, but reared to manhood by his maternal uncle, a resident of the mountainous district of Covibia, Portugal, Paoli had taken his degree in philosophy at Paris, had joined the Society of Jesus, and in 1612 formed one of a company of fifteen Jesuit missionaries that left Lisbon for the far-off island-empire of Japan. None of his brethren had become so much loved or so deeply hated as he. From Yezzo, in the far north, to Riu Kiu, in the extreme south of the empire, every island and every province became in turn the scene of his labors, and was full of the fruits of his quenchless zeal. It was natural, therefore, when the suspicions of the Japanese government were aroused against the foreign religion, and its propagators were thought to be plotting to bring the country under the authority of the Pope, that the foremost missionary in the field should be subjected to a jealous surveillance and have his every movement noted by spies appointed for that purpose. In the midst of the dangers by which he was now encompassed, Paoli showed himself as courageous as he was devoted. He conscienciously believed in the universal supremacy of Rome. To him the Pope was a king of kings, before whom it was just and proper and the bounden duty of all the rulers of the world to bow in submission. With unflinching fidelity to this belief, he organized an association among the Christian princes to labor for the official recognition of the Church. Failing in this, they sought to form alliances with the Catholic powers of Europe. Paoli was seized by the government, imprisoned for a time, and then banished from Japan, with strict orders never to return. At the first opportunity he again entered the country, and, in various disguises eluding his foes, he became the secret leader of the Christians during the successive persecutions that swept over the Church, threatening her very existence.

Finally convinced that the hour had come to seek foreign help for the liberation of the faith in Japan, Paoli returned to Europe to procure, if possible, armed assistance from Portugal or Spain. But the time was inauspicious. The great religious struggle known as the Thirty Years' War was raging, and all Europe was either already involved or waiting in expectancy. At such a time ships and soldiers could be ill spared, even for so worthy an object as the one that Paoli represented. At Rome, however, he was granted an audience by the Pope, who created him Bishop of Japan, and with this slight token of interest in the cause for which he was laboring, Paoli returned to Manila, where, disguised as a Japanese and under the name of Anjiro, he took passage with Shiro for Nagasaki.

His detection aboard the *Spuyten Duyvil* was the result of no accident. Cruger, the second officer, had been boatswain upon the ship that carried Paoli from Nagasaki to Goa on the occasion of his banishment from Japan. He, therefore, knew the priest well. Carefully as the latter was now disguised, Cruger's suspicions were aroused, and he felt convinced that the so-called Anjiro had also recognized him. Cruger determined to watch the two Japanese and, in the meantime, to keep his suspicions to himself. On the night preceding the day in which the events narrated in the last chapter took place the officer at a late hour crept cautiously to the place where Shiro and Anjiro slept, and found the two engaged in a whispered conversation, speaking for the greater safety in Japanese. Cruger's acquaintance with that language was slight, but he caught enough to assure him that Anjiro was none other than the famous Jesuit missionary, Francesco Paoli. At the first opportunity on the following day he informed the captain of the discovery he had made, and the latter, as the reader has already learned, calling Beaumont to his cabin and hearing Shiro's story from him, in turn revealed to the young Englishman what had been made known to him respecting Anjiro.

The Englishman advised Van Neist to call in Cruger, Shiro and Anjiro and to have a conference with them. The captain approved the plan, and when the three men were brought together and Anjiro was charged with concealing his true name and character, to the surprise of all, instead of denying the accusation, he frankly acknowledged its truth.

"I have deceived you, Señor Captain," he said, humbly. "And I ask you, was not the deception justifiable? The cause with which I am heart and soul identified has now reached its supreme crisis. My presence and the presence of my companion is imperatively called for in Japan. No Spanish nor Portuguese ship now goes to that country; my only resort was to take passage with you. Had I, as the banished missionary, Francesco Paoli, sought to have gone aboard the *Spuyten Duyvil*, you, Señor Captain, though you might have been willing to receive me, would not have dared to do so. Is it not so, Señor? I disguised myself as a Japanese, and you took me cheerfully enough. Had I escaped discovery, neither you nor

THE ISLANDS IN NAGASAKI BAY.—*See Page 52.*

my enemies would have ever afterwards suspected the truth, and what harm could the deception, which I was compelled to practice, have done you or the interests of your countrymen in Japan? On our first day out, however, I recognized Señor Cruger, and from that hour I expected detection. My fears have now been realized; you know who I am. I am at your mercy."

Beaumont was deeply touched by the frankness and the simplicity of the man, and even the stern, matter-of-fact Van Neist was visibly moved. It was evident he was much more disposed to be lenient than he had been a short time before. Turning to the second officer, who was on the point of leaving the cabin, he said briefly:

"Cruger, for the present, let this go no further. Neither the other officers nor the crew are to know that Bishop Paoli is aboard." And then, addressing Shiro with some degree of sternness in his voice: "As for you and this man, I shall reserve what I have to say until we approach Japan. It is a useless precaution to put two unarmed men in irons so far away from land; nevertheless you are to consider yourselves prisoners, liable to be handed over to the government officials upon the arrival of the *Spuyten Duyvil* at Nagasaki."

VI.

A VISION OF WAR.

A week of fair weather with favoring winds passed by, and the *Spuyten Duyvil* drew near her destination. Marmion Beaumont was awakened one morning at daybreak by the voice of Van Neist:

"Land ahead! Up, Mynheer Beaumont, if thou wouldst

look upon one of the fairest sights to be seen on the earth."

Nothing further was necessary to arouse the young Englishman; and hastily dressing himself, he hurried on deck. The bishop and Shiro were already there, both gazing ahead to where, some twenty miles distant, the green summits of the outlying islands of Japan were visible. The morning was bright and beautiful, and a fresh breeze drove the *Spuyten Duyvil* through the water, the bank of plunging foam under her bows bearing evidence to the speed with which the good ship bore on her way.

" Yonder islands on our larboard quarter," said the captain, addressing Beaumont, "are the Goto Islands, and ahead you perceive the mainland with a belt of small islands lying in close to the coast; and that long stretch of open sea is the outer entrance to Nagasaki bay, the city and harbor being both hidden from sight by yonder high range of hills. If this breeze stands by us we ought to be inside by noonday."

As the morning hours wore on, and the *Spuyten Duyvil* lessened the distance between her and the entrance to the bay, Beaumont constantly found fresh occasion for admiration in the beauty of the prospect before him. Islets of all sizes, grouped together in picturesque confusion, seemed, as they advanced, to hem them in on either side. Towering rocks of every conceivable shape— some mimicking the tall pointed spires of a cathedral, others the frowning ramparts of some mighty fortress— appeared to rise up out of the water as they advanced. At the rocky bases of these beetling cliffs the surf broke with a sullen roar, dashing its wreaths of fleecy foam high into the air. Beyond the islands, the mountains on the mainland seemed to roll away from the coast in a long succession of billowy swells, rising higher and higher as they receded from the shore, their rugged sides everywhere clothed in a mantle of vivid green.

Marmion Beaumont, turning finally from a contemplation of the fair scene before him, looked toward Bishop Paoli and his companion, who were standing aloof from the others, both silently gazing at the land ahead. The young Englishman had already gained Van Neist's promise not to give them over into the hands of their enemies, and he thought that their safety now depended upon themselves.

"Your land is indeed a most beautiful one," he said, coming up to the place where the two were standing together, and addressing his remarks to Shiro, "I am not surprised that you Japanese are so proud of your country and so jealous of her honor."

"The more it is to be regretted that in such a paradise man's hand is raised against the hand of God, and his cruelty blights the beauty of nature." Shiro spoke in his usually quiet tone, his eyes never leaving the shore.

"Fair as yonder land is," broke in the bishop, "fairer still will it be when its millions are clothed in the beauty of holiness."

"You see nothing but sin where others see only loveliness," responded Beaumont, with a smile. "But it is, I presume, because of your calling. Men can seem to you to be only brands in the burning, and you think it is your mission to pluck them forth from the midst of destruction. Honesty of purpose in a heathen, like the fairest of landscapes, has no beauty in your eyes and no place in your thoughts."

"Nay, you are mistaken. Righteousness in even an idolator is to be commended. But of what value are all the glories of natural beauty if they but make alluring the way to hell? What terrors can the deadliest clime or the most barren desert contain if there souls mount upward from the midst of misery and privation to the paradise of God?"

The bishop's voice died away in a hoarse whisper. He staggered, and would have fallen had not Shiro sprung forward and with Beaumont's help, seated him upon a heap of cordage.

"A trance," said Shiro, in reply to the young Englishman's look of inquiry. "You will now learn the source of my knowledge of events that are at present occurring in Japan."

Paoli's face was blanched to a deathlike paleness. His eyes were closed, and his breathing, at first, was heavy and labored, but soon became as gentle as that of a sleeping child. Shiro knelt by his side, and taking the bishop's hands in his own, inquired, in a clear, low voice:

"Good father, speak! What dost thou see?"

"I see," replied Paoli, his voice sounding hollow and far away—"I see a castle, and above it float the standards of the heathen. Wait! I know this village and yonder mountain—yes, it is the castle of Tomioka."

"And our brethren?" asked Shiro, anxiously. "Good father, dost thou see aught of them?"

"No. But hold! What is that that meeteth mine eyes upon the Shikino plain? It is the camp of an army, and —Mother of God be praised!—I behold upon their banners the figure of our Christ and his cross! It is the camp of the Christians prepared to do battle for their holy faith!"

A silence followed. Both Shiro and the young Englishman waited in breathless impatience for Paoli to continue. Over the face of the bishop flitted an amazed expression, and an exclamation of surprise burst from his lips.

"Speak again, good father," cried Shiro, no longer able to control his anxiety. "What dost thou now behold?"

"The Christians are pouring from their camp, and are marshaling themselves in battle array upon the plain! And—O saints and angels defend them!—they are now rushing in three solid columns upon the castle! Madness! madness! to cast away their lives in so forlorn a hope! How bravely they sweep forward to the assault? Now they near the castle walls; with a wild cry they dash on at redoubled speed! And now! now! Oh, merciful God!"

With a cry of anguish, Paoli struggled in the arms of the two men, as if he was endeavoring to shut out some terrible picture from his sight. Still clinging to the bishop's hands, Shiro, trembling with his own intense emotions, pleaded with passionate earnestness:

"Again, again, O father! Look once more, and tell me what it is that thou seest."

The bishop shuddered as he responded:

"A moment ago and the cloud of the foemen's arrows and missiles of death darkened the air. I saw the ranks of our brethren melt away before that pitiless storm of destruction as might melt a snowdrift before a river of flaming lava. For an instant methought I saw them attempt to rally and again prepare to rush to the assault, but what happened then I know not. I heard a savage shout of triumph from the castle, a ringing cry of defiance from the Christians; again came the crash of musketry and the fierce tumult of battle. Then a dizziness came over me, and now, when I look, only a blood-red haze meets my sight, but what it conceals I know not —I know not!"

Paoli was now fast falling into that comatose condition that frequently follows a trance; nevertheless, with the assistance of Beaumont and Shiro, he was able to go below. The Englishman, it may well be believed, had been greatly amazed at what he had just seen and heard, and, as he and Shiro were returning to the deck, he said in a low voice that the seamen standing by might not hear:

"These trances—does the bishop frequently fall into them? And can he summon them whenever it may please him to do so?"

Shiro seemed reluctant to discuss the subject, but at length he whispered back:

"They are wholly involuntary. He has been subject to them I have heard ever since he was a child, but they come only when some deadly peril or a great crisis affects the fortunes of those in whom he takes a profound personal interest. You saw how it was in the instance we have just witnessed. Evidently our brethren were endeavoring to carry some infidel stronghold by storm, and were in danger of defeat."

"And this battle was taking place at the very time the bishop beheld it in his vision?"

"Even so."

"Strange! strange!" said Beaumont; then fixing a keen look upon Shiro, he asked suddenly:

"Have you ever known the bishop to exercise a mesmeric power over others, throwing them into a trance or causing them involuntarily to obey him?"

The Japanese youth's face flushed and his eyes fell before the questioner's gaze.

"Ask the crew of the *Spuyten Duyvil*," he replied, as soon as he recovered from his confusion, "they all believe Father Paoli to be a sorcerer. But excuse me, Señor," he continued nervously, "I must return to the bishop; he may need attendance;" and Shiro hastened below.

Beaumont smiled as he looked after his retreating figure.

"So, so," he mused half aloud, "the conclusion, then, to which a week's study of those two had brought me is correct. Nirado Shiro is nothing more than a voice and hand of Francesco Paoli, and should this rebellion, which they declared has already begun, be successful, and should this youth become, as he believes himself destined to become, the ruler of Japan, it will not be he who shall govern but this strange being who has gained so complete and so mysterious a power over him. Truly, they are two men of destiny."

And pondering upon these things, the Englishman went forward to hunt up his friend, Captain Van Neist.

BOOK SECOND.

TAKABOKA.

I.

CAPTAIN VAN NEIST RECEIVES A LETTER

"IN the name of all that's wonderful, Heer Santvoort's boat is coming out to meet us!" Captain Van Neist lowered his glass, and, with a perplexed expression on his face, turned to Beaumont. "I do not understand this," he exclaimed, "something has happened."

The Englishman took the glass and looked in the direction the captain was indicating with his outstretched arm. There some little distance ahead he saw a small boat directly in the course of the merchantman. Three picturesquely dressed natives were slowly urging the strange-looking little craft toward the *Spuyten Duyvil*. The combined speed of the ship and the boat itself was rapidly lessening the distance between the two, and in a short time the *sampan*, as this species of craft is called, was under the vessel's bows. A well-dressed Japanese issued from the tiny cabin, built in the middle of the boat, and, observing Van Neist looking down at him he drew something white from the bosom of his loose flowing dress, and, waving it above his head, shouted out a few words in Dutch to the captain.

"Ah!" exclaimed Van Neist, "Heer Santvoort, the private trader at Nagasaki, has sent me a letter. Strange that he should meet us so far out, and stranger still, that if there is anything of importance to communicate, he has not come himself. Believe me, there is something wrong. That young man in the boat, if I mistake not, is Asuga, Santvoort's interpreter."

In a few minutes Asuga—for he it proved to be—was upon deck and had delivered the letter to the captain, who hastily broke its seal, and after running it through, read it aloud in English to Beaumont:

"To Heer Van Neist, Honorable Master of the Spuyten Duyvil : *Sir*—The look-out reports a foreign ship approaching this coast, and as no other vessel is expected, it must be you. I regret to say that I am unable to come to you in person, that being expressly forbidden by His Excellency, the Governor of Nagasaki. I am, however, permitted to send you this letter to acquaint you with the condition of affairs in this part of the empire, and also to inform you of the measures that His Excellency has decided upon taking with regard to any Japanese passengers you may have on board.

"About a week ago the Christains of Amakusa, a large island lying southeast of here, rose in rebellion against their prince, and the insurrection has already assumed a most serious aspect, having spread to the neighboring province of Shimabara. A number of battles have been fought, and thus far the government troops have been unsuccessful in their efforts to surpress the insurgents. Fears are entertained that the doctrines of the foreign priests have a large following throughout the country, and that the victories gained by the Amakusa and Shimabara rebels will encourage many secret sympathizers to rise with them in an endeavor to overthrow the government. On this account the authorities feel compelled to resort to extreme measures to avert any such danger. A few days ago a Spanish priest was discovered in a village near the city disguised as a Japanese, and to-morrow he is to be put to death. To-day the government officers, with a large body of soldiers, are hunting out any that may be Christians in the villages north of us and among the mountains across the bay.

"His Excellency the Governor commands me to inform you that he will send Kanshin, his deputy, with a number of officials, to the *Spuyten Duyvil* to examine such Japanese passengers as you may have with you, and to compel them to trample on the cross—a very successful method of inquisition the Japanese have invented to find out who are Christians, since no true believer will consent, even on pain of certain death, thus to insult the sacred symbol of his religion. I need hardly say that the Governor's officers will be afforded all the assistance in your power to make their examination of your ship as thorough and satisfactory as His Excellency may wish. Information has lately come to Nagasaki that some Japanese Christians now in the Philippines contemplate a return to Japan for the purpose of stirring up their fellow-believers to a revolt. You remember, I presume, that famous Jesuit missionary, Francesco Paoli; nothing has been heard of him for above two years, and the government now breathes freer, being convinced that that arch-enemy of their peace and safety is either dead or has returned to Europe to trouble them no more. I would God that I could be as confident of this as they appear to be, for I greatly fear that the crafty Jesuit is still alive, and, wherever he may be, is plotting against the quiet of the country. A letter yesterday from the factory at Hirado brings the welcome intelligence that Mynheer Nicolass Koeckenbacker will be in Nagasaki to-morrow.

"May we soon have the happiness of seeing you. Your honor's most humble servant,

"MELCHIOR SANTVOORT."

When the captain had finished reading the letter, he and Beaumont looked at each other for a time in silence. Both men realized the difficulty of the situation. The Englishman was the first to speak.

"Whatever may happen," said he, "this can be affirmed —the captain of the *Spuyten Duyvil* is free from suspicion. You had no means of knowing that Shiro was an openly avowed rebel, or that the man calling himself Anjiro was a Jesuit in disguise; and the voyage was more than half over before their true characters were discovered. I can vouch for that. But what of them— Shiro and Paoli? It seems now, indeed, that there is no escape for them. Would that there were! Is it not possible that even yet something might be done?"

"No, nothing can be done," replied Van Neist, curtly, and with a trace of impatience in his voice. "They took the risk of being discovered when they came aboard this ship, and now, when detection threatens them, they must abide the consequences of their own rashness."

II.

THE GOVERNOR'S DEPUTY LOSES HIS SWORD.

The traveller of the present day, standing on the deck of one of the many steamships that enter the little landlocked bay of Nagasaki, is certain to have a rocky islet, just outside the harbor, pointed out to him, with the remark: "There, that's Pappenberg!" The little island thus so familiarly known to all tourists as to need no furthur introduction in order to enlist their deepest interest, is, to the European, one of the classic spots of the Far East. More than two centuries ago the Dutch gave it the name of Pappenberg, for reasons which the readers of this history are soon to learn; but the Japanese have always called it Takaboka—this word meaning, Tall Spear. The name is very appropriate, for the island-rock does resemble a gigantic spear head set upon its base. The islet is, perhaps, a half mile in circumference, and its highest point rises somewhere in the neighborhood of six hundred feet above the water. The southern side is precipitous almost from the summit, and from the top one gazes down on the sharp, black rocks, over which, in storms, the waves churn themselves into white drifts of seething foam. To the northward there is a thickly wooded slope leading down with a gradual descent to the water's edge, where it terminates in a wide, white, sandy beach. The island is now frequented as a picnic resort by the foreign residents of Nagasaki, and, during the summer months, the beach is used as a bathing-ground. The distance from the city is but a league, and the ride down the bay, hemmed in on either side by the green beauty of the inclosing hills, and out into the wider waters of the outer passage to the pretty little island, is a delight not soon to be forgotten by those who have once enjoyed it.

As at present, so also at the time of which we are writing, vessels entering Nagasaki Bay passed close under Takaboka. It happened that, as the *Spuyten Duyvil* came before the island under a full spread of canvas, the wind, which, for some time past, had been blowing in light, fitful gusts, gave unmistakable evidence of dying away altogether. And this it did do, just as the ship lay before the entrance to the harbor. Finding that his vessel had lost way, and that the tide was setting out with a strong current from the bay, Van Neist ordered the anchor to be dropped, and soon, with her sails thundering against the shrouds, the *Spuyten Duyvil* swung round to the tide, her bow rising and falling on the broad, deep swells that set in from the open sea. The captain fretted and grumbled at the unexpected turn matters had taken.

"Too bad, too bad, I say, Mynheer Beaumont! that just as we are in sight of port the wind must play us such a trick as this. But," he added, casting his eye around the sky, "if I mistake not, there is plenty of wind over there," pointing to a ragged bank of black clouds that was slowly rising in the south-west. "So, perhaps, we ought to be thankful that we are so near our haven, for methinks a full-grown typhoon is brewing out yonder."

"If that should be the case," asked Beaumont, "will there be breeze enough before the storm bursts to put us inside?"

"Oh, yes; these storms usually begin quite moderately and increase in violence. As soon as we feel the first puff we shall weigh anchor, and run in, and shall be safely anchored again before the storm really breaks upon us. Even here, unless the typhoon is one of unusual fury, we are quite secure. But what is that?"

Asuga, who was standing by, answered his question.

"That, Heer Captain, is the boat which is bringing the governor's deputy and the officers to examine the Japanese passengers."

"Indeed!" responded the captain, in by no means a gracious tone of voice. "Then I shall go forward to receive them."

The officers, eight in number, were already on deck by the time Van Neist and the young Englishman had reached the ladder. Beaumont was interested in noting their quaint appearance, so different from anything he had ever before seen. They had thought it necessary to equip themselves in full military accoutrement, their heads protected by helmets and their bodies by heavy quilted armor. Each bore two swords—a long and a short one—and their whole appearance struck the Englishman as extremely savage.

As Van Neist and Beaumont approached, instead of the usual low bow of salutation, they all stood stiffly erect, and their interpreter, stepping forward, made known their errand:

"His Excellent Highness, the Governor of Nagasaki, demands that you deliver up, for examination, such of his subjects or other Japanese that may be aboard your ship;" and, having given his message in his most measured and pompous tones, he stepped back into the ranks of his comrades, who had formed themselves into a line of scowling faces along the deck.

"Curse his insolence," growled the captain beneath his breath to Beaumont, in English. "I would like to give him a taste of my cat-o'-nine-tails. There's something in the wind. The last time I was here they were all

cringing and scraping the deck, their mouths full of the softest flattery. But it is the way with this accursed nation—all flattery and abject humility if they have anything to gain, but all overbearing insolence if they think they have the upper hand. Curse them, they'll not lord it over me!"

Van Neist knew well enough, however, that any display of resentment upon his part was just what the haughty officials would have welcomed the most as another excuse for drawing the lines stricter upon the already restriction-burdened Dutch merchants of Nagasaki and Hirado. He, therefore, simply replied to the officers, through the interpreter, that he granted their request, and, turning to Cruger, he ordered him to call Anjiro and Shiro.

The young Englishman could not repress a shudder as he reflected that in a few minutes the two friends must meet whatever terrible ordeal these pitiless inquisitors might have in store for them; and he grew sick at heart as he imagined the hapless Jesuit, his disguise torn off, standing bound in the midst of his ruthless foes. What triumph would swell these savage hearts when they discovered that the feared and hated missionary, Francesco Paoli, upon whose head a price had been set for more than ten years, was at last in their hands!

After a delay of several minutes Cruger returned, his face wearing a bewildered look.

"What it the matter?" demanded the captain. "Where are Anjiro and Shiro?"

"Mynheer Captain," responded the officer, "I have searched the ship thoroughly, but Anjiro and Shiro are not to be found."

"Anjiro and Shiro not to be found!" exclaimed both

Van Neist and Beaumont simultaneously, the latter with mingled amazement and relief.

"Anjiro and Shiro not to be found!" cried the horrified interpreter in Japanese.

"Anjiro and Shiro, two subjects of Japan, not to be found!" growled forth the line of scowling officials, and as every sword was drawn from its scabbard, the growl continued: "Anjiro and Shiro must be produced!"

This threatening movement was too much for the hot-tempered Van Neist and his crew that now formed a close circle around the officials. As Kanshin the deputy with a hostile gesture stepped up to the captain, the latter, with a roar of rage, threw himself upon the Japanese, and before the officer was aware of his intention, tore his sword from his grasp. The crew now dashed in between their captain and the deputy's companions, and, for a moment, Beaumont thought a conflict unavoidable. But a glance at the fierce, resolute faces about them, convinced the Japanese officials of the folly of provoking a quarrel with such odds against them, and, returning their swords to their scabbards, they sullenly fell back and stood in a little group by the vessel's side.

"Tell this officer and his companions," Van Neist shouted to Asuga, who had been a terrified spectator of the scene, "that if they do not immediately leave my ship I shall give orders to have them seized and thrown overboard."

Seeing no way of escape, Asuga did as he was ordered, and when the deputy had spoken he interpreted to the captain the meaning of his speech, which was that they agreed to quit the ship as soon as Van Neist returned Kanshin his sword.

"Tell him," the captain ordered, "that I shall keep

the sword as a *souvenir* of the courtesy of Japanese officials."

The deputy, when he learned what Van Neist had said, seemed to be greatly agitated, and renewed his pleadings with touching earnestness. But the captain was obdurate; and finally, the officials, vanquished and crest-fallen, took their leave.

III.

THE FIRST OFFICER MAKES AN EXPLANATION.

"Shiro and Paoli have escaped," said Beaumont as soon as the Japanese officials had left the *Spuyten Duyvil.*

"I am glad they got out of a very difficult place just in the nick of time. But how did they get away?"

"I can tell you that, captain," broke in the first officer, who had overheard Van Neist's question. "About an hour ago, I observed a small boat, partially filled with water, drifting out to sea with the tide. It became lodged against the side of the ship, and it then occurred to me that if our Japanese passengers wished to get ashore quietly and as soon as possible, here was their chance. I remarked as much to them, and they at once fell in with my suggestion"—and here a broad smile overspread the officer's honest face—"so in a short time they had their baggage in the boat, and were off."

Van Neist had listened to the officer with a face that threatened to break into a smile, despite his efforts to look severe.

"It would have been more in accordance with the discipline of the ship, Van Sylt, if you had first consulted me. But it is too late now to undo what has been done. Hereafter, however, be more observant of our rules," and with this rebuke, the captain accompanied by Beaumont, left the group of officers and seamen.

"Van Sylt," said Van Neist to the Englishman, as the two walked aft side by side, "is the best officer I ever had, but he is a Catholic withal, and, I doubt not, he knew all about Shiro and Paoli long before we did."

Just then a sound was borne over the water from the hills to the west.

"What can it be?" exclaimed the captain. "It surely is not thunder."

The sound swelled louder and louder, every now and then breaking into a sharp, explosive rattle.

"Musketry!" cried Beaumont.

"And the shouting of men!" added Van Neist.

"A battle!" exclaimed both together.

A battle it certainly was; for now could be distinctly heard the sharp report of fire-arms, the frenzied shouts of combatants, and above all the uproar, the piercing shrieks of women. The high peak of the rocky islet, Takaboka, intercepted their view, but it was manifest to the listeners that the conflict was rolling nearer and nearer, for the sounds were constantly becoming more audible. Summoning Asuga, the captain asked him if he knew what it meant.

"This morning the governor dispatched a large body of soldiers to seize the Christian farmers dwelling in the Inasa mountains and in the Murakami valley north of the city. I presume the Christians were, in some way, made aware of the governor's intention, and have gathered together and are resisting the officers and their men."

"See yonder!" cried Beaumont, pointing toward the

entrance of the harbor. "A fleet of boats full of armed men is coming down the bay!"

Van Neist and the interpreter looked in the direction indicated by the Englishman, and beheld the water literally covered with *sampans*, bearing straight down upon the *Spuyten Duyvil* with all the speed that the rowers could command. Each boat contained from ten to fifteen soldiers, in full armor—some bearing bows, others long spears, and not a few carrying muskets.

"They are making straight for us," exclaimed the captain. "What can it mean?"

"I do not know," answered Asuga. "But let us wait quietly, and," he added, casting his eyes about the ship, and upon the officers and men, who were now regarding the approaching boats with suspicious alarm, "I advise you to make no efforts towards resisting them, should they wish to board your ship. I cannot think that they have hostile intentions upon the *Spuyten Duyvil*, but resistance might provoke them and make trouble."

Van Neist turned impatiently from Asuga, and addressed Beaumont in English:

"A fine thing, Mynheer Beaumont, that a ship captain must needs let his hands hang idle by his side, and permit an army of armed barbarians to swarm over his deck! And this fellow, like all the commoners in Japan, trembles at the sight of a *Samurai*. Forsooth, he would have us stand tamely by and be butchered if those swaggering scoundrels yonder take it into their heads to draw their swords upon us. But he'll see whether we'll cringe like craven cowards before a horde of savages!"

And the captain, his eyes blazing with anger, sprang upon a heap of cordage, shouting:

"Men, to arms! On with your cutlasses! Have the muskets brought on deck; unlimber and load the guns!"

Instantly the deck was a scene of wild confusion, the men hurrying to arm themselves and make preparations for the conflict that now seemed to them inevitable.

The reader will remember that in the days of which we are writing, the waters of both the Eastern and the Western Seas swarmed with pirates. It was thus a necessity for merchant ships to have a strong and well-trained crew, and to carry a very arsenal of arms for defence. Often the larger merchantmen fell but little short of the men-of-war of the times in the number of their guns, and some of the most desperate sea-fights of the age were those fought between merchant ships and the pirates. The *Spuyten Duyvil* carried twelve heavy guns, and her crew had shown their bravery in more than one hard-fought engagement. In her early career she had borne the name of *Goede Vrouw*, but it had happened that after a fierce encounter with two pirates off the African coast —a battle in which she had sunk the one and captured the other—the conquered chief of the freebooters had told Van Neist that the *Goede Vrouw* was a veritable *spitting devil*, and, from that time, *Spuyten Duyvil* the good ship had been called, and the name was well-known among the pirates of both the Indies.

IV.

A CONFERENCE.

Asuga, the interpreter, perceiving the preparations for battle that were being made aboard the *Spuyten Duyvil*, sprang into his boat and was rowed off in the direction of the approaching soldiers. Beaumont pointed him out to the captain, who now appeared upon deck fully armed and said:

"Yonder goes our timid adviser to inform his countrymen, I presume, of what they may expect. We shall soon know what they intend to do. And, captain, I have a request to make: If there should be a conflict I desire your permission to fight by your side. You see, I am armed and ready."

"Thank you," responded Van Neist, gratefully. "Every man will count, and especially so since we are to meet an enemy that so heavily outnumbers us. But look yonder! Asuga is speaking to that officer in the foremost boat, and, as I live, they are resting on their oars, and the interpreter is hurrying back to us!"

In a short time Asuga was within hailing distance, and he called out to Van Neist:

"It is all right; they are friends; let them go aboard!"

"We are ready for action," Van Neist shouted back. "The men are at arms, and every gun is loaded and ready. If those soldiers come a yard nearer my ship, I will give the order to fire. If they wish to consult with me let their leader with six men come aboard and I shall talk with him. But the rest must remain where they are."

Asuga returned to the officer with whom he had previously been speaking, and another consultation was held, the men upon the *Spuyten Duyvil* watching the proceedings with anxious interest. As they stood awaiting developments, the sound of the conflict beyond Takaboka continued without intermission, and, seemingly, was still moving in their direction. But for the present they had eyes and ears only for what was taking place before them.

Finally, after a long parley, Asuga was seen to again turn around and make towards the ship, followed by the officer's boat, the others remaining where they were.

"Let us aboard; your proposal is accepted."

In answer to Asuga's request the ship's ladder was lowered, and he, together with the officer and six of the latter's chief retainers, were received on board. A very marked difference was observed in their behavior from that of those connected with the governor's deputy. The firm stand made by Van Neist had had a wholesome effect upon the officer and his men, who, had they been tamely allowed to board the ship, would have conducted themselves with as much arrogance and insolent swaggering as the others. They were quick to preceive, however, that they stood in the presence of brave and determined men, who would tolerate no blustering or bullying, and they conducted themselves accordingly.

Approaching the captain with low bows, the officer, whom Asuga introduced as General Hosokawa, at once proceeded to address him in Japanese, which, although unintelligible to his listeners, Van Neist judged to be some request, from the speaker's frequent low bows which he always accompanied with a long, audible suction of his breath. When he had finished, Asuga conveyed the purport of his speech to the captain and officers of the ship, who had gathered round eager to hear the cause of so much hostile display.

"It seems," said the interpreter, "that what I surmised concerning the cause of the battle that we hear over there is correct. The Christains dwelling among those mountains were just on the point of rising in rebellion and joining the insurgents now assembled, more than thirty thousand strong, at the village of Arima, some twenty-five miles to the east of here. Thus it happened that when the governor's officers with their soldiers arrived this morning at Inasa they found every house deserted. Pushing forward, they at length discovered tne entire population, numbering some five thousand men, women and children, gathered on the shore behind yonder long, rocky island. They were just in the act of embarking in boats to sail around the point of the cape to join their friends on the other side.

"The officers called upon the Christians to surrender, but the latter replied to the summons with a volley of arrows and stones, and some armed with guns, fired upon the soldiers, killing a number and wounding many more. The soldiers were then ordered to attack the rebels, and the fight has been going on ever since. From a deserter, who came over to the officers, it has been learned that having seen the foreign ship anchored here, the rebels have formed the daring plan of seizing her for the arms and other munitions of war that she may contain, and compelling her captain to transport them to Arima. As soon as this intelligence reached Nagasaki, His Excellency the Governor dispatched General Hosokawa, with a thousand picked men, to help you in defending your ship against the rebels. General Hosokawa, therefore, begs that you will allow him to place five hundred of his men aboard the *Spuyten Duyvil*, while the remainder will be drawn up between your ship and the enemy."

Van Neist listened attentively to what Asuga had to say. The truthfulness of the story he had no reason to doubt ; and had he been disposed to do so, visible proof of the officer's veracity was at hand. A more than usually heavy burst of sound from the scene of battle drew his eyes in that direction, and there in full view, rounding the point of the island that Asuga had pointed out, came a fleet of small boats and junks, propelled by oars, while the government troops appeared simultaneously upon the land, firing into the boats of the Christians, that seemed to be densely crowded with persons of all ages and of both sexes. Thus far it had been impossible for the insurgents to get out of range of the destructive fire of their enemies, but now, as they passed the island, upon the southern point of which rises, in our day, the white walls of a mission chapel, they pushed out from the shore, and were soon beyond the reach of the troops. In the struggle at the place of embarkation, and in the running fight along the shore, nearly a third of their numbers had fallen, and the spectators upon the deck of the *Spuyten Duyvil* saw the survivors, after they had shaken themselves free from their foes, steer out into the open channel, and there pause as if for deliberation.

General Hosokawa, who had been nervously uneasy during the few minutes that Van Neist and his officers were deeply engrossed in watching the movements of the Christians, now again addressed the captain. Asuga, interpreting his words, said that the officer was awaiting with anxiety the captain's answer. Would he be so kind as to permit the soldiers to come aboard at once, as the danger was alarmingly near.

Ven Neist, though, no longer doubted but that the proffered assistance was offered for the reasons which the officer alleged, had observed the good effect his firmness had thus far had upon the domineering spirit of Japanese officialism, and he resolved not to do anything that might look like a surrender of his position. He therefore told Asuga to inform Hosokawa that he considered the help of his soldiers unnecessary, as his crew were well able to protect the ship against any force whatsoever; and that, while thanking the governor for his kind offer, he could not allow his men to come aboard the *Spuyten*

Duyvil. He would promise the governor, however, that the rebels would not be allowed to seize the vessel.

With a scowling face, Hosokawa listened to Van Neist's answer, and, without vouchsaving anything in reply, he turned upon his heel and left the ship, his retainers sullenly stalking after him. Asuga, evidently fearing the consequences of the captain's decision, begged leave to be excused, saying that Heer Santvoort would be anxiously awaiting his return to learn how matters stood with the *Spuyten Duyvil.*

V.

THE BATTLE.

As soon as General Hosokawa and the interpreter had left the ship, Van Neist ordered the ladder to be drawn up, the deck cleared for action, and the men to stand by their guns in readiness for anything that might happen.

"Not that I think that it will come to a conflict between us and the insurgents," he remarked to Beaumont, as the two walked forward where they could command a better view of affairs upon the water. "There are soldiers enough in Hosokawa's force to compel the surrender of that mob of untrained farmers, incumbered with their women and children; nevertheless, it's well for us to be prepared."

"Do you observe what they are doing?" asked Beaumont, who was intently regarding the Christians. "They are putting their wounded, together with the women and children, in the junks, while the able-bodied fighting men are taking to the small boats."

"See, they are dropping their dead overboard!"

"There! they are ready! The whole force is moving this way."

"'Sdeath! They are going to attack us!" cried the captain. "Van Sylt," he shouted to his chief officer. "Ready there! They are moving down upon us. Curse them!" he added impatiently. "I don't want to hurt the fools. Why isn't Hosokawa up here with his men before this?"

"He is getting his forces into position," answered Beaumont, glancing towards the government troops. "It seems as if he has some trouble; now it is all right—but no, they have stopped again."

"A plague upon him!" shouted the captain, furiously. "The insurgents will be swarming about the ship before the fellow gets in motion. Van Sylt, give those boats a broadside, and let every man fire his musket. Fire low so as to strike the water just in front of them. I don't wish to kill them," he added, speaking to the young Englishman. "And, perhaps, when they see that we are armed and ready to resist them, they will hold off."

Scarcely had Van Neist stopped speaking, when the air was rent with the mingled roar of cannon and the crash of musketry, and the water just before the advancing Christians was torn into foam. One boat had been struck in the bow, and it quickly filled and capsized, but there was no evidence that any lives had been lost. As the smoke rolled away the crews of the other boats were seen busily engaged in picking up their friends, who were struggling in the water.

"Finely done!" exclaimed Beaumont, as he saw the effect of the shot. "That delay will be sufficient to enable Hosokawa to bring up his men."

"Yes; and our hands will be clean of blood," returned the captain. "This is going to be an ugly piece of business before it is over with, and I wish to have nothing to do with it."

Beaumont's prediction proved to be a correct one. The Christians spent considerable time in picking up their men, but no sooner was this done than, with a fierce shout, they dashed their boats forward toward the *Spuyten Duyvil*. They had just perceived Hosokawa's force and they seemed to realize that all depended upon their reaching the ship before their foes. But the government troops were now urging their *sampans* at full speed through the water, and, though they had the greater distance to traverse, their boats were superior to those of the Christians and better manned with rowers.

The heaver craft of the insurgents, conveying the wounded, together with the old men and women and children, were now seen to turn into Takaboka, where a large number of people poured out upon the beach from the junks and began swarming up the sloping side of the bluff from the northern shore of the island, until they reached the summit, where they gathered in thick, black clusters watching the movements of their friends and foes on the water below.

The men aboard the *Spuyten Duyvil* were likewise intently gazing upon the exciting spectacle. Nearer and nearer came the insurgents, the water furrowed into foam by their rushing boats, the click of their oars ringing out fast and sharp; but still quicker came their enemies, and when the Christians were within a stone's cast of the ship, five or six of Hosokawa's boats shot in between it and them. In another instant the foremost *sampans* of both parties clashed together, and the men, standing up in their boats, engaged in a sanguinary hand-to-hand struggle.

The impetuosity of the charge of the Christians and

their desperate valor for a time carried everything before them, and the government troops, despite their overpowering numbers and savage bravery, were hurled back toward the entrance to the bay, their boats driven one upon another, and the water filled with struggling men. Then, rallying at the call of their leaders, they, in turn, crowded the insurgents slowly backward towards the *Spuyten Duyvil*, until the struggle was raging by the very side of the ship. The superior arms of Hosokawa's disciplined soldiers now began to tell upon the brave but poorly-equipped and untrained yeomen; and soon the tide of victory set in strongly upon their side. Beaumont, as he watched the progress of the fight, was horrified at the ferocious cruelty of Hosokawa's men. Even after whole boat-loads of the Christians had cast aside their arms and cried out for mercy they were cut down, their murderers hacking and mangling the still quivering bodies. He saw one boat, commanded by a fine appearing youth armed only with a club, fight its way through the thick press of the government troops to the ship's side, and the young leader, turning an imploring look at Van Neist, who was watching him from the deck, cried out in Dutch:

"For the love of Christ, Heer Captain, help us! Are you Christians and can you see brethren butchered like this? For God's sake—"

But the sentence was never finished; a hostile sword cut him down, and his body was quickly hidden from sight by the mangled corpses of his heroic companions.

Sickened by the sight of the brutal massacre—for such the struggle had become—Beaumont turned away and looked toward the rocky island, where the agonizing women and children were gazing down upon the slaughter of their husbands and fathers and brothers.

THEY WERE ON THE EXTREME EDGE OF A LEDGE OF ROCK.—*See Page* 91.

Two or three boat-loads of fugitives from the fight were hastening toward the island, and, in close pursuit, followed twice as many of their enemies; and soon the whole body of Hosokawa's men, having finished the massacre of the Christians on the water, with a fierce yell of triumph, turned their course toward Takaboka.

VI.

INE TANAKA.

"The idolators are driving our friends back against the foreign ship! Alas, Ine Tanaka, the day has gone against us!"

"See, see! they are killing them all—even those who have thrown down their arms and are pleading for mercy!"

"And we, Ine Tanaka, we, too, shall be murdered! Woe, woe!"

A wild shriek of terror went up from the group of trembling women as they heard the words of the last speaker, and their pallid, tear-stained faces were turned, in an agonizing appeal toward the tall, queenly figure of a young woman standing upon a rock that rose up out of the plateau-like top of Takaboka:

"Ine Tanaka, Ine Tanaka," rose their wailing chorus, "What sayest thou? Is there no hope? Must we perish?"

The woman thus addressed looked down into the terrified eyes of the people below her, and her face, superbly beautiful despite its present death-like pallor, bore an expression of inexpressible tenderness and pity. The vast throng of aged men, women and children, gathered more closely around the foot of the rock upon which she stood, and bent forward in breathless anxiety to hear her answer. Clear and firm, thrilling with a holy fervor, and awful in its solemn calmness, rose the woman's voice:

"Yea, friends, we shall perish. Vain were it to hope for mercy from yonder infidel; sinful would it be to desire it. We shall be slain, but let not that dismay us. Blessed are they that die in the Lord. God, in his infinite goodness, permits our blood to be shed that the righteousness of our cause may be the more firmly established. But we, O my friends, we but exchange earth for Paradise, sorrow for rejoicing, a cross for a crown."

Some one who had been looking in the direction of the *Spuyten Duyvil*, now cried out:

"Merciful Mother! The soldiers are coming!" and a low shuddering wail rose from the lips of the hundreds gathered on the summit of the rocky islet, as they realized the nearness of their doom.

Ine Tanaka had turned and was also looking down upon the water, and, as her gaze rested for a moment on the scene of the now finished massacre, a look of terrible anguish swept over her fair face:

"O my brother," she murmured, with a quick, hard sob, "Would that we might have died together! My brother, my brother!"

Then regaining her composure, the woman descended from the rock, and, passing among the terror-maddened people, she exhorted them to fidelity to their faith and to fortitude in the trying ordeal just before them; and the resolute firmness of her own bearing and the expression of heavenly peace that rested upon her beautiful features inspired, as much as did her comforting words, a like firmness and resignation in the hearts of those who looked upon her. Even in the midst of their agony of fear, there were those to whom she was a stranger who gazed after her, as she passed away from their side, and wondered who this angel of consolation, so forgetful of self, so brave, so calmly possessed, might be.

"Knowest thou, Kane, who she is that just now spoke to us so tenderly?" asked a sad-eyed woman, whose husband and son had perished in the massacre on the water.

"Nay, nay, I never saw her until last night when she and her brother came from Shimabara to warn us to fly to Arima," returned the woman spoken to, lifting a wild terrified face upon her questioner. "And, Blessed Mother, would that we had never seen either of them!" she continued, sobbing bitterly, "It was they who urged us to rise in revolt against the governor. Had it not been for them we should still be safe—"

"Hush, Kane, hush!" interrupted her companion, "yield not to temptation, dear sister. In the very shadow of death, with our eternal reward in sight, let not Satan rob thee of thy soul! The infidel were already on our track, the governor had ordered his officers to seize us. Lay not our destruction, then, upon the heads f those who risked their own lives to save ours, and who are now dying with us!"

An old man standing by had heard the conversation of the two women. His dim eyes sought the face of the last speaker, and his tranquil features lit up with an approving smile as he listened to her words:

"Well-spoken, woman," he said, in a low, calm voice, "honor and praise to those to whom honor and praise are due! Yet I marvel that thou knowest not Ine Tanaka; hast thou, then, never heard of Nirado Shiro?"

"Yes, yes, we have!" cried the two women in unison, both turning an interested look upon the old man; and the woman called Kane added: "He it is who shall yet return to Japan to deliver the church from the power of the infidel."

"Even so, friend," responded their companion. "Our divinely appointed deliverer he is, the first Christian ruler of our nation he shall be; and Ine Tanaka was to have been his wife. In childhood did their parents betroth them, the good Father Paoli approving and blessing the union. Alas, now—"

The old man's words were here drowned in the loud cry that rose from those about him. Through the grove that covered the sloping side of the hill to the northward the Christian fugitives from the fight upon the water were seen hastening up the steep ascent, and after them, in close pursuit, came hundreds of their savage foes. In a minute more, the foremost fugitive—a young man armed only with a short lance—had reached the summit, and Ine Tanaka, with a wild, joyful cry had dashed through the thick press to the place where he stood.

"Ine, Ine! O my sister!" and the strong arms of the youth gathered the woman to his breast.

"Mother of Mercy! I thank thee for this! O my brother! Long have we labored together, now shall we die together! I am content."

"It was for that, dear sister, that I fled hither as soon as I saw there was no hope for us. Be strong, my noble, faithful Ine! it will soon be over; lean upon me; they come!"

A cloud seemed suddenly to pass before Ine Tanaka's eyes, and her ears were filled with a sound like the roaring of a mighty storm in a forest. She saw the terrified faces of the Christians around her, but they appeared to be half-hidden in a blood-red haze; she beheld Hosokawa's savage warriors as they gained the plateau, and with their naked swords dashed upon their trembling victims, but their stature seemed to be twice the stature of men, and their faces shone out of the all-pervading mist, shadowy and ill-defined, yet fierce and unspeakably cruel. Then she was dimly conscious of the horror of a pitiless massacre—infants tossed into the air and caught on spear-points, human fiends trampling and leaping upon the breasts of gray-haired sires and grand-dames, mothers, youths and young girls hurled shrieking from the high cliff into the sea, and the many-voiced wailings of the terror-stricken and the dying sounded to the ears of the dazed, half-unconscious woman like the chirping of frightened birds in a storm. She felt that they were being driven backward—she and this strong, heroic brother, whose left arm encircled her waist and whose right hand made the keen-pointed lance a shield for the breasts of both.

On the very brink of the precipice they paused, and while the mists that had clouded the vision of the fainting Ine seemed at length to be darkening into utter blackness, she was conscious of a tall, terrible form that suddenly rose up out of the gloom behind them, and one wild, piercing shriek of terror pealed from her lips as she saw her brother sink beneath the swiftly descending sword. The awful sight roused her into a momentary possession of full consciousness; she beheld the lifeless body at her feet, the ruthless murderer at her side. Then she dashed herself against the soldier, and, before he could recover himself, she had seized his arm in a vise-like grasp. A loud cry of terrified amazement broke from the man's lips as he realized the peril of his situation. For an instant the two swayed back and forth upon the brink of the precipice, and then, Ine Tanaka, putting forth all her failing strength in a final effort, sprang out, dragging with her the murderer of her brother.

BOOK THIRD.

BISHOP PAOLI AND NIRADO SHIRO BEGIN THEIR LABORS.

I.

IN THE STORM AMONG THE DEAD.

HE STORM that had been all day gathering in the west burst at night-fall in full fury over sea and land. Long before it came, fitful, eddying gusts, sweeping over the face of the water, and marking their paths with broken lines of foam, heralded its approach. Van Neist, watching his chance, weighed anchor, and the *Spuyten Duyvil* glided swiftly amid the gathering blackness through the entrance to the harbor, casting her anchor again far up the bay before the city, where she would be safely sheltered from the fury of the coming gale.

These fierce storms, called typhoons, so frequent in the eastern seas, are usually accompanied by rain, though seldom by thunder and lightning. The wind blows in fierce gusts, and the rain is driven forward in almost horizontal lines, the roofs of houses are wrenched off, forests upturned, junks and the smaller sailing craft destroyed, and the largest ocean steamships im-

Paoli; the Last of the Missionaries. 89

periled by the mountainous waves that are heaped up and driven hither and thither by the mad fury of the wind. The staunch-built ships of our day are generally able to outride the storm, provided they are not caught too near land and driven ashore; but in the early days of European commerce in the East, shipwrecks were terribly frequent—so frequent, indeed, that it was considered a fortunate expedition if more than four ships out of a fleet of twelve returned from Japan.

In the gathering gloom that fell upon sea and land, like a shadow from the coming tempest, a small Japanese boat might have been seen, on the evening of which we are speaking, crossing the narrow strait of water lying between Takaboka and a little island nearer the mainland, called Nedzumi-shima, or Rat Island. There were two men at the oars, and they often cast anxious glances toward the fast approaching storm, and then would measure with their eyes the distance yet to be traversed before they reached the opposite beach.

"Faster, a little faster!" whispered the taller of the two. "The storm is at hand, and, once upon us, it will be impossible to make headway against it."

The two men bent to their oars with redoubled effort; but the wind was already strong against them, and, despite their most heroic labors, they made but slow progress. They rowed on in silence for a time, and then the younger man spoke:

"Do you think we will find any alive? and do you believe that we are safe in thus exposing ourselves? It is not yet wholly dark; we could still be seen from that hill where we last saw the soldiers who pursued our poor friends along the shore."

"Do not fear!" his companion returned. "They did their work too hastily to have killed them all outright.

We are safe. God is throwing around us the shelter of his storm, which our enemies will not dare to face."

"I am almost exhausted," panted the other. "But we are nearly there."

A fierce blast, accompanied by a heavy dash of rain, announced that the typhoon had at last burst upon them. The moaning of the sea, that had for some time been growing louder and more fearful, now changed into an angry hiss, and this again was quickly followed by the crashing and booming of the breakers upon the rocks on the other side of the island. The two men labored frantically at their oars, and, with an almost superhuman effort, they succeeded in running their boat upon the beach. Hastily drawing it up upon the sand, out of the reach of the waves, Bishop Paoli and Shiro, for they it was, turned and began to feel their way through the dense darkness, that had now settled down upon them, along the shore to the southward in the direction of the place where they knew the bodies of the slaughtered Christians must be lying.

"The roar of the storm is so deafening," shouted Shiro in the ear of his companion, "that we could not hear any cry for help. We are risking our own lives, and, I fear, to no purpose."

"Mother of God!" cried the bishop, as a terrific gust swept past them, deluging them with the spray that it had torn from the waves; "I verily thought it would loose my hold upon the rock and carry me away!"

"We can go no further," called out Shiro, who was a few feet in advance; we have reached the end of the ledge of rocks. I can feel only the perpendicular face of the cliff to our right, while to our left and in front I hear the rush of water."

Just as he spoke, there happened one of those rare occurrences in connection with a typhoon. A blinding flash of lightning flamed across the sky, illuminating the whole scene, and revealing to the two men a spectacle that neither of them could ever afterwards forget. Shiro had been right in his conjecture. They were on the extreme end of a ledge of rock skirting the base of the cliff. Right before them the sea had made a large indenture in the land, forming a sheltered cove, dry at low water but submerged at high tide or when a storm, like the present, drove the sea in upon the shore.

It had been from the rocks, overhanging this cove, that hundreds of the victims of the massacre had been flung, and their mangled bodies had been heaped up upon the bare rocks. The storm and the incoming tide had now flooded the place, and Paoli and Shiro, clinging to the side of the cliff, just out of reach of the waves, saw before them, in the dazzling gleam of the lightning, a vast cauldron of eddying, boiling, surging waters, foaming and hissing, ever rushing outward as if to escape into the open deep, and always hurled back by the mad, white-crested breakers pouring in from the sea. In the midst of this seething abyss of waters gleamed out the pale faces and stark forms of the hundreds who there that day had met their death, their bodies now the prey of the angry surges that dashed them hither and thither in their fierce eddying currents.

With the lightning's flash, the terrible sight blasted the eyes of the two beholders, and with the expiring gleam it again vanished into the blackness of the storm. Shuddering at what they had just beheld, Paoli and Shiro clung to the rock, while a gust of wind, fiercer than any that had preceded it, rolled a heavy wave up to their very feet.

"We must get out of here!" shouted the bishop, as

soon as there came a momentary lull in the uproar. "Another such a breaker may wash us off the rock—back, Shiro, back! I hear it coming! back!"

With a bound the two men plunged backward through the darkness. And none too soon; for, with a deafening crash, a huge wave dashed itself against the cliff at the very point where, a minute before, they had been clinging. Again the lightning glared out.

"This way," the bishop called to his companion. "Here seems to be an opening in the rocks that may afford us a shelter from the storm. Here, stand by me, and let us wait for another flash."

"It is useless for us to continue our search any further," said Shiro, as he and Paoli, holding each other's hand for the greater safety, pressed close to the face of the cliff. "We shall not be able to find any alive. Those who might possibly have survived their fall, have long ere this been drowned in the waves, and, even if some are beyond reach of the sea, they cannot live exposed to such a storm as this."

"I fear not," sadly replied the bishop. "I had hoped that we might come across some one who could have informed us of the whereabouts of our friends, and how things stand with our cause. But there is a flash, look quickly under the rock, Shiro! What did you see?"

"A cave! good father bishop," cried the young man excitedly. "And I fancied I saw a woman sitting at the farther end. Wait, I shall call," he added, and bowing down, he shouted into the opening he had discovered: "Fear not, we are Christians! Who art thou?"

"A servant of the Lord," came back the clearly spoken response.

II.

THE STORY OF A CHURCH MILITANT.

With a simultaneous cry of joy the two men hastened to enter the little cavern. As they did so, another flash of lightning lit up the woman's face, and Shiro, seizing Paoli's arm as if to support himself from falling, cried out to his companion:

"Good father, it is Ine Tanaka!"

"Ine Tanaka!" cried the bishop in turn, "she upon whom I bestowed the baptismal name of Phebe, your betrothed wife! Impossible."

"It is she! It is she!" returned the other, confidently. "You remember her portrait, which the good Father De Castro painted and sent to me? She who sat for that portrait is here before us in this cave."

The woman heard the conversation of the two men; a low cry broke from her lips.

"Speak quickly," she cried, in a voice trembling with intense emotion, no less than with physical pain and weakness. "In the name of our Lord, speak quickly! Only two men upon the whole earth could speak of me as ye have spoken—Father Francesco Paoli and Nirado Shiro."

"And we are they," returned Paoli, joyfully. "Then, indeed, Shiro is not mistaken. Thou art none other than Ine Tanaka."

The woman made no reply; she was weeping for very happiness. In silence the men waited; the bishop kneeling on the rocky floor of the cavern, breathed forth a fervent prayer of thanksgiving.

At length Ine spoke:

"And yet I live! Joy does not kill! The hour to which thy suffering church, O God, has for so long looked forward has come! Thou hast answered the prayers of thy people! Shiro, Thy appointed messenger of deliverance is here."

She spoke as if the effort gave her pain; she paused for a moment to gather strength, and then, with a pitiful wail, she continued:

"Ah, but I am dreaming, dreaming! I am bruised and wounded, faint and sick at heart with what I have seen and suffered, and the delirium of fever is upon me! the voices, methought I heard, were but the mocking delusions that haunt the maniac. Speak to me again, if flesh and blood ye are! reach forth thine hand, Nirado Shiro, and touch me! Tell me again that it is thou and that thou hast come back to thy brethren, and to me!"

"It is indeed I, dearest Ine," answered the young man, his voice choked and husky with the emotions he strove vainly to suppress. "I have come back to thee, never to leave thee again. I have come back to my brethren, to stand by their side until God giveth us the victory over our foes."

Another flash of lightning illuminated the little cavern and springing forward, Shiro clasped the wounded women gently in his arms. She was cold and trembling with weakness from loss of blood.

"Merciful Heaven!" cried Shiro, aghast. "Thy hands are cold as those of the dead, and is this blood that I feel upon thy arms? Thou art sorely hurt I fear."

"I know not," replied Ine, faintly. And the woman proceeded to tell the two men how she had avenged the murder her brother and, in conclusion, she said: "I must have lain out there unconscious for hours. The rain beating upon my face revived me, and, creeping on my hands and knees, I, by chance, found the entrance to this little cave. I came in here and laid myself down to rest or to die, as God might will. Your voices aroused me, and you know the rest."

"Heaven be praised for such heroism as thine," cried the bishop fervently.

"Another Judith, thou has been God's instrument of vengeance upon another Holofernes."

"Nay, speak not of it, good father," the woman rejoined, "yet the Lord did strengthen my heart and arm to smite His enemy. The soldier lies lifeless out yonder."

Again the lightning blazed out through the darkness, and Paoli and Shiro saw the pale face of the woman turned eagerly towards them as she strove to catch a glimpse of their features in the passing flash.

"Thou art disguised, good father," she said, as the darkness again fell upon them. "Thou art disguised as a Japanese, but I recognized thy face, notwithstanding."

"Let us hope, daughter, that the eyes of strangers may not prove so keen as thine. But rest, Ine, rest. Thou art exerting thyself too much, I fear."

"Nay, not so. It is balm to my wounds to hear thee speak. Thy words strengthen me. Tell me, good father, how you came to Japan."

In reply, the bishop narrated the story which the reader is already acquainted with, the woman listening with rapt attention.

"Tell us, dearest Ine," Shiro now broke in, "what has thus far been done for the deliverance of the church; for the good Bishop Paoli saw in his visions the battle between our brethren and their foes; and he beheld the host of the idolators fleeing before the banner of the cross."

"The story is one of thrilling triumph for the truth, marred for the first time by to-day's pitiless massacre of

God's people," Ine responded. "Nearly a month ago the Christians of Oyane, in Amakusa, gathered together one Sabbath morning to worship in the house of Jimboye, where the good Father Massilla, before his martyrdom, had set up the crucifix and a figure of the blessed Virgin. While our people were engaged in their devotions, they were surprised by the visit of six armed officers, who said that they had been sent thither with orders to destroy the image of the God of the Christians, and to forbid any further assemblages. A struggle ensued, our people throwing themselves between the officers and the crucifix and Virgin, to defend these from the touch of profane hands. In their efforts to do this a Christian was cut down by the sword of one of the officers, and immediately our brethren attacked their foes with great fury, slaying three of them, and compelling the others to seek safety in flight.

"When the Christians perceived that they had shed the blood of the government officials, and that, consequently, not only would this be used by their enemies as a pretext for a new persecution, but also that their own lives would pay the forfeit, they resolved to take up arms against their oppressors. They therefore issued a call to all the Christians of Amakusa to assemble at the village of Oyane, with arms and munitions of war. The rulers, finding their forces too few to cope with our friends, shut themselves up in Tomioka castle, and dispatched messengers to the Prince of Karatsu, begging for assistance. The prince himself, at the head of one thousand men, hastened to Amakusa.

"Our people saw the boats of the Karatsu men approaching the coast, and they laid a trap for the friends of their enemies. They made signals for the troops to land at the village of Muriki, where they prepared a

A CONFUSED CLAMOR OF VOICES AROSE IN THE GOVERNMENT BOAT.—*See Page* 103.

great entertainment for the prince and his followers in the grounds of the Buddhist temple. They conducted themselves with so much cunning dissimulation that the infidel never suspected the trap into which they had fallen. They ate and drank and made merry until midnight; and then, piling up their arms in the temple, they sank into a drunken slumber. Noiselessly our brethren removed such of the weapons as they could obtain without awakening the enemy, and then, firing the temple in a dozen places, they burst in upon the sleeping troops. The advantage was all upon their side, and before those of the Karatsu men who still had arms could lay their hands upon them, a large number of their comrades were cut down. For almost an hour the fight raged with great fury about the burning temple, until, just as day was breaking, the government troops succeeded in cutting their way out of the little village, and began their retreat over the country to Tomioka Castle, the Christians pursuing them to the very gates."

"A glorious victory!" exclaimed Shiro.

"And our people, daughter?" inquired Paoli. "Was the loss of life great upon our side?"

"Only fifty men killed and about twice that number wounded, while of the one thousand of the enemy scarcely two hundred made their escape.

"Last week the Christians in Shimabara maddened beyond further endurance by the cruelty of Prince Matsukura, and inspired by the success of their brethren across the bay in Amakusa, refused to pay their taxes. The Prince dispatched six hundred men to accompany the tax-gatherers, with orders to arrest all who refused to pay, and to bring them before him in his castle in Shimabara. Night before last this force was surprised in one of the mountain passes, and cut to pieces by a body of Christians."

"Your story, Ine," said Paoli, "is indeed marvellous in our ears. The future of our cause is as bright as are the promises of God. But, friends," he continued, rising to as nearly a standing position as the overhanging rocks would allow, and peering out into the storm, "we are in need of some safer retreat than this little island can afford when daylight and a calmer sea brings the throng of curious sightseers from the city, and, as soon as possible, we must leave the island."

III.

TAKABOKA AND VENGEANCE, IN THE NAME OF THE LORD."

Bishop Paoli, creeping out from under the rock that had sheltered them, made a careful scrutiny of the sky.

"The storm will soon be over," he called back to Ine and Shiro. "The stars are shining through the rifts in the clouds, and I fancy I can see the dim outline of the mountains to the east. The waves are still running high, and will continue to do so, I presume, for hours to come. Dangerous as it seems, we must soon make the attempt to cross over to the mainland."

The little party waited, however, until it was nearly midnight, and then the two men, gently lifting the wounded woman, bore her to the place where they had left their boat some hours before, the faint light cast by the stars enabling them to make their way without much difficulty over the rocks. Placing Ine in the little cabin, and making her as comfortable as they could, they pushed off.

Under the strong, steady strokes of Paoli and Shiro

their *sampan* made rapid progress. The wind, that had now settled down to merely a brisk breeze, was in their favor, and by hoisting the sail their speed was greatly increased. When they were about half way across, Shiro suddenly seized the bishop's arm and said in a whisper:

"Look yonder, good bishop. Is not that a boat approaching us on our right?"

Paoli gazed intently for a moment in the direction indicated. A boat it certainly was. Its course was at right angles to their own, and it was heading toward the city. As it rose high on the crest of a wave, he perceived that it was full of soldiers, their polished armor and long spears being now distinctly visible in the dim starlight.

The two men rested for a minute on their oars, closely watching the hostile boat. Then Shiro addressed his companion, speaking in a whisper that the wounded woman in the little cabin might not hear:

"They see us, for look! their faces are turned this way! We cannot escape them. What shall we do?"

Paoli seemed not to hear the words of the younger man. He spoke and his low, rapid voice was like the voice of one communing with himself:

"Yonder boat is overloaded. There are, at least, thirty men in it, when there ought not to be more than twenty. The three rowers are hardly able to keep it afloat in this heavy sea. Moreover, they have no sail, and are making but slow progress."

"Very true," assented Shiro, as if the remark had been addressed to him. "With the wind in another quarter, we could easily make our escape."

The Jesuit laid his hand on the young man's arm; his eyes blazed with suppressed wrath, but his voice was steady enough:

"Who are those soldiers, Shiro? Let me tell you. They are the murderers of our brethren. Shiro, when our enemies have been placed in our power shall we allow them to escape?"

"No!" cried the other aloud, startling Ine in the little cabin. "No! *Yaso-Maria*, Takaboka and vengeance, in the name of the Lord!"

"What is it, good father!" inquired Ine, anxiously. "What is it, Shiro? You have been whispering together; there is some danger threatening us! Tell me what it is?"

In a few words Shiro informed her of the situation.

"Good Father Paoli, what do you intend to do?"

"With God's help, daughter, we shall send those merciless murderers to the bottom of the sea!"

Under the brisk breeze, the little boat, bearing the bishop's party, was now fairly flying over the heavy swells, shooting from the crest of one wave, and falling with a loud splash against the rising bosom of the next. A short distance ahead, and still a little to the right, the larger craft, carrying the government troops, was laboring slowly through the high waves that continually threatened to swamp it. In a minute or two more the two boats would cross each other's course at right angles, and a collision seemed unavoidable. Standing by the side of the little cabin, Shiro now hailed the government boat:

"Boat ahead, ahoy! Who are you?"

"Prince Kaneko and his retainers!" came the reply.

"Where are you from?"

"We have been at Inasa, hunting out the rebel Christians. But beware, there! You'll run us down!"

The two boats were now alarmingly close together. A sudden gust of wind dashed the Jesuit's *sampan* forward with furious speed. Paoli stood erect, his tall form towering up in the dim starlight like some avenging Nemesis. The kindly expression that his face habitually wore had disappeared, and a terrible look of vengeful hatred distorted his countenance. Guiding the course of his flying boat with the long scull oar that he held in his iron grasp, his eyes never for a moment left the fated craft before him. He was working his boat so as to strike the enemy's in the middle, that he might capsize it. Again Shiro called out:

"Have you any prisoner's aboard?"

"No! Be careful there! We are overloaded. Bear off! bear off! Who are you?"

"Christians! and the avengers of our murdered friends! I am Paoli, returned to Japan! *Yaso-Maria*, Takaboka and vengeance, in the name of the Lord!"

A confused clamor of voices arose in the government boat. Some of the soldiers sprang for their arms, others to the assistance of the rowers in the vain attempt to swing their craft around out of the course of the oncoming danger. In the commotion the boat careened and threatened to capsize. At that moment, as they sank into the trough of the sea, the *sampan* of the two daring Christians appeared on the crest of the wave above them. For one breathless moment it seemed to hang there, and then, with a swift plunge, it dashed down on the overladen and struggling craft below.

There was a crash of boat upon boat, mingled with a cry of terror from the soldiers, and a shout of triumph from Paoli and Shiro, as they beheld the government boat disappear beneath the waves, and saw the water about them filled with their struggling foes. In another moment their own *sampan* had righted itself and was bearing them quickly away from the scene of death.

IV.

AMONG FRIENDS.

"So perish all the enemies of the Church of Japan!" exclaimed Paoli, looking back at the place where the encounter had occurred.

"Will not some be able to reach the shore?" Ine asked.

"Possibly the *sendos** may swim to land," replied Shiro. "They are as you know at home in the water; but not one of the soldiers will escape. Their heavy armor will soon drag them under in such a sea as this."

"And now," said the bishop, his countenance and voice assuming their accustomed gentleness, "we must decide upon a place of refuge. There are many Christian families along the shore, but we shall have to exercise caution in approaching them lest we arouse the suspicions of their heathen neighbors."

"Let me guide you, good father," broke in Ine. "My sister lives at Kayaki, a little village but a short distance down the coast. Turn your course thither, and we shall soon be among friends."

In a short time the *sampan* of the three Christians was opposite the place the woman had mentioned, and when they had run in near enough to the land for the eye to distinguish objects in the faint starlight, Ine, with Shiro's assistance, emerged from the cabin and closely scanned the shore ahead.

"There!" she said, "to our right you see a steep cliff, and beyond it a little valley running down from the hills. Put the boat upon the beach at that point, and we shall be within a short distance of the house to which I shall take you."

* Boatmen.

In the course of a few minutes they were at the place indicated, and not very far back from the water a small house, half hidden beneath some wide-spreading trees was faintly discernible. The two men lifted Ine out of the boat, and set her upon her feet upon the shore, but she was unable to move.

"My limbs feel benumbed," she said, "and I am too weak to stand. Ah, that terrible fall!"

"We must make haste and get thee where thou canst have rest and care," said the bishop, "but are you sure, daughter, that this is indeed your sister's house? And are all connected with the place faithful to our cause? Remember, Ine, there is much at stake."

"Fear not!" the woman replied," this is the place, and you may depend upon all here. This household has been rich in martyrs for the faith. They will shield us with their own lives if it should be necessary."

"Then are we fortunate indeed! But do you rest awhile, Ine, and Shiro, you remain with her. We must proceed with the utmost caution. I shall go up to the house and reconnoitre. If the family be known to the infidel to be zealous Christians, it may be that the government has set a watch upon them. It will be best, therefore, to move carefully."

When he had said this, Bishop Paoli crept stealthily away in the direction of the house, concealing himself in the shadow of the trees. Cautiously approaching the dwelling, he fancied that he heard the murmur of voices from within. As he stood listening, he saw a dark shadow flit along the wall of the house. Paoli at once divined the situation. "Some Christians have met here to-night to consult together," he thought," and that lurking fellow is a government spy."

Creeping noiselessly forward toward the figure before

him until he was sufficiently close, the Jesuit sprang upon the spy and with a quick movement, hurled him to the earth, pinioning his arms across his breast with one hand, while with the other he held a dagger at his throat. The fellow's shriek of terrified surprise at being thus so unexpectedly assailed, brought Shiro running from the shore, fearing the bishop had been attacked. At the same time three or four men rushed out of the dwelling, armed with swords, and thinking that the two figures that they saw bending over the prostrate spy were enemies seizing some friend, they fell upon them with drawn weapons, and had not Shiro shouted : " Hold there, we are friends ; this fellow is a government spy !" it is hard to say what might have been the result.

However, the men, now reinforced to the number of a dozen or more, quickly surrounded the three strangers, and thus making sure that they had them in their power, seemed disposed to listen.

"Will some one bring a rope and help me to bind this fellow?" panted the bishop, still holding on to the struggling spy.

There was a moment's consultation among the men. Then one ran into the house and brought forth the desired rope. Two of the bystanders came forward and assisted Paoli and Shiro in securely binding the prisoner. When this was done, the Jesuit stood up and spoke to the still doubtful men :

"You are, apparently, uncertain as to how you should receive us. My companion has told you that we are friends, and so we are. But it is not necessary that you take our word only, for there is another person with us— a young woman, whom some of you know. You will find her down on the beach. If the master of the house is here, and will go to her, he will be rejoiced to find that a friend, whom he thought was killed in to-day's massacre, is still alive, though sorely hurt and needing care."

An exclamation of surprise ran through the group of listeners, and after another short consultation together, three men started off in the direction of the beach. Soon those waiting at the house heard a glad cry of recognition, and the sound of voices in rapid conversation, and then silence again ensued. In a short time the men were seen returning, bearing Ine with them.

"Take her into the house, Oyama and Naro; her sister is mourning her as dead. Joyful, indeed, will be their meeting!" Then, after the two men had disappeared in the house with the woman, the speaker turned to Paoli and Shiro and said heartily: "Brethren, we welcome you in the name of the Lord. My sister did not give me your names, but she said you were Christians whom we could trust. We thought at first that you were enemies, and, therefore, we came out against you with swords in our hands. In these days of persecution and bloodshed, we must needs suspect every man until he proves himself a friend of the faith."

"I would counsel you, brethren," the bishop responded, "not merely to suspect, but to watch as well. Had I not chanced along just as I did, and caught this fellow with his ear glued to a chink in your wall, a few hours hence might have witnessed an end to your suspecting anybody."

"We ought, indeed, to have stationed sentries, and have always done so heretofore. We thought, however, that no one would be out in such a storm as was the one to-night."

The speaker, who appeared to be the master of the house, now gave some orders in a whisper to some of the men standing by, and immediately two of them seized the prisoner and dragged him into the dwelling. Once again their host addressed the bishop and Shiro.

"Pray come within, brethren, there are many of our people here to-night, and they will be glad to meet you and to hear any report you may have for them."

Shiro shot a quick glance at Paoli. The latter perceived it, and, as they were passing in together through the open doorway, he whispered in Spanish to his companion:

"Prepare, Shiro, to take thy place as leader of our brethren. Sooner than we hoped for has the time come."

V.

THE CAVE-CHAPEL OF KAYAKI.

Once within the house, Shiro looked around to see Ine, but she was nowhere in sight. Even the men, who had entered just before them, had also disappeared, and evidently they had taken the prisoner with them. The master of the house closed the door securely, and then taking up a small oil-lamp, asked the Jesuit and Shiro to follow him.

"Are you a Christian, and have you never heard of the cave-chapel of Kayaki?" said he, in answer to the questioning look of the younger man.

"I have often heard of it," responded Paoli. "But I never suspected to-night that Ine was guiding us to it. Have the enemy, then, never discovered it?"

"Our people are faithful; for ten years we have worshipped here in safety."

As their guide spoke, he raised a trap-door in the floor, revealing what appeared like a small cellar cut in the solid rock. The party descended into this, and when the door above was closed, their host applied his shoulder to one of the walls of the cellar and immediately the rock began to roll back, disclosing a long passageway leading to the entrance of a large cave-chamber beyond.

"We are having a conference to-night," said the guide. "A few of us, however, were up in the house when that fellow's shriek called us out. We have been discussing what course to take in the present state of affairs."

Neither the bishop nor Shiro made answer to this information, for each was too busy with his own thoughts. Hurrying along the passage, the party soon emerged into the chapel, a large, lofty cavern, fitted up with a high altar, crucifix, and other paraphernalia of worship. The immense chamber was filled with an assembly of men and women. At the entrance those who had the captured spy in custody were awaiting the coming of the others. Here, too, in the shadow of a huge stalagmite that rose from the floor of the cavern, the bishop and Shiro paused:

"Let us wait here a moment," Paoli said ; "and will you," he continued, addressing himself to three of the men, "take this spy into some side-chamber, and learn from him all you can? Listen!" he added, addressing Shiro in a whisper, "that's Ine's voice ; she is speaking to the people."

The bishop and Shiro stepped out from behind the rock that concealed them. It was as the former had said : Ine was addressing the assembly. She had been placed on a high dais by the side of the altar, and half sitting on a broad mat, and half reclining in the arms of a woman, whom the two men recognized, by the likeness of her features to those of Ine, to be her sister, the wounded woman was telling the listening people the terrible story of the past day. As she concluded her narration a great sob of mingled grief and anger swept over the assembly.

"*Yaso Maria!*" cried one. "The infidel must be made to suffer for this! Let us rise in arms against them!"

"Nay, nay! What can we, a handful against millions, do?" interposed another. "Better to cling to our faith and to die, if need be; but never let it be said that the Christians of Kayaki rebelled against their rulers."

"Friend, hast thou forgotten so soon the good Father Paoli's teachings?" responded the first speaker. "Did he not tell us that the church had the first claim on our obedience, and that it is our duty to oppose and overthrow those who deny her authority? How much the more, then, ought we to rise up against a government that has leagued itself with hell for the destruction of our holy faith?"

"Ay, and to set up Christian governors to rule over us in the places of these confederates of Satan, who count us but wild beasts to be hunted down and butchered!" exclaimed a third, springing to his feet. "O! fellow Christians! would that our good father, Francesco Paoli, who for so many years was leader of our cause, were here to-night!"

"And he that is to deliver his brethren, and rule the people of his nation," broke in a woman's voice from a distant part of the chapel, " Nirado Shiro, our promised leader—would that he, too, were here!"

The effect that the mention of the names of Paoli and Shiro had upon the people was electrical. Women's sobs and prayers mingled with the deep murmurs of approval that broke from the lips of the men. The two watchers by the rock gazed with anxious interest upon the assembly before them, but their faces betrayed nothing of the emotions that thrilled their souls.

"We are forgetting Ine," said the man who had spoken first. Then, turning to the woman, he added:

"Perhaps you have still other tidings for us."

Ine had caught sight of the bishop and Shiro, where they stood by the entrance. Paoli made a few rapid motions with his hand, signifying that he wished her to call him before the people. The woman smiled back an assent, and again addressed the people before her.

"I have, indeed, other tidings for you, dear friends; a few hours ago I lay at the foot of the cliff on yonder island. Around me, thick as the leaves that strew the earth beneath a winter forest, were the mangled bodies of the Christian multitude that had been flung by the savage infidel from the heights above. Returning to consciousness, I crept away from the ghastly scene, and sought shelter from the storm in a little grotto beneath the overhanging rocks. Whom think ye Heaven sent thither to my rescue? Ah, ye cannot guess; and yet methinks ye can. It was but a minute ago that I heard one of you pronounce his name; a name feared beyond every other by the enemies of the church; a name precious as life to the thousands who have learned to call him their father in the Lord."

"Father Paoli! Father Paoli!" was the cry that burst from the lips of hundreds throughout the assembly. "Father Paoli hath returned! is now in Japan! Is it not so, Ine?" and the excited people rose to their feet, and would have crowded around the dais on which she was reclining, had not the young woman waved them back as she replied to their eager questions:

"Be seated, I pray you, good friends. Father Paoli hath indeed returned to us. He was one of the two who rescued me on the island; he came to Kayaki in the boat that brought me hither; he is here with you in this chapel."

Before Ine had ceased speaking, Paoli was standing on

the dais by her side, and as the loud, joyful cry of recognition which greeted him echoed through the rocky recesses of the cavern, he stretched out his hands to invoke silence, and then, dropping on his knees, he broke forth into prayer. Into the troubled souls of the now kneeling men and women before him the words of his supplication breathed the spirit of a new life. The prayer itself was an impassioned psalm of praise and thanksgiving for the Divine mercy and goodness that had again brought together the pastor and his hunted flock; a trustful pleading for strength in the coming hour of trial, for faith and patience in the midst of suffering.

Without change in attitude of body or tone of voice, the bishop turned from his prayer to Heaven to an address to the still kneeling people.

"Dearly beloved children, now is not the time for me or for you to speak of the joy of this reunion. It behooveth us to put self aside and to be up and doing in the name of the Lord. And what we do must be done quickly. We are oppressed; we are persecuted; we are hunted down and slaughtered. Day and night the sword of the pagan is reddened with the blood of our brethren. The stake, the cross, the living grave, the fiery mouths of volcanoes have witnessed again and again the dying testimony of the Christian martyr. The midnight surprise and massacre have blotted out whole villages. It is counted an honor among the idolators for a man to be known as one who has slain his Christian. Brethren, what shall ye do? To-morrow, or the next day, or the day following, your turn may come, as to-day came the turn of the Inasa Christians. I bring you this night the summons to arm yourselves, while yet there is time; to leave your homes and to flee for your lives to the stronghold of our

SHIRO HAD STOLEN NOISELESSLY TO THE DAIS, AND WAS NOW STANDING BY THE SIDE OF PAOLI.—*See Page* 115.

brethren at Arima. The gallant little army that has there unfurled the banner of the Lord needs your assistance. Fear not, our cause shall conquer. I heard you here to-night speak of him who is ordained of Heaven to be your leader and deliverer, the destroyer of your foes, and the first Christian ruler of Japan. What if I should tell you that Nirado Shiro was on his way back to his native land ? Would ye not be armed and ready to welcome his return ? And what would ye say if I told you that he was already in Japan ? Ah, would ye not hasten to his side to follow whithersoever he might lead ? But what will ye do when I tell you that Nirado Shiro is even now in Kayaki, within sound of my voice, in this very chapel, standing here before you ?"

An indescribable scene followed the Jesuit's closing words. The people had arisen from their kneeling posture; the speaker himself was upon his feet. Shiro had stolen noiselessly to the dais, and was standing by the side of Paoli. As soon as the first moment of breathless amazement was over, and the people fully realized the situation, neither the bishop's attempts to maintain order nor Shiro's shouts to them to remain seated prevailed to curb the outburst of enthusiastic rejoicing that took possession of all.

Paoli leaned forward and, grasping Shiro's hand, whispered :

"Said I not that thy time had come ? But now do thou speak to the people, as soon as quiet is restored, while I go to discover what our friends have learned from the spy."

A considerable time elapsed before the excitement had subsided ; and Shiro, as he finally rose to speak, perceived the bishop approaching him. At a signal from Paoli, Shiro descended from the dais, and the two men were engaged for a few minutes in a whispered consultation by the side of the high altar. A death-like silence now pervaded the assemblage, and every eye was turned upon Paoli and Shiro with anxious eagerness. Soon the young man again ascended the dais and began to harangue the assembly. He dwelt upon his own divine appointment as the chief who was destined to lead his brethren to victory over their foes, the unprovoked persecution of the church that was raging throughout the nation, the present crisis, the necessity of a revolution, and the certainty of success. His fiery eloquence and impassioned earnestness swept away all opposition to an open declaration of war. He called upon those who favored a revolt to rise, and, like one person, the whole assemblage sprang to their feet amidst the wildest excitement.

"And now, in conclusion," said Shiro, "let me tell you what we have just learned from a spy, whom the officials sent hither to watch our movements. The governor has been seizing the Christians of Tokitsu, and even now more than three hundred of them are lying in the city prisons. To-morrow night it is his purpose to burn and crucify these, together with all others that may in the meantime be discovered. The day of their execution is to be declared a public holiday. Brethren, shall it be that we will stand tamely by and allow this immolation of our fellow-Christians to be accomplished? It is in our power to raise a force strong enough to rescue our friends and to bear them off to Arima. Shall it not be done?"

Again a loud shout of approval echoed through the cavern-chapel, and a chorus of cries went up from the lips of the assembled multitude:

"*Yaso-Maria!* To the rescue! To the rescue! Woe to the infidel!"

BOOK FOURTH.

THE STRANGE ADVENTURES OF MARMION BEAUMONT.

I.

MYNHEER VAN SYLT HAS SOMETHING TO SAY.

THE morning after the storm dawned clear and beautiful on the ancient city of Nagasaki. Not a cloud marred the deep blue of the sky, not a breath of air stirred to break the tranquil calm that rested upon the town and bay and encircling hills. Both foreign and native dwellers in the Nagaski of the seventeenth century, like their successors of our own day, believed that theirs was the fairest spot on earth. This reputation for beauty the place has always maintained. With a bay surpassing the far famed one of Naples, and equalled only by that of Rio Janeiro, and inclosed by towering hills, the green loveliness of which sheds the charm of perpetual spring upon the landscape, her surroundings render Nagasaki peerless for situation.

So thought Marmion Beaumont, as he stood on the deck of the *Spuyten Duyvil*, this calm, bright morning, catching the first rays of the sun as it appeared above the range of hills east of the city. The greater part of the quaint old town lay on the northeastern shore of the bay, running back into a broad valley, shaped somewhat like a horse-shoe. Skirting the eastern boundary of this valley, and a considerable elevation above the rest of the city, Beaumont saw a long succession of temples, all apparently of recent erection. The first officer, Van Sylt, was just then passing by, shouting out orders to the seamen aloft, who were spreading out the sails to dry. Van Sylt, noticing that Beaumont was looking at the distant line of temples, said to him :

"You are looking at those heathen temples, I take it, Mynheer Beaumont. Ah, the sight of them, sir, makes sore the eyes of a good Christian !" Here Van Sylt crossed himself devoutly. "Why, Mynheer, when I used to visit Nagasaki twenty-five years ago there was not a temple to be seen in the entire city. The place was as much Christian as any town of like size in Europe."

"The city, then, I take it, has lapsed into heathenism," said Beaumont.

"Just so, sir," the other replied, "the people that now inhabit the city are filled with the bitterest hatred against all that savors of our religion. The former Christian population being entirely destroyed, the government has filled their places with persons who have distinguished themselves as successful oppressors of the hated foreign faith and zealous adherents of the old paganism."

"It is a terrible story."

"Ay, ay, sir, it's the truth you are saying, and, Mynheer, yesterday, when that poor fellow fought his way up to us, and cried out for us to help them that were Christians just like ourselves, it made my heart sick, sir, not to be able to do something for them. It seems to me, sir, that we Christian men were worse than pagans to stand there and to see all that slaughtering of helpless folk go on unhindered."

"You must remember," rejoined Beaumont, who, in truth, felt in regard to the matter not very differently from Van Sylt himself, but considered it incumbent upon him to speak otherwise, "Master Van Sylt, you must remember that Captain Van Neist is in the employ of a company, whose interests might have been greatly injured by any such rash procedure on his part."

"Perhaps so, sir, perhaps so," and Beaumont detected a trace of impatience in the officer's voice, "but, Mynheer Beaumont, let me tell you of a resolution that I have made. Perhaps, sir, I was wrong in making such a vow as I did this morning, but, sir, I could not help it, and as soon as it was made I felt easier here;" and the big fellow laid his large, brawny hand over his heart. "Yes, sir, much easier." Then, after a pause, he continued: "You see, Mynheer, those awful sights of yesterday kept coming back to me all night, and I could not sleep. The noise of the wind seemed to my ears just like the shrieks of those poor women and children we saw pitched from that big rock down there into the sea; and then the voice of that youth, who called on us Christian men to help him, kept ringing in my ears after the storm had gone, and I saw his brave looking face staring up at me, just as he looked yesterday, when those savage murderers cut him down. Well, sir, I got to thinking over the matter, and I thought something began a-talking to me, and it said: 'Van Sylt, do you think that you took up your cross yesterday, like a good Catholic, when you stood there and saw the merciless idolators butchering your brothers and sisters in Christ?' I said nothing in reply, and the voice went on :

"'You were a coward, Van Sylt, and not worthy the name of Christian. It was your duty to put away all thoughts of self, and taking your good sword, to jump into that youth's boat, and to die fighting by his side.'

"I confess, sir, that the voice gave utterance to just what I had myself been thinking upon the subject, and so I closed my eyes right there where I lay, and I said :

"'O, Lord, hear my petition and forgive my great sin ! O, Christ, I am not worthy to be called by Thy blessed name ! O Holy Mother, register my vow in heaven ! I promise to no more look on and behold the slaughter or persecution of Christian folk without interposing my life in their behalf. So help me God !'

"Then, sir, as soon as I had made this vow, it seemed as if a great load was taken off my heart ; I heard those terrible shrieks and saw that youth's pale, pleading face no more. I fell asleep, sir, as soundly and as sweetly as I used to do, when a child, in my mother's house at Ryswick."

Beaumont looked keenly at the officer as he finished his narration, and he was fully convinced of the man's earnestness. In his own way, Van Sylt was as sincere as were Shiro and Paoli, and the Englishman was satisfied that if occasion should call for the sacrifice the vow would be kept, regardless of consequences.

"Master Van Sylt," he said, earnestly, "I trust you counted well what such a vow may possibly cost you ? I doubt not but that before the *Spuyten Duyvil* leaves Japan we shall be called upon to witness again, and more than once, perhaps, sights similar to that which horrified us all yesterday."

"Yes," returned the other, slowly, "it is quite possible we may; yet, sir, I do not regret what I have done."

"And have I really found you at last, Mynheer Beaumont?" broke in the captain's cheery voice behind the speakers, "I have been searching for you. Heer Santvoort, with the company's agent from Hirado, is coming off to the ship, and I need hardly say you are longing to stretch your legs a bit on shore. So I shall bespeak an invitation for you to dine to-day at the trading-house."

"Many thanks, indeed," responded the young man, "I shall be highly pleased to go."

"Come with me, then," Van Neist returned, "the *sampan* is alongside by this time; let us go forward and meet our visitors," and linking his arm within that of the Englishman, the captain and Beaumont hastened to the gangway, where a group of officers were already gathered in readiness to receive the two merchants.

II.

THE PLOT OF KANSHIN, THE DEPUTY.

Never to forget an injury, never to forgive the perpetrator, never to rest content until revenge had been obtained—this was an important part of the code of honor prevailing among the *Samurai* of Japan. Kanshin, the governor's deputy, by both natural disposition and education, was a typical *Samurai*. The humiliation he had suffered at the hands of Captain Van Neist, though nothing more than a just rebuke to his insolent bullying, aroused all the savage thirst for revenge his ferocious nature was capable of. On the way back from the ship, his mind was busy with schemes for the accomplishment of his supreme desire, and, by the time he had reached the governor's palace in the heart of the city, he had decided on a course of action which needed but his superior's sanction to insure him the attainment of his wished-for vengeance. Entering the building in his stocking feet, the deputy passed noiselessly through room after room until he reached the governor's audience-chamber. This was a larger and more richly finished room than the others, and was embellished with many articles of European manufacture, that had found their way hither through the agency of the Dutch traders. At one side of the apartment the floor was raised a foot or more above the level of the remainder of the room, and here, dressed in the rich official robes of his station, sat Lord Oda, Governor of Nagasaki, engaged in conversation with two men, who, from the profusion of decorations that covered their armor, were evidently military officers of a high rank. Such they were; one being General Itakura, the commander-in-chief of the government troops assembled at Shimabara, for the suppression of the Christians, and the other, Prince Ogasawara, the second officer in command.

The three men were seated on the mats that covered the floor of the room, a small charcoal brazier before them, and close beside Ogasawara stood the ever present tea service; for in Japan nothing, from the most frivolous neighborhood gossip to the weightiest affairs of state, can be discussed without oft repeated libations to the great god, Tea.

As Kanshin opened the sliding doors that separated the audience-chamber from the adjoining room, and, perceiving the guests, he prostrated himself on the floor in a low obeisance, then, rising to a sitting posture, he awaited in silence the will of the governor. Oda and his guests acknowledged the deputy's low bow with a slight inclination of the head and continued their conversation. General Itakura was speaking:

"As I said a moment ago, the rebellion had already become too formidable for the small military force then in Kiushiu to subdue. Nearly all of our princes were in Yedo, and their principal retainers were with them. As soon as the insurrection occurred in Amakusa therefore, Terazawa dispatched messengers to the Shogun acquainting him of the fact. I was present in the conference of the Kiushiu princes that followed. The prevailing opinion among those present was that the trouble had been caused by the tyranny of Terazawa and Matsukura, and that they, in order to shield themselves, pretended that the uprising was wholly due to the rebellious spirit of their Christian subjects."

"These dogs of Christians have always been a thorn in our side," cried Oda, savagely; "and how could our princes mistake so concerning the cause of the trouble!"

"They knew both the Lord of Amakusa and the Lord of Shimabara to be violent men," said Ogasawara, with a quiet smile. "And more than once have complaints of burdensome taxation come from their subjects."

"Be that as it may," General Itakura resumed, "it was decided in the council that the Kiushiu princes, with their retainers, should hasten to the scene of the disturbance, and that I should be entrusted with the leadership of the campaign for the suppression of the insurrection. A week ago I arrived in Shimabara, and I found Matsukura and his retainers feasting and drinking in the shelter of their castle, the rebels having driven them to its very walls and compelled them to close their gates. He had done nothing to check the progress of the rebellion. During the past week a few unimportant engagements have been fought, but, owing to the advantage of position which they hold, the rebels have generally been the victors. Yesterday morning they met their first reverse. A detachment, under two of their leaders, made an attack on Tomioka castle, and was repulsed with considerable loss."

"I heard," said the governor, "that the Christians are repairing Hara Castle, with the intention of making it their stronghold. Have they yet entered it?"

"They have," Ogasawara replied. "And, in addition, they hold the whole line of country from Mt. Unzen to the castle, and out to the small islands in the gulf. They have a strong position."

"And that is the very reason why we must have foreign artillery," Itakura added. "I understand that the ship which has just arrived in the outer bay is the heaviest armed merchantman that comes to Japan. She would, therefore, most admirably suit our purpose. With her help, our fleet of war-junks could dislodge the Christians from their defenses on the islands, and then bombard the castle from the sea, while our army storms it from the land side. No means must be left untried to secure that ship."

"You may depend that no effort shall be spared to secure her," Lord Oda responded promptly, and then, with a significant smile, he added: "Without her captain and officers if that be at all possible."

General Itakura bent an approving look upon the governor. "Be it as you say. The ship can be used to greater advantage if she should be wholly under our control. Nevertheless, let a sufficient number of the crew remain to navigate her. We might otherwise have trouble."

"It shall be as you wish," Oda replied briefly, and

then, as his guests arose to take their departure, he continued: "Can I not prevail upon you to remain until to-morrow night? You, of course, have heard of the contemplated execution of the Christian prisoners now lying in our dungeon. If you stay, I can promise you a spectacle, the equal of which has not yet been seen in Japan. More than three hundred of the accursed *jashiu mon*,* after we are through with them to-morrow night, will no longer menace our peace and safety."

"You are kind to invite us," Itakura responded, "but it would be impossible for us to remain. Within a day or two Prince Nabeshima of Kai is expected at Shimabara, and, as soon as he arrives, I am intending to move upon the enemy. In the meantime, preparations must be made."

"Nabeshima will be here to-morrow evening," the governor said. "He and his body-guard are to form my escort to the execution."

"Indeed! Ah, that Nabeshima is destined to be one of our nation's greatest warriors. It would have pleased you had you seen the joyful excitement among the troops when they heard, the other day, that the Prince of Kai was to take part in the campaign. No leader in Japan so fills the soldier's ideal of a brave, gentle, and chivalrous chieftain as does Lord Nabeshima."

"He seems to me to be too gentle for the sort of work we are now engaged in," Oda said, with a shrug. "He would spare the women and children of this hated *jashui mon*, and that, we know, would be folly if we desire to rid the country of the pernicious doctrines of the barbarian priests."

"I like him not," Ogasawara remarked, with a frown. "Lord Nabeshima may be brave and courteous, but

* Corrupt sect.

wherever he is, his excessive praise and flattery of his men make the other princes' retainers look for the same from their lords, and be dissatisfied when they do not receive it."

"I did not mean to raise a discussion respecting the military character of the Prince of Kai," interposed General Itakura, with a smile. "I am aware that there are persons that do not look upon him in the manner in which I am inclined to do. But, Lord Ogasawara, we must be on our way at once; the afternoon is already far spent, and a long journey lies before us."

The guests, with many profound bows, now took their departure. As soon as they had passed out, Oda turned to the deputy and motioned him to draw near.

"Thy report, Kanshin!" he said, briefly, pushing the tea-service toward him.

The deputy, in a subdued voice, and with frequent low bows, recounted his experience aboard the *Spuyten Duyvil*. When he had finished, he once again prostrated himself on the floor before his superior, who scarcely acknowledged the obeisance, so deeply buried in thought was he, not, however, over Kanshin's report that the two Japanese passengers aboard the *Spuyten Duyvil* had escaped to the shore, but over an endeavor to discover some way to secure the coveted vessel.

"Your Excellency!" It was Kanshin who spoke, and once again his forehead was bowed to the mat on which he was sitting.

"Well, what is it?" Oda inquired, absently.

"A few weeks ago Gonroku, the robber-chieftain, was captured. He is now in the city dungeon awaiting his execution that is to take place the day after to-morrow."

The governor turned a frowning countenance on the deputy. What had Gonroku, the robber, to do with the problem that was now perplexing his brain? With another low bow, the speaker continued:

"Which would you prefer: that Gonroku have his life and you the foreign ship which General Itakura has just commanded you to secure, or that Gonroku die and the ship be lost to you?"

Oda was now interested.

"I do not comprehend you, Kanshin," he said, his amazement plainly visible in the look that he turned upon his companion. "What relation can a prisoner in our dungeon have to the capture of the *Spuyten Duyvil?*"

Kanshin was silent for a minute or two. His naturally unprepossessing countenance wore a look of crafty cunning.

"I have a plan," he said, at length, "that will place the ship in your possession. Will your Excellency hear it?"

The governor laid his hand on the deputy's shoulder.

"I shall gladly welcome any scheme that will bring about what you say; and, mark you, Kanshin, if your plan be successful, rich shall be your reward."

Kanshin's evil eyes glittered. He was thinking of the humiliation that he had suffered at the hands of Van Neist, and a look of ferocious hatred swept over his savage face. Bowing low, he said:

"It is for a reward; but, perhaps, not such a one as you may think, that I have devised this plan."

"Your reward will be what you wish," Oda returned, divining by the expression on the deputy's countenance what that reward was to be. "Only go on and explain your plan. What is it?"

"The barbarian captain—may the wrath of the eight hundred thousand gods of Japan seize him!—is now angered against us. Early to-morrow morning I must go back and apologize for drawing my sword upon him this afternoon."

"What is the object of this?"

"To conciliate the foreign devil withal, and to make your victory over him the more certain."

"Proceed."

"Then—" But the deputy's courage here seemed to fail him. He hesitated to suggest the next step. "Your Excellency, I fear, will be angry with me."

"Kanshin," and again the governor's hand was laid on his companion's shoulder, "we must have that ship. Whatever plan promises to secure it must be followed, regardless of our personal feelings."

Thus encouraged, the deputy proceeded to unfold his scheme.

"I beseech your Excellency, then, to go in person to Santvoort's house to-morrow, and, in whatever way you can, to win the good-will of the barbarian captain. When this is secured, offer to hire his ship to assist us in subduing the rebels at Arima. Plead the necessity of having his co-operation at even the greatest cost, and let him make his own terms. Have the agreement at once drawn up and signed."

"What makes you think that the Dutch captain will consent to enter into such a contract?"

The other's lips curled in a contemptuous sneer.

"Do not fear that. We know the Dutch. Bait your trap with gold, and they will walk into it with their eyes open."

"And that is your plan?"

"A small part of it only. With this agreement between you, the barbarian will be less suspicious. Then invite him and his officers to attend the execution to-morrow night, promise them an armed escort. Ask him, more-

THE THREE MEN WERE SEATED ON THE MATS THAT COVERED THE FLOOR OF THE ROOM.—*See Page* 122.

over, to allow thirty or forty of his crew to come ashore to assist your guards in keeping order ; for this, likewise, offer a liberal compensation. Secure also, if possible, the loan of the small arms of the ship. Be free with offers of money ; it will be but promises ; you will never be asked to pay it."

The governor's face wore a puzzled expression. "You interest me. If the ship can be had for promises of money only, pray let me know how."

The deputy leaned toward Oda ; a smile of diabolical triumph made his countenance seem like the face of some savage beast.

"A short time ago, I heard you promise Itakura to secure him the Dutch ship without her captain and officers should it be at all possible to do so. My plan will enable you to fulfill your promise even in this. I just now mentioned the name of Gonroku, the robber-chieftain. Give him his liberty, and promise him a liberal reward upon the performance of certain things." The speaker paused, and keenly regarded his companion.

"Proceed !" said Oda, calmly. "I am listening."

"The city is filling up this afternoon with hundreds of lawless characters from all the surrounding country, attracted, no doubt, by the approaching execution. All day to-morrow they will probably continue to come. Among these there will be many of Gonroku's followers, and scores of other outlaws, whom he knows. Turn him loose among these, and in a few hours he will have a force more than able to do what is wanted of it. After the execution to-morrow night, let Gonroku make a riot, let the officers and the crew of the foreign ship be attacked, let the guards about Van Neist be instructed to flee, as if in terror, and leave the rest to Gonroku and his outlaws."

III.

TEN THOUSAND RYO REWARD, DEAD OR ALIVE.

"Were I a Captain Van Neist's friend I should warn him to beware of the governor's deputy."

The speaker was Asuga the interpreter, and the person to whom he addressed his remark was Marmion Beaumont. The two were just entering one of the principal streets of Nagasaki, whither the young Englishman had gone to have his first glimpse of Japanese life. Asuga had kindly volunteered his services as guide.

"Why so?" Beaumont inquired, in answer to the interpreter's hint of danger. "Is Kanshin, as I believe you call him, likely to do the captain harm?"

"Even so, Heer Beaumont, Asuga replied with a profound obeisance, "that officer will dog Van Neist's footsteps wherever he may go until he has an opportunity to avenge himself for yesterday's humiliation."

"Thank you for the hint; I shall warn the captain, that he may be on his guard."

The interpreter's caution, however, was soon forgotten in the interest which the strange life about him aroused in the young Englishman. The quaint rambling street, through which they were passing, lined on either side by open shops with their dingy wood-colored and weather-beaten fronts, were thronged with people. Here a *betto*,* running ahead of some mounted official, shouted to the pedestrians to clear the way; there a lady of rank, clad in rich, flowing robes, was seen seated in her luxurious *norimono*,† borne on the shoulders of four picturesquely

---

* Groom.   † Palanquin.

attired men-servants. The more humble wayfarers, men and women, young and old, jostled against each other with the utmost good-humor. Street venders, bearing large baskets slung from a pole laid over the shoulder, were noisily announcing the names of their wares ; children, scarcely more than four or five years old, bearing still younger children bound on their backs, darted here and there under the very feet of the horses and through the thick press of the hurrying crowds ; beggars, standing at the street corners, or lying on the numerous bridges, besought a *tempo*,* from the passers-by ; and dwarfish, surly-looking ponies, their backs heavily freighted with rice from the distant plains of Higo, or with charcoal from the mountains close at hand, staggered through the streets after the almost nude rustics leading them.

After walking a considerable distance, Asuga led the young Englishman into an open space at the foot of a broad flight of stone steps, that led upward in successive stages to a small plateau on the hillside above them, where rose the picturesque roof of a large temple. On either side of the entrance to these steps public notice-boards were erected, and before one of these a number of soldiers and citizens were assembled.

"The temple that you see above us on the edge of that grove is dedicated to Suwa, the patron god of Nagasaki, and is, consequently, the most frequented one in the city," remarked the interpreter to Beaumont, as the two men paused for a moment at the corner of the little street whence they had just emerged. "Therefore, the government officials use this place for any special proclamation, knowing that more people will see the notices here than anywhere else in the city. Here, of late years, the government's utterances respecting Christianity have con-

* A small sum of money equal to about 1¼ mills.

stantly been published : that large announcement, placed above all the others, being Iyeyasu's edict, issued twenty-three years ago, proclaiming a profession of the foreign religion upon the part of a Japanese subject to be a capital crime. Just under it is another edict declaring all European priests to be enemies of Japan, and forbidding any Japanese to shelter them. On this other side you perceive a new board. That was set up by order of our governor some two weeks ago. It gives official announcement of the fact that the Christians of Shimabara and Amakusa have taken up arms against the government, and states that if any one in Nagasaki or its vicinity dare to join the rebels, or in any way to give them assistance, that person, with all his kindred, shall be put to death. I presume some new proclamation has to-day been posted up, as the people ahead of us seem to be reading a notice, and something unusual, too, it must be, for, see! they are greatly excited."

"Would it be possible for us to join them and discover what it may be?"

"Certainly ; let us walk up a little closer."

The two soon found themselves before the proclamation that was attracting so much attention. It was written with various colored inks and in large characters upon a newly erected board. The interpreter gave utterance to an exclamation of surprise.

What is the notice, may I ask?" inquired Beaumont.

"The governor makes official announcement that he has received trustworthy information that Francesco Paoli, the Jesuit missionary, has returned to Japan, and is now in the city or its immediate neighborhood," cried the interpreter, breathlessly. "He calls upon all who value the good of their country to make untiring efforts to hunt down the hated priest, and offers ten thousand *ryo** reward for his capture, dead or alive."

The Englishman heard Asuga's words with a sinking heart. Paoli's return, then, was known to his enemies, his capture, he feared, was as good as accomplished, for with such a price as this set upon his head, his detection could only be a question of time. Nevertheless, assuming as indifferent an air as he could command, he said to his companion:

"Is this anything new? I understood that for the past ten years a reward has been offered for his capture."

"Very true, but this is double the reward formerly offered."

"I presume that it will be no more effectual, however, in bringing about his capture than was the earlier offer."

"It may be so," replied the interpreter recovering somewhat from his excitement. "Our people say the Jesuit is an *oni*,† and that his life is, consequently, proof against all manner of weapons and poison. And if he now escapes, with this price set upon his capture, I, too, shall be inclined to believe that he is more devil than man."

IV.

AN ENGLISH RAPIER ENCOUNTERS A JAPANESE SWORD.

Just then one of the bystanders touched Asuga on the shoulder.

"Fellow, I would speak with thee," said the stranger haughtily.

---

* A sum of money equal to about fifty thousand dollars at the present day.   † Demon, or devil.

The interpreter turned a quick, startled look upon the speaker, and saw a *Samurai*, dressed in a soldier's ordinary suit of armor, coldly regarding him. Instantly Asuga dropped upon his knees, and, touching his forehead to the earth, said in a humble tone :

"May it please thee to speak to thy servant."

"Rise!" said the other, even more disdainfully than he had previously spoken.

Asuga sprang to his feet.

"Who is thy companion, fellow?"

"An Englishman ; his name is Beaumont."

"When did he arrive in Japan?"

"Yesterday, aboard the foreign merchantman now lying in the harbor."

"Ah! the ship that is suspected of bringing the accursed priest, Paoli, to Nagasaki," said the other, motioning with his hand in the direction of the notice-board.

Asuga was silent.

"Fellow, I would speak to thy companion," continued the soldier, "but wait. Dost thou know this crest upon my helmet?"

"Is it not the crest of the valiant Prince Kaneko, of Ishihaya?"

"Fellow, it is. I am Uyemon Yamada, and yesterday I was proud to be called a retainer of my Lord Kaneko. Mark, fellow, I say *was*, for to-day I am a *Ronin ;** last night I lost my prince."

Asuga did not dare to make any reply to this information beyond a low bow. The speaker continued :

"The Jesuit, Francesco Paoli, killed my lord."

The listener could not repress an exclamation of astonishment.

---

* A retainer who has lost his lord and wanders about the country.

"Silence, fellow, silence!" the *Ronin* said, haughtily. "Where are thy manners? Wouldst thou have me carve thee with my sword? I said that the hated priest killed Prince Kaneko; he likewise slew twenty-eight of my fellow-retainers. The Jesuit ran down their boat, and they perished in the sea. A single *sendo* swam ashore; he heard the barbarian declare himself to be Paoli, and this morning he came and told me. I have sworn to avenge my lord. Day and night shall I follow on the track of this priest until I hunt him down. No disguise shall hide him from my eyes, no number of friends secure him from my sword. This companion of thine, I would see him; he has moved off yonder; let us go to him. Come, fellow, lead on!"

The Englishman had moved a little distance away from the notice-boards, and was patiently waiting until the soldier might be pleased to allow his companion to rejoin him. As he stood watching the noisy concourse before him, his attention was attracted by an old man in the white garb of a Buddhist pilgrim, who was slowly making his way through the crowd that jostled him roughly from side to side. The upper part of the pilgrim's face was entirely covered with the drooping rim of his hat, a rosary hung suspended from his neck, and he carried in his hand a staff, on the upper end of which was affixed a small bell. The old man walked slowly, frequently pausing to ring his bell and mutter over in a chanting monotone the words of the Buddhist prayer:

"*Namu mio ho ren ge kio!*"*

Approaching Beaumont, the pilgrim reached forth his hand and began to examine the clothing of the foreigner, until, under the pretext of closely scrutinizing his doub-

---

* Glory to the salvation-bringing Buddha.

let, the old man bent his head over the Englishman's shoulder, whispering in Spanish as he did so:

"Hush, Señor, not a word! It is I—Paoli. Meet me to-day on the hill-top above us alone; I wish to speak with you. Hush! for the love of God, Señor, be quiet!"

But the shock of surprise was too great. Beaumont sprang back, barely checking the cry that rose to his lips. Asuga was close behind him, with the *Ronin* at his side.

"Heer Beaumont," said the interpreter, "this soldier wishes to speak with you."

He pointed to Yamada as he spoke; but the *Ronin's* eyes were fixed on Paoli, and, with a tiger-like spring, he leaped upon him, felling him to the earth.

Then turning to Asuga the soldier spoke a few words in the same haughty tone that he had used in his previous conversation with the interpreter. The latter stepped forward to Beaumont, whose alarm for the safety of the bishop was now greater than had been his surprise a moment before at finding him in the guise of a pilgrim.

"Mynheer," the interpreter said to him, "the soldier wishes me to inform you that he saw this old man molesting you, and evidently making you afraid. He has, therefore, struck down the offender, as you have perceived, and, if you desire it, he will give him a beating."

The Englishman drew a long breath of relief. The *Ronin*, then, had not detected Paoli. He had only been defending a foreigner from, as he supposed, the meddlesome inquisitiveness of the old pilgrim.

Paoli had fallen face downward. Divining at once the cause of the assault, he remained in a prostrate position until the interpreter had conveyed the *Ronin's* words to Beaumont, and then rising to his knees and bowing his forehead to the ground at the feet of Yamada, he said in an abject tone:

" Thy servant, great sir, meant no harm. May it please thee to let him depart in peace. And will the honorable foreigner, likewise, grant the miserable offender his pardon?"

Asuga briefly made known to the Englishman the meaning of the pilgrim's words.

"Assure this soldier that it is not my wish that he further punish the old man. Let him go in peace, as he desires. Nevertheless, allow me to thank your companion for his promptness in ridding me of what he conceived to be an annoyance."

Beaumont's reply pleased the *Ronin*. With a threat of a severer punishment to follow his second offence, the pilgrim was dismissed with a rough push. The Englishman saw him move off slowly, as though decrepit with age, stopping every now and then to ring his bell and to repeat his prayer.

Beaumont moved after him, followed by Asuga and the soldier. When they had arrived at the great gate of the temple, the *Ronin* said to the interpreter :

"Invite thy companion, fellow, to go up with me to one of the tea-houses by the temple ; what I would have the foreigner say is made for my ears alone."

Beaumont, when acquainted with the invitation, hesitated, remembering the bishop's request for a meeting on the hill. The other perceiving this, and mistaking it for fear, said, scornfully :

" Tell this cowardly barbarian, fellow, that he is safe. The sword of Yamada is reserved for a better cause than to be stained upon him."

" Let him not mistake," retorted the Englishman, coldly, and touching the hilt of the rapier that hung at his side, he turned upon the *Ronin* a look as proud and haughty as his own ; "I am not afraid. Yet for his insolence, let him know that I refuse his request. If he has aught to say to me, let it be said here, where his comrades, if he have any, can be at hand to assist him in defending himself, should he be foolhardy enough to provoke a quarrel."

This defiant speech stung the *Ronin* into a furious passion. With a cat-like movement, he snatched his sword from its scabbard, but quick as he was, the Englishman was still more rapid in unsheathing his weapon. One moment the slender rapier glittered before the breast of the soldier, and the next, as the latter raised his heavy blade to smite the foreigner, there was a dexterous turn of the Englishman's wrist, and the *Ronin's* sword was sent flying from his grasp.

A cry of surprise burst from the spectators. "*Kekko! Kekko!*"* shouted one, and others laughed. It was plain that some of the bystanders enjoyed the haughty *Samurai's* discomfiture. A soldier, among the spectators, returned his sword to the *Ronin*, and the latter, uttering a fierce yell of rage, threw himself with redoubled fury upon Beaumont.

The young Englishman's heart beat as though it would break through his side; not from fear, but from a sort of mad delight in the desperate struggle he was waging. He was an expert swordsman, and, in the present emergency, despite his excitement, his eye lost none of its quickness, his hand none of its cunning. Like a flash, the slender blade darted forth just at the proper instant, and once again the *Ronin's* sword was torn from his grasp and fell with a sharp ring on the stone pavement. This time the keen point of the Englishman's rapier had pierced his adversary's wrist,† severing one of the larger muscles and rendering his hand helpless. The shout that greeted this

---

* Excellent, well done. † See frontispiece.

second achievement was more hearty than the one before; even some of the soldiers joined in the applause.

The fight was now ended. The *Ronin*, defeated and foaming with rage, picked up his fallen sword with his uninjured hand, and, without a word, withdrew. Beaumont, also, beckoning to the terror-stricken Asuga to follow him, passed out into the street. The spectators, parting right and left, made a way for him, watching his movements in respectful silence.

The Englishman and his companion took their way along a broad avenue, skirting the base of the hills. Asuga, as soon as he had recovered from his fright, congratulated Beaumont on his victory, and then added:

"Nevertheless, Mynheer, I fear it will prove to be a bad piece of work."

"How?" the other inquired.

"The *Ronin* is now your relentless enemy, and will seek revenge."

Beaumont laughed. "So, so! Captain Van Neist is to have the governor's deputy hunting him, and now this fellow will be thirsting after my blood! Marry! but we may be looking out for sport ahead."

The timid Asuga failed to see anything like sport in the situation.

"I am sorry, Mynheer, that you angered him."

The Englishman ignored the interpreter's remark.

"You seem to know the fellow," said he. "Who is he, and what did he wish of me?"

In reply, Asuga informed him of all that the *Ronin* had said, and continued:

"I presume he wished to question you respecting the two missing Japanese passengers, one of whom, it is believed in the city, must have been the Jesuit priest, Paoli, in disguise."

Beaumont became very thoughtful. He perceived how narrow an escape the bishop had just had.

V.

THE STORY OF A MARTYRDOM.

At length the Englishman recalled Paoli's desire to meet him on the hill above the city, but he was at loss to know how he might first rid himself of his companion's presence. Even while he was pondering over the problem, the interpreter halted, and, turning to him, said :

"Heer Beaumont, I have some business with a friend in a street close by us. With your permission, I shall let you climb this hill upon our left alone. From its summit you will have an excellent view of the entire city, the harbor, the islands along the coast, and a wide stretch of the surrounding country. I assure you, you will feel amply repaid for the labor of the climb. This path that branches off to our left will lead you to the top of the hill. I shall meet you at this place at sunset. If you do not care to go, however, I shall first conduct you back to the factory, and visit my friend later in the evening."

"Nay, I shall be delighted to climb the hill," cried Beaumont, rejoiced beyond measure at the opportunity, thus so unexpectedly given him, for meeting Bishop Paoli. "I shall join you here at the time you have set."

The two men now separated. In a short time, the Englishman reached the hill-top, where he seated himself on a stone, at the foot of a spreading tree, and gazed long and delightedly on the fair scene before him. Before long he heard the tinkling of a bell somewhere near, and, rising to his feet, he beheld the bishop approaching him. The disguise was perfect, and, as Paoli joined him, Beaumont, with a smile, said :

"He who detects you in that disguise, Bishop Paoli, will earn, methinks, his ten thousand *ryo*."

"No name, please Señor," the other said, resting upon his staff. "Yes, it will be difficult to discover me in this garb, I think. After disguising myself, I always go first among friends, and if they do not recognize me, it is safe to presume that strangers will not."

"Why did you select this particular disguise?"

"I have always found it safe and convenient," the bishop responded. "At times, it is true, the pilgrim falls into the hands of some quarrelsome *Samurai*; but otherwise he can travel from one end of the country to the other with the utmost safety. You see, the Buddhist pilgrim, on his way from one famous shrine to another, begs his food and shelter, and the people, believing that his prayers are peculiarly acceptable to Buddha, are usually very liberal in their donations, and vie with one another in the readiness with which they welcome the wayfarer to their homes. The pilgrims, also, are among the most efficient spies upon the Christians that the government possesses, and that is an additional reason why, in the past, I so often donned their garb, since thus I have frequently been able to discover what dangers threatened my people, and to warn them early enough for their escape."

For a time the two men looked down in silence upon the quaint old town and the pretty little bay nestling between the two ranges of fronting hills. Then the Englishman spoke.

"Yesterday I learned that a foreign priest had been

detected in his disguise, and, if I remember rightly, he was to be executed to-day. Have you heard anything about this?"

A shadow crossed Paoli's face, as he replied:

"Yes, it is but too true. The sole survivor of a once numerous and devoted company of apostles of the faith has to-day fallen, leaving me, Señor, the last of the missionaries, to labor alone in this broken vineyard of the Lord. Poor Father Sotero! And yet, why do I call him poor? for surely he did die most triumphantly, to the confusion of the heathen. I was just returning from his execution, Señor Beaumont, when we met at the temple below, where that accursed pagan soldier had need, as he thought, to punish me for being too close to you. Last night I heard of Father Sotero's arrest and of the determination of the officials to put him to death to-day. Early this morning, disguising myself as you now see me, I hastened to a little mountain hamlet a mile or so to the north of us, where the execution was to take place. As I drew near the village, I perceived a vast concourse of idolators gathered on a hill-top. Pressing toward them, I found that Father Sotero, with five other victims, had just been brought from prison. To increase the anguish of the venerable father, the officials tortured and put to death before his eyes the five native Christians. But the designs of the heathen were foiled. Father Sotero, though agonizing in spirit with his perishing converts, joined them in their praises to God for thus crowning their past services with the honors of martyrdom.

"Defeated in their attempts to make him display any signs of pain, the idolators, shrieking in their baffled rage, rushed upon Father Sotero, and bore him to the earth. Throwing myself among the mad wretches, I

THE OLD MAN BENT HIS HEAD OVER THE ENGLISHMAN'S SHOULDER.—*See Page 138.*

succeeded in reaching the prostrate form of my friend. The fiercest of his assailants were religious pilgrims, dressed like myself, and I knew that I was safe from discovery. I allowed the surging crowd to trample me down by the side of the venerable father, until, with my lips close to his ear, I whispered my name, and told him that Shiro had come. How can I describe what followed! Was it a momentary return of the Samson-like strength of his youth, or was it a miracle of Almighty God? I know not. But I beheld him as he sprang to his feet, bursting the cords that bound him as though they were but straws, and shaking his enemies off from him as a lordly lion might cast off a pack of yelling curs. I saw his gigantic form towering above his murderers; and they, confounded at the unexpected energy he displayed, shrank back, cowed into silence. His clothing had been torn off him, his right eye was dashed out, and his head and body were streaming with blood. I heard his deep, strong voice, thrilling with triumph: 'Lord, now lettest thou thy servant depart in peace, according to thy word; for mine eyes have seen thy salvation.' Then, with a heart-piercing cry, he plunged forward upon his face. The bloodthirsty mob again closed over him, but only to wreak their fury on a corpse. Father Sotero was dead!"

VI.

THE BISHOP OF JAPAN APPEARS IN A NEW RÔLE.

Beaumont had listened to the impassioned recital with visible emotion. Ignoring the effect that he perceived his words had had upon the Englishman, Paoli added, quietly:

"Pardon me, Señor, for dwelling thus upon the death of my friend. What are your plans for the immediate future, may I inquire?"

"I cannot say," Beaumont replied, with a smile. "I would be safe, I suppose, in saying that I shall return to Europe on the *Spuyten Duyvil*."

"Even what you appear to take for granted as certain is not entirely beyond the range of doubt, is it, Señor? Are you sure the *Spuyten Duyvil* is ever going back to Amsterdam?"

Something in the tone in which Paoli asked the question aroused the Englishman's attention. He at once felt that the bishop had learned of some danger threatening Van Neist and his ship. His anxiety was plainly visible in the inquiring look he turned upon the Jesuit.

"You have heard of some plot against the *Spuyten Duyvil*, Bishop Paoli; pray tell what it is."

"First let me hear, Señor, what happened aboard the ship yesterday morning, after Shiro and I so unceremoniously took our leave of you," and the Jesuit's face was lighted with a quiet smile.

In answer to the bishop's request, Beaumont told him of the deputy's visit and what had come of it. "But surely there can be no danger from that quarter," the young man said, "for early this morning Kanshin came off to the ship with Kœckebacker, the Dutch agent from Hirado, and tendered Van Neist a most humble apology for his rudeness yesterday. An hour or so ago Governor Oda himself called upon the captain at the trading-house; and, when I left, he, the agent, and Van Neist were closeted together, discussing some proposition the governor had to offer. This much I heard, but nothing more."

The bishop listened in moody silence. When Beaumont concluded his narration, he looked anxiously at the Jesuit, expecting that he would now inform him of any rumor he might have heard ; but Paoli seemed to be lost in thought. His face wore a deeply troubled expression, and when at last he spoke he appeared to be unconscious of the presence of another.

"Then the report among the people is correct ; I was trusting that it might be but an idle rumor. And yet what is it but one more straw that the infidels are flinging against the bulwarks of Heaven ?"

Paoli's words increased the Englishman's alarm ; he could wait no longer.

"Bishop Paoli, you are perplexed, troubled ; you have heard some ill-tidings—"

The sound of his companion's voice aroused the Jesuit.

"Pardon me, Señor," he cried, interrupting Beaumont, "I have been selfish enough to allow my own anxiety to make me forgetful of yours. What I have heard is briefly this : the governor has been ordered by the commander-in-chief of the infidel army at Arima to secure the *Spuyten Duyvil*, by fair means or foul, to assist him in suppressing the insurrection of the Christians. There is also a vague rumor afloat that some mischief to all the foreigners in the city and upon the ship is intended, but just what it may be I have been unable to discover. It was to warn you of this that I desired to see you here."

"Thank you, Bishop Paoli," was the grateful response. "We are intending to go aboard again this evening ; the captain can then make preparations for defense."

"Then you are not to be present at Lord Oda's entertainment to-night ?"

"I do not understand you ; I have heard of no entertainment."

A strange smile flitted over the bishop's face.

"Is it possible? Then, I shall tell you, Señor, for, perhaps, when you have heard all you may wish to be present. The entertainment I refer to, is to be on yonder hill opposite us. Hundreds of Christian prisoners are to be dragged from the city dungeons, and there executed. This afternoon the governor's officers are going through all the streets of the city, and through every village in the neighborhood, visiting each house, and giving orders that at least one person from every home be present at the execution. It is the determination of the governor and his councilors to strike such terror to-night into the hearts of his subjects that those who may secretly favor our cause shall never dare openly to espouse it, and that all others may shun and hate our holy faith as they would the most loathsome disease."

This was the first intimation that Beaumont had received of the impending tragedy, the magnitude of which appalled him.

"Merciful God!" he exclaimed. "What barbarity! Can nothing be done to defeat the scheme of this inhuman butcher?"

"The arm of the Lord is not shortened," said the bishop, devoutly crossing himself. "Something has been done, Señor, that, with the help of Heaven, shall not only frustrate the designs of the idolaters, but make those very plans by which the governor is seeking to terrify his people into a hatred of the truth, to redound to the encouragement of secret believers and to the strengthening of the cause of the church."

"Thank Heaven!" the Englishman exclaimed earnestly. "How is this to be accomplished?" he inquired eagerly. "What plan is there afoot? What do you propose to do?"

Not heeding Beaumont's interruption, the bishop continued :

"There shall, indeed, be a carnival of blood to-night, but the blood that is to flow will be that of the infidel."

"Ah, I understand!" cried the young man, excitedly, "there is to be an attempt to rescue the prisoners ; Shiro is to lead an attack upon the government officials at the execution grounds. Am I not right?"

"There is to be rescue, even as you say ; but it is I, and not Shiro, who is to lead the attacking force."

The young Englishman's entire experience with Francesco Paoli had been full of surprises ; but this was the greatest of all. A priest, a bishop to be a leader of armed men, his own hands, doubtless, to be reddened with blood! Impossible!

The Jesuit was closely regarding his companion.

"You are doubly surprised, Señor. First, you are astonished that the Christians should contemplate so daring an enterprise, and, in the second place, you marvel that I should exchange the gown of the churchman for the armor of a warrior."

He again looked at Beaumont. The young man said nothing. He was awaiting to hear what would come next.

"I am trusting you, Señor. It is as safe to do so now as it was aboard Van Neist's ship, is it not?"

"You may be assured that it is."

"Then I shall more fully outline our plan of action. Last night the Christians of Kayaki decided to rise in revolt. They number about five hundred able-bodied fighting men. Half of these are to convey the women and children to-night by water around the cape to Arima. With the others I shall do what you have just said. This morning, long before daybreak, messengers were dispatched to the leaders of the Christian army, informing them of the return of Shiro and myself, and requesting them to send at once five hundred well-armed men to assist in the rescue."

"Bravo! Your plan is a bold one. May it be successful."

"It cannot fail," was the quiet response. "The work of torture and death is not to begin until midnight; the preceding two or three hours will be occupied in games and various sports. The officials will not dream of such a thing as a rescue. We shall be well armed. A hundred or more of our party are to mingle in various disguises among the spectators taking care to remain near the prisoners. The relief from Arima will be nigh at hand awaiting our signal. The struggle will be a desperate one, but, Señor, we shall conquer."

"Pray Heaven you may! But how is it that you, instead of Shiro, are to lead the rescuing party?"

A strange smile passed over Paoli's features, then as he observed the Englishman keenly regarding him, his face assumed its wonted gravity and he quietly said:

"Shiro is at present stopping at the house of a friend in Kayaki. Last night we found among the dead on Takaboka, Ine Tanaka, the woman to whom he has been betrothed since his childhood. She had most wonderfully escaped the otherwise universal destruction; but nevertheless, was so severely injured that she needs a few days rest. Shiro will remain with her, and the two will join us later at Arima. But, Señor, the sun draws near to his setting, and I must be hastening on my way to Kayaki. The friends there will be anxiously awaiting my return; much remains to be done in preparation for to-night. We shall probably see each other again. The governor, I hear, intends to invite all the foreigners in the city. Be there, for you'll see some hot work, I assure you. Farewell!"

VII.

MARMION BEAUMONT FALLS INTO ANOTHER ADVENTURE.

Beaumont and Paoli now sought the city below by different routes; the former bearing to the right toward the bay, and the latter taking the same path that he had followed in the ascent. The Englishman found the interpreter at the place where they had parted, and the two men now turned their steps in the direction of the trading-house. As they were passing through one of the larger streets they perceived a crowd of people approaching.

"What can it be?" inquired Beaumont, as the madly screaming mob drew nearer.

"I cannot say," Asuga answered, "but perhaps I may be able to learn."

So saying, he stepped to the side of the street and accosted a shopkeeper, who, in common with his neighbors, was standing before his door and gazing in the direction of the approaching procession. The interpreter, after a minute's conversation with the man, rejoined Beaumont, who had remained in the middle of the street.

"It is a company of officials," he reported, "taking a number of people, who are suspected of being Christians, to the cross ordeal."

"And what may that be?"

"A large cross is placed upon the ground, and the people, having been formed into a procession, are compelled each, in turn, to walk over it. If they trample upon the cross, that is taken as proof either that they are not Christians or that they thereby renounce their adherence to the foreign religion. But those who refuse to go over it, by so doing, publicly declare themselves to be believers in the foreign creed, and they are at once hurried off to prison, or to immediate execution."

The Englishman could not repress a shudder at the cool, matter-of-fact way in which his companion spoke of what so appalled him. The frequent sight of such scenes as the interpreter was now describing had robbed them of the horror they would have otherwise inspired in him. A strange desire to see the ordeal took possession of Beaumont's mind. He turned to Asuga, and asked:

"Where does this ordeal take place?"

"Heretofore they have always been upon Higashi-yama, the hill just south of the city. I presume the present one will be in the same place."

"Will it be possible for us to witness it?"

"I think it would be perfectly safe for us to be present. Other foreigners frequently have witnessed not only the ordeal, but also the execution of those who were convicted of being Christians. In fact, the officials are rather pleased to have foreigners behold with what hatred they regard Christianity, in order that they may be intimidated from attempting to introduce it anew. Does Heer Beaumont wish to see the ordeal?"

"Yes."

"Then let us turn into this street, and walk on ahead of the crowd. If we keep straight on over the hill before us, we shall get to the grounds before they are filled with the rabble. The officers, I perceive, intend to take the road running along the shore of the bay."

The two hurried on in the direction indicated. In a short time the uproar of the mob grew fainter, as the officers, with their prisoners, turned off into another street, taking the course that Asuga had predicted they would. The sun had now set behind the mountains across the bay, and the shadows of the coming night were fast settling down upon the city. In a few minutes Beaumont and the interpreter had reached the long flight of stone steps that still lead up the steep northern slope of Higashi-yama from the Hirobaba market. They ascended these, and soon they stood on a commanding eminence, looking down on the city and the bay, both now but faintly discernible in the gathering darkness.

The uproar of voices, growing constantly louder, and a long line of waving torches and lanterns slowly ascending the steep hill-side, fronting the bay, announced the approach of the officers and prisoners, followed still by the tumultuous and madly roaring mob.

"A little to the right and we shall have a good position from which we can look down on the whole proceedings," said Asuga, leading the way to a tall pine tree that stood but a short distance from the road.

They did not have long to wait. The officers soon appeared and took up their position on a piece of level ground that lay just below the place where Beaumont and Asuga stood. Toward the bay this level stretch broke off in a precipitous cliff overhanging the low land that bordered upon the beach. In still another direction it was bounded by a deep cut that had been excavated for a public road that here pierced the hill and wound up along the western side of Higashi-yama.

The officers conducted their prisoners to the edge of the cliff to shield them from the violence of the howling rabble that had dogged the procession up the hillside, and were now savagely calling for the blood of the Christians. A rope was stretched across the only side of the ordeal ground to which access was possible, and fifteen or twenty soldiers were detailed by the officer in charge of the proceedings to keep guard and to hold the populace back. The mob, howling in its rage, now covered the entire hill-side, and the air was rent with their repeated demands for the destruction of the prisoners. The latter, numbering, perhaps, fifty persons, included both sexes and all ages. Youths and maidens, strong men, middle-aged matrons, and hoary-headed grandsires and granddames—all were huddled together, and plainly oblivious to both the savage outcries of the mob and the preparations being made by the officers for the ordeal.

Beaumont perceived a venerable-looking old man standing in the midst of the Christians, and from his gesticulations it was evident that he was addressing his fellow-prisoners, though nothing could be heard, the uproar of the mob drowning his voice. In the light of the flaring torches, Beaumont could see the old man's face, and its calm, peaceful expression in the midst of those terrible surroundings haunted him long afterwards.

While the Englishman was watching the Christians, the interpreter was anxiously regarding the mad throng of spectators that now completely hemmed them in. Never before had he seen so dangerous looking a mob. The news that a great execution of Christians was to take place that night had spread far and wide through the country, attracting to the city the lawless element of the entire province. Scores of these desperate characters were now mingled with the city rabble about them, and Asuga's heart leaped into his throat as four or five half-drunken ruffians came up to the tree beneath which he and Beaumont were standing, and one of them shouted :

"Iya, iya, comrades, here's a foreigner! Down with the foreigner! Down with Christians and foreigners! Ho, help, here! Down with the foreigner!"

The cry was taken up by others, and hundreds of eyes were turned upon the Englishman, and a mad roar went up:

"The foreigner! Down with the foreigner!"

The terrified Asuga looked at Beaumont, who, unconscious of his peril, was still intently watching the Christians. The interpreter reached out his hand to touch his companion's arm, but some one struck it down, and, turning a frightened look in the direction whence came the blow, Asuga beheld the savage face of Yamada, the *Ronin*.

"Silence, fellow!" hissed the soldier in the ear of the interpreter. "A word to thy companion, and I shall plunge this knife into thy heart! Thinkest thou," he continued, in a hoarse whisper, "I shall allow this rabble to tear the accursed foreigner to pieces without myself striking the first blow? Remember what happened at the Suwa Temple this afternoon, fellow, and stand aside."

There was no mistaking the *Ronin's* intention. The interpreter saw his right hand bandaged and hanging by his side, but in his left Yamada held a keen, double-edged knife. The mob, it was plainly to be seen, would soon attack the foreigner. The *Ronin* was determined, in revenge for the defeat he had suffered, to anticipate the others in their designs.

A shout of "Down with the foreigner!" louder and more savage than any that had yet preceded it, startled Beaumont, and caused him to turn around to inquire of Asuga the meaning of the cry. A single glance at the frightened interpreter and the scowling face of the *Ronin* at his side was sufficient to inform the young man that some serious danger threatened him. Quickly springing backward, he placed himself in a defensive attitude, with his back against the tree. The *Ronin* saw the movement, and not daring openly to attack with his left hand one with whom, even when uninjured he had been unable to cope, he tore the bandages from his wrist, and as the blood gushed forth afresh from the wound, he held up his bloody hand and shouted to the mob:

"Ho, fellow-countrymen! Ho, comrades! Behold the work of the barbarian! He has drawn his sword on a *Samurai* of Japan! He has destroyed my hand! Down with him, comrades! I call for vengeance! Down with the foreigner!"

The mob was already prepared for any sort of mischief. They were of themselves meditating an attack on the Englishman, and the words of the *Ronin* excited them to open violence. With a savage roar, they closed around the tree. Beaumont needed no interpreter to tell him the meaning of the *Ronin's* words. The shower of clubs and stones that rattled about his feet, the wild, vengeful yell of the mob, and the fierce, merciless faces that glared out upon him from the frenzied throng, told him enough.

At this moment of deadly peril, while he stood with drawn rapier, awaiting the onslaught of his foes, he became aware of a commotion in the rear of the screaming rabble before him. Casting a glance over the heads of the mob, he beheld a company of mounted warriors urging their horses through the press towards him. The strangers were vigorously plying their short spears upon the heads and shoulders of the rabble, whose savage cries for the blood of the Christians and the death of the foreigner were now changed into shrieks of terror, as they cowered under the blows of the new-comers. The roughs that had gathered around Beaumont, as they saw the cavalcade heading for the place where their intended victim stood, slunk silently away into the darkness. The *Ronin*, however, remained until the others were gone, and then, in a voice choked with baffled rage, said to the interpreter:

"Fellow, the gods have again stood upon the side of thy companion! But let him beware! No man has yet incurred the hatred of Uyemon Yamada and lived. Mark you, that accursed barbarian shall not escape!"

VIII.

THE ORDEAL OF THE CROSS.

By this time the party of mounted warriors had reached the open space before the pine tree. Beaumont still stood where he had taken up his position to defend himself against the mob, his naked rapier yet in his hand. The peril to which he had just been exposed had come upon him suddenly and unexpectedly; and now, with no less quickness, this unlooked-for deliverance had been wrought. Scarcely believing his eyes, he gazed on the horsemen before him as if he expected the vision to depart, like something created by his own imagination. Still more inclined was he to think the whole spectacle before him to be nothing more than some fantastic illusion of his excited mind, when the leader of the cavalcade, dismounting, approached and addressed him in the accents of his native English speech:

"Put up thy sword, friend; there shall be no need of it for the present. Strong and fearless as thou seemest to be, it was yet fortunate for thee that I and my guard chanced here just when we did. This savage mob is mad for blood."

Beaumont was too much astonished to speak. The

new-comer looked doubtfully at him for a minute, and again spoke :

"Am I mistaken ? I took thy face to be the face of an Englishman, and, therefore, I spoke to thee in the English tongue. Art thou, then, the native of some other country and understandest not my words ?"

"Nay. I understand thee. I am an Englishman," replied Beaumont, recovering himself sufficiently to answer the stranger's question. "Pardon me," the young man continued. "I was too much surprised to be able to speak. I cannot tell thee which astonishes me the more : the rescue of a minute ago—for which, sir," he added, with a low bow, "my most grateful thanks are due to thee,—or now the sound of my native speech."

The other laughed lightly.

"I ought, methinks, to understand your language. My earliest and dearest friend was one of your nation, and three years of my youth were spent in England. But of all this we may speak later. You came here, I suppose, to witness the ordeal ; the same object brought me. I perceive they are about ready to begin. We shall stand here together and watch the proceedings, and, after the examination is concluded, I and my guards will accompany you to whatever place you may be stopping. It would scarcely be safe for a foreigner to go through the streets to-night without an armed escort."

The stranger's guards had arranged themselves in a semi-circle around Beaumont and their chief, leaving the space in front of them open, that their view of the ordeal ground might not be obstructed. As the leader stepped aside to give some orders to his men, Asuga whispered to Beaumont in Dutch :

"You are fortunate, Mynheer, in your rescue to-night. Your deliverer is none other than Lord Nabeshima, the

SHE KNELT REVERENTLY BESIDE THE CROSS.—*See Page* 168.

Prince of Kai, the noblest and bravest general in Japan. I heard to-day that he was expected in Nagasaki this evening, and, most luckily, he came here just in time to save you. He is on his way to Arima to fight the rebel-Christians."

With this introduction to his preserver, the young Englishman directed his eyes towards him with increased interest. Lord Nabeshima was evidently about thirty years of age, and was a much taller and heavier-built man than the average Japanese. His frame was well-knit and muscular with broad, full chest and powerful arms. He was clad in a full suit of armor of a rich crimson color and profusely ornamented with gold. His weapons, consisting of a short spear and the universal two swords, were likewise brilliantly mounted with the precious metals. The prince's firmly-cut features, keen, piercing eyes and lofty forehead betokened him to be the possessor of as much mental strength and force of character as physical prowess. His kindly countenance lit up with a graciously winning smile as he turned and saw the Englishman earnestly regarding him, and his voice was soft and musical as he spoke:

"I was instructing my guards to be on the watch, and, should they perceive any one of the ruffians here trying to excite the mob against foreigners, to ride him down and seize and bind him. The city is full of desperate characters this evening, and, once aroused, there is no saying where their violence may stop."

"Allow me to thank you again for the timely rescue that you brought me, and also for your present watchful care," said Beaumont, delighted by the other's charming manners. "My companion has just now made me acquainted with your name, and, believe me, Prince, the honor that I have in meeting you to-night shall remain one of the pleasantest memories of my life."

"Say no more, I entreat you," Lord Nabeshima answered. "I consider myself most happy in the privilege of serving one of a nation I so deeply respect. But, see! the officer has mounted the rock, and is calling for silence!"

All eyes were now turned toward the ordeal ground. The preparations were at last completed. A large wooden cross had been laid down in the open space between the prisoners and the rope stretched across the entrance to the place of examination. The chief officer, having secured silence among the spectators, descended from the rock and approached the prisoners. The old man who had been haranguing his fellow-captives stepped out, and a short colloquy ensued. The voices of both speakers, however, were so low that neither the prince nor Asuga could make out what was being said. At its conclusion, the officer again mounted the stone, and waving his hand to the vast multitude that covered the entire hillside, he cried out:

"All ye who uphold the hands of your princes in destroying the roots of contention among our people, give attention!" and then turning toward the prisoners, who were watching him no less intently than the populace, he continued:

"You are here, charged with believing in the doctrines of the hated foreign religion, which it is the determined purpose of our government to utterly extirpate from the soil of our Japan. You have the choice, here and now, either to renounce, in the presence of your countrymen, all allegiance to the teachings of the barbarian priests by trampling on this cross, the symbol of the prescribed religion, or, by refusing to do this, to stamp yourselves as traitors to your nation, meriting the destruction which we, in the name of our princes, and for the safety of our native land, will this night visit upon you."

The speaker stopped, and the uproar of the mob, that broke out in a fierce burst of applause, rose too loud for the prince to hear what the old man, who was again addressing his companions, was saying. One of the soldiers, however, seized him in the midst of his speech and hurried him toward the cross. Here the soldier relinquished his hold, and retreating, left him to do as he would. The old man gazed for a time on the cross before him, and then raising his face toward the breathless multitude, which the thrilling excitement of the moment had hushed into a deathlike silence, he cried out:

"Behold, ye idolators and slayers of the innocent, whom my God shall judge!—behold thus, thus does Mampei Fuji trample upon the cross of his Lord!" And throwing himself prostrate on the earth, the old man clasped the cross to his breast; then, springing to his feet, raised it above his head.

A roar of rage burst from the spectators; and the soldiers, seizing the old man, dashed the cross from his grasp, and hastily binding his hands, hurried him aside, and made ready for another.

The next to be led forward was a young woman. She could not have been more than seventeen years of age, and she was beautiful with that fresh picturesque beauty, so difficult to decribe yet so thoroughly charming to the eye, often seen among the daughters of Japan. With bowed head and reluctant step she advanced to the cross, the soldier at times dragging her roughly forward. When she had at last come to the place where the sacred symbol of her faith lay just before her feet, she paused, and having looked calmly around upon her friends, the officers and soldiers, and the vast sea of faces on the hill-side, she knelt reverently beside the cross, covering her face with her hands. For a moment, she remained thus; then slowly rising to her feet, she moved to the side of the old man, and, with a smiling, averted face, held out her hands to the officer to be bound. The spectators had looked upon the pathetic scene in breathless silence, even the most savage feeling a momentary touch of pity; and, as they beheld her refuse to trample upon the cross, a low cry arose from the multitude: "She is lost!"

Of all that followed Marmion Beaumont was unconscious. The pale, resolute faces of the prisoners, the angry commands of the officers, the savage screams of the mob, he saw not, heard not. His thoughts were dwelling upon Bishop Paoli and the heroic rescue the Jesuit was soon to attempt. Alas! in the face of a trained soldiery and this vast throng of rough and desperate men, the daring scheme of the little band of Christians, be they ever so brave, could appear but a forlorn hope. In his own mind Beaumont endeavored to picture the scene: the preparations for the execution; the secret signals; the thrilling battle shout; the surprise of the heathen; the exultation of the Christians; the sudden hope kindled in the breasts of the prisoners; the resistless onslaught; the momentary triumph; the rallying of the soldiers; the unequal conflict; the inevitable defeat; the massacre of the gallant little army, and the ten-fold more savage fury of the executioners.

"What wonderful constancy these Christians have displayed! Out of all this party to-night, only three renounced their faith, and of these, one afterwards repented and gave himself up to suffer with his fellow-believers.

It is sad to think that the evil has grown so great that the remedy must needs be so severe!"

It was the voice of Prince Nabeshima that recalled Beaumont's mind to a realization of his present surroundings, and as he looked up into the face of his companion he fancied that the nobleman's eyes were misty with tears. As he perceived the Englishman keenly regarding him, the Lord of Kai hastened to say:

"The ordeal is finished, and it is yet two or three hours before the execution begins. It will not be safe for you to wait here; mount this horse, therefore, I pray, and we shall conduct you to whatever place you may wish to go."

BOOK FIFTH.

THE HOUR OF THE CHRISTIANS' WOE.

i.

INE TANAKA'S STRANGE LOVER.

N the early part of this same memorable evening, the Christians of Kayaki and the adjacent villages made preparations for their intended flight. Chijiwa, one of the generals in the Christian army at Arima, had come to Kayaki to assume command of the division that was to conduct the women and children around the cape to Hara Castle. Shiro, also, had donned a full suit of armor, and, seated on the lofty dais in the cave-chapel, he received the reports of his assistants and consulted with them as to the best methods to be adopted for the carrying out of their plans. The time proved to be very propitious for their undertaking. Shortly after sunset, nearly all the heathen population of the village set out for Nagasaki to be present at the execution. The few idolators that remained were quietly seized and imprisoned in the cavern-chapel, and the same course was pursued with such travellers as entered the place on their way to the city.

The preparations for embarkation were, in the meanwhile, hastened forward with the utmost secrecy and dispatch; and thus it happened that neither officials nor citizens in Nagasaki had the slightest intimation of the formidable uprising that was taking place at their very doors.

In the principal room of the house, to which the evening before she had guided Nirado Shiro and Bishop Paoli, Ine Tanaka, still sore and bruised from her terrible fall, reclined on a couch spread out upon the mats that covered the floor of the apartment. She was alone, her sister being busily engaged in her preparations for departure. The woman's delicately moulded features were lit up with a smile of peaceful happiness, for her thoughts were dwelling upon the swiftly approaching time when the Church of Japan would be redeemed from her cruel bondage to the infidel. In that great day of deliverance Ine Tanaka was to have part. The central and grandest figure in all her visions of the coming triumph was that of her returned lover; and by his side she was destined to stand, sharing then his honor and glory as for years she had shared the trials and the perils of his people.

Ever since her childhood had Ine Tanaka been the betrothed wife of Nirado Shiro. Their parents dwelt in the same village, and had long been faithful and zealous disciples of the Romish missionaries. In the storm of persecution and bloodshed, which for more than two score of years had been desolating the church of Japan, both families had been rich in martyrs for the faith. Prominent in every undertaking that promised to be of service to the cause of their religion, and recognized as leaders among the Christians throughout the country, it was but natural that the two families, in conformity to the time-honored custom of their race, should seek an alliance the one with the other through the betrothal of their children.

Shiro, it was confidently believed, was the deliverer whose coming had been foretold in the prophetic inscription on the rock that had long overhung the village, and which on the night of his birth, had been torn from its resting-place by the earthquake and had been lodged before his father's door. Ine's parents, with the assistance and counsel of the missionaries, had endeavored to bring up their child in a manner befitting one who was destined to occupy the lofty position of consort of the first Christian ruler of Japan. Shiro was sent to Manila, that he might be safe from his enemies, and receive the training which the troubled condition of the Japanese church rendered impossible for him to obtain in his native land.

During these years of his absence, Ine, from a girl of twelve, had grown to be a woman of twenty-one. To her pure and gentle nature had been added the powerful influence of an ardent belief that she was elected of Heaven to the nigh and noble position as wife of the future ruler of Japan ; and this faith, together with her sincere piety and spiritual temperament, had molded her character into one of queenly dignity and gracious sweetness, making her the idol and the hope of the persecuted church. Her name was known and loved in every Christian home in Kiushiu, and everywhere throughout the church of her nation she wielded an influence scarcely less potent than Francesco Paoli himself.

Amid all her labors in behalf of her fellow-Christians, Ine's heart went out in a passionate love for him to whom her hand was bound in plighted troth. Such a nature as hers is capable of an untold depth of affection, and with all the powers of her pure and earnest soul did she love Nirado Shiro. It was a love that was patient, bearing the long years of his absence without a murmur. It was best for him, for the cause to which his destiny was indissolubly linked, and, perchance, also for her, that he should be far away.

Not only among the Christians, but throughout the nation at large, had Ine Tanaka won the distinction of being the most beautiful and highly gifted woman of her time; and this renown had brought her many suitors. Among these had come Lord Nabeshima, Prince of Kai. Ine knew this nobleman's popularity among the people; his family was an influential one; many of his friends had been Christians; the prince himself was opposed to the wanton persecution of the church. By marrying him, therefore, she would gain not only a most honorable position, but, as Princess of Kai, she would be able to wield a powerful influence in behalf of the church. Yet, it is needless to say, that Ine and her family were unmoved by these considerations. Courteously, but firmly, Nabeshima's suit was declined; and so the years dragged slowly by, until, as the reader remembers, on the night of the storm, in the little grotto on Takaboka, Ine Tanaka awoke to the joyful discovery that Shiro had come back to his work and to her.

A soft step in the adjoining apartment aroused the woman from her dreams of coming victory and happiness, and as she turned her gaze in the direction of the sound, the sliding doors opened and she beheld the tall form of Bishop Paoli. He had just returned to Kayaki and had not yet laid aside his disguise. Removing the pilgrim hat which he wore, the Jesuit entered the room, his countenance lighting up as his eyes fell upon Ine.

"Heaven be praised!" cried the woman, joyfully. "Thou hast at last come! Our people, good bishop, were growing anxious about thee."

"Little cause had they to trouble their hearts about me," Paoli responded. "The dear people, how prone to unbelief they are! Know they not that those who are given a work to do shall be protected in doing it? But, daughter, thou art here alone!" the speaker continued, bending a questioning look upon Ine. "This is strange; where is Shiro?"

"In the chapel, good bishop, with Chijiwa and the other leaders. Ah, he comes even now!" the woman exclaimed, a pleased look irradiating her features.

As she was speaking, the young Christian chief entered the apartment, and, perceiving his warlike equipment, the Jesuit said in a softly grave tone:

"Thou art yet a man of peace, my son; is there need, then, for thee to put on so soon the armor of the warrior?"

The fine face of the Japanese youth was glowing with excitement and enthusiasm.

"I know, good father bishop, that thou hast advised me to permit you to lead the rescue of our brethren at Nagasaki to-night; but, good father, ought not I, who am, by divine appointment, the commander-in-chief of the army of the church, brave whatever perils my office may expose me to? The brethren here expect this of me; Chijiwa and the other leaders say I ought to lead the rescue to night; I, also, feel that it is my duty to do so. I have, therefore, prepared myself to go; good father bishop, I myself must lead to-night—"

And then Nirado Shiro suddenly paused.

Ine had been listening in rapt attention to her lover's words, and she cordially approved his desire to assume at once his position as leader of his people. His, and none other's, was the place at the head of the rescuing party, and it was his duty, as it was his right, to fill it. She had no fear of the perils that might encompass him. "Those who are given a work to do shall be protected in doing it," had been Paoli's language, only a few minutes before, when assuring her of his own immunity from harm. To Nirado Shiro, likewise, Heaven had given a great and holy work, and until this was done he, too, was safe.

When her lover had uttered the words: "I myself must lead to-night," and then abruptly paused, the woman looked up in surprise. The two men before her were looking into each other's faces; the Jesuit's calm features wore a strangely resolute expression and she perceived that his steady gaze was exerting an influence over the younger man. She saw the ardent enthusiasm, which but a moment before had been blazing in Shiro's countenance suddenly fade away and a look of tranquil submissiveness come in its place. For a short time the two men stood thus, and then the astonished Ine beheld a soft smile wreathe the bishop's face as he made a slight gesture of his hand toward the couch whereon she was lying. The next instant Shiro had flung himself upon his knees by her side.

"Forgive me, dearest Ine!" he cried, and the woman was amazed at the change in his voice—a minute before so full of passionate ardor and manly daring, now so irresolute and pleading, "Forgive me! In my foolish excitement, I forgot thee."

"Nay, nay, Nirado Shiro, speak not thus, I pray!" the woman returned, distressed beyond measure at this sudden transformation. Then a glow came to her pale cheeks and a fine light to her large, lustrous eyes, and, raising herself to a sitting posture, her voice rang out with all the fervor and enthusiasm that but a short time before had marked the bearing of the man now kneeling at the side of her couch. "Nirado Shiro, heed not me! My wounds are not dangerous; let me go with my sister and the other women in the boats to-night. Do thou be the leader of our friends in the coming conflict, as they expect thee to be. Thou knowest it to be thy duty to go, and Ine Tanaka would not have thee stay."

For a moment it seemed as if the woman had succeeded in inspiring in her lover's breast a resolution as ardent and an enthusiasm as intense as those which had formerly possessed him. He raised his head proudly, and as his eyes met Ine's he felt her gaze thrill him like a draught of strong wine. He would have spoken, but the calm, even voice of the Jesuit broke the breathless silence.

"Shiro is right, Ine; thou shouldst have a day or two more of rest. And can you think it strange, my daughter, that thy betrothed husband desires to remain by thy side to shield thee from possible peril? Such is your wish, is it not, my son?" and as the eyes of the two men again met Shiro bowed his head, and, turning to Ine, yet never raising his eyes to her face, he said in a low, rapid voice:

"Even so. My place for the present is by thy side, and it is folly for us to talk of my leading the rescue to-night or of your going with the other women. You are not yet able to leave your bed, and the exposure of a night sail to Arima might harm you beyond recovery."

"Be it then as you both desire!" Ine replied, striving hard to conceal the regret and disappointment that she felt. "Saints and angels go with thee and shield thee, good father, as thou leadest our brethren to-night against the cruel idolators."

"Amen, to that prayer of thine, daughter!" cried the bishop, crossing himself, and Shiro exclaimed: "The arm of the Lord, is it not with us? Is it not the promise of Heaven that we shall succeed?"

"Fitly spoken, Nirado Shiro," said the woman, fixing her clear, earnest eyes upon her lover's face. "O my lord and dearest, let our hearts be strong, our faith steadfast! In this supreme crisis of our cause, it behooves us who are leaders to be patterns of fortitude to the people."

Bishop Paoli had thus far during the conversation remained standing in the middle of the room. He now came and seated himself near the lovers, but in such a position that he and Shiro faced each other. Ine fancied that she caught the glimpse of an interchange of glances between the two men, and she noted a look of sullen defiance flashing from her lover's eyes. This rebellious outburst, however, went no further than the passing glance which the younger man shot at his companion, and then an expression of beseeching appeal settled over his handsome face. But no trace of emotion disturbed the placid and sphinx-like calm of the Jesuit's countenance, as, ignoring both Ine's look of mystified surprise at the strange actions she had just witnessed and the mute entreaty that was written upon Shiro's features, he spoke in his calmest and most gentle tone:

"Yesterday, thou, my daughter, wert most wonderfully saved from death, and likewise, thou, Shiro, providentially escaped destruction at the hands of the governor's officials," and Paoli proceeded to relate the story of Kanshin's visit to the *Spuyten Duyvil*, as he had that afternoon heard it from the lips of Marmion Beaumont. "And, now, my children," he said, in conclusion, "what does it mean, your miraculous preservation and your equally marvellous meeting upon Takaboka last night? Let me tell you. It was, my son, that thou, who art destined to be, with the help of Heaven, the deliverer of the church, and thou, daughter, since thy childhood the betrothed wife of Nirado Shiro and long the consolation of our suffering people, should, by your union, now at the beginning of our struggle for freedom, realize the hopes the Christians have ever cherished concerning you, and give our sacred cause the inspiration of your united leadership. To-night, dear children, I am to exchange, perhaps forever, my priestly office for the sterner duties of the soldier ; but before this is done permit me to announce to our people here, ere they go forth to their brethren at Arima, or to do battle for the rescue of their friends, that at last their prayers have been answered, their long desire fulfilled ; that Shiro, their leader, and Ine Tanaka, their well-beloved Ine, are man and wife."

The woman had heard with bowed head Paoli's concluding words. She felt her cheeks burn and her heart throbbed as if it would break through her side. Not daring to look up, she waited to hear her lover's answer. A minute passed and the silence remained unbroken. The wild intoxicating joy that had thrilled her soul at the bishop's mention of her union with Shiro died away, leaving an indefinable foreboding of evil. Intuitively, Ine felt that these two men before her were again gazing into each other's eyes, and that once more a conflict of mind with mind, of will with will, was being waged between them. At last Shiro spoke :

"Dearest Ine, let it be even as the good bishop says !"

The words were spoken with the voice of Nirado Shiro, but the wish they expressed was the wish of another.

And Ine Tanaka was conscious of this.

She raised her head, and her face seemed to the two men before her as the face of some fair and saintly queen, whose love had been proffered and declined. Her womanly dignity felt keenly the humiliation put upon it, but there was no resentful clamor for redress. The vague dread of something still worse to come, which had al-

HIGASHI-YAMA.—AS IT WAS IN THE SEVENTEENTH CENTURY; RESTORED FROM A MODERN PHOTOGRAPH.—*See Page* 139.

ready oppressed her, settled closer and more heavily upon her aching heart. The love she cherished for this man could endure much, patiently awaiting in hope. But until she was satisfied that he spoke the feeling that inspired his own heart and not the will of another, she would stand between him and a union, from which, when master of himself, he might shrink.

"Good Father Paoli," and she bowed herself before the bishop, "I have something to say, may I speak?"

The Jesuit's face grew strangely tender as he looked down upon the kneeling woman, and his voice was as gentle as her own as he addressed her.

"Rise, Ine, and speak what thy heart prompts thee to say!"

Was it for the better or the worse that the woman was not granted an opportunity to unburden her heart to the men now sitting before her in expectant waiting? Obata, the master of the house, appeared in the open door.

"Good Bishop and Shiro," he cried, "you are needed at once in the cavern-chapel! The brethren are assembled there; and it is time both for the women and children to embark and the rescuing party to set out for the city."

Paoli was on his feet and leaving the room before Obata had ceased speaking.

"We have forgotten ourselves, Shiro! Do thou, my son, assist the women to their boats. I must haste to arm myself," and, turning to Ine, he added, "Ponder well, my daughter, what thou wouldst say to us; we shall hear thee in Arima."

And Ine Tanaka, left alone, bowed her queenly head and wept.

II.

LORD ODA'S PLACE OF ENTERTAINMENT.

The section of the modern city of Nagasaki, assigned by the Japanese government as the foreigners' quarter, extends southward from the native town about a mile along the eastern shore of the bay. Its breadth varies, but at no place are foreign residences to be found further than two thirds of a mile from the water's edge. This foreign concession, known generally by its Japanese name of Oura, consists of two hills with the intervening valley, through which runs a little stream of water, that flows down from the mountains further inland. The southern hill is now called Sagaru-matsu, and the most conspicuous object on it is the large, white Roman Catholic Cathedral, erected on the site of the Jesuit college of three hundred years ago. The opposite height, Higashiyama, or the Eastern Hill, is, in our times, covered with foreign buildings, principally the residences of American missionaries and the schools that they have established. The very spot where the Christian prisoners underwent the cross ordeal is now a missionary's home ; and the place where Beaumont and the Prince of Kai stood is, at present, included in the grounds of a large and flourishing Christian female seminary, its imposing building and terraced grounds being the most conspicuous object that greets the traveller's eye as his ship steams into the little land-locked harbor.

At the right of the seminary, the sloping hill-side, which thus far has an easterly trend, turns sharply toward the south, and for some distance follows that direction. The hill thus forms an admirable natural amphitheater, its sloping sides commanding an excellent view of the level tract of ground, thirty or forty acres in extent, that stretches from the base of the hill to the little stream on the south, and westward to the waters of the bay. It was on that part of this low-lying plain, that stretches along the foot of Higashi-yama, that many of the Christian martyrs in the early years of the seventeenth century met their death; and it was here that the larger number of men and women, that lay in the city prisons, were doomed, upon the night of which we are speaking, to afford their savage foes "a spectacle," to use the words of Governor Oda to General Itakura, "the equal of which had not yet been seen in Japan."

After the ordeal of the cross had come to an end, the spectators did not disperse, but seemed to prefer waiting where they were until the time set for the execution should arrive. As soon, therefore, as the officers with their prisoners had passed down the hill to the execution grounds, the mob hastened to secure positions that would command an unobstructed view of all that was to take place below.

The execution grounds were brilliantly lighted from hundreds of gayly colored lanterns, suspended from ropes that were stretched across the open space between high posts. In addition to the lanterns, other pillars had been erected at regular intervals, and these bore large oil lamps, that flared and sputtered, emitting a close, fetid odor. Beyond the grounds toward the bay, a large pavilion, open upon the side facing the hill, had been put up, and within this, rising tier above tier, successive stages had been erected and covered with soft mats. Here would Lord Oda, with his staff of government officials, military officers and especially invited guests, sit and behold the torture and death of his victims. On either side of the governor's pavilion, ruder, uncovered platforms had been constructed for the accommodation of the large body of inferior officials, both civil and military. The open space, between the pavilion and the stout wooden railing that had been erected along the base of the hill to hold back the common throng, was reserved as the place of execution. Here the ghastly preparations for the approaching horrors met the eye. A double line of rude wooden crosses extended along the entire length of the grounds on the side nearest the hill, and at the foot of each cross lay a heavy hammer and the requisite number of nails. Directly in front of the crosses were the stakes. These, also, were arranged in a double row, each with its pile of faggots and coil of cord. Before these, in turn, yawned a wide and deep open pit, prepared to receive those whose doom it might be to be buried alive. In the yet large space remaining, between this pit and the pavilion, were gathered all the engines of torture that cruelty could devise to make life intolerable, and to render even the stake and the cross a relief to the sufferer. Lord Oda had indeed reason to commend the entertainment that he had prepared for this night as one never before equaled.

The officers, leading their prisoners down the hill-side from the ordeal, crossed the execution grounds, and, placing them in a large walled enclosure that had been prepared for the condemned, took up their position as guards at the entrance, there to await the coming of the main body of the Christian captives from the city prison.

Eleven o'clock came, and the great bell in the Suwa temple boomed out in a heavy volume of sound, that rolled over the town and harbor and far away into the dark recesses of the neighboring hills. It was the signal for the government troops to bring forth the prisoners from the dungeon in the city and to begin the mournful march to Oura. Scarcely had the fainting notes died away on the still night air, when a simultaneous crash of sound burst forth from all the Buddhist temples clustered along the eastern hill-side, and soon, across the bay, and far up the Urakami valley and down the coast, among the villages of the fishermen, and far back among the mountain hamlets, wherever there was a temple and a bell, were the tidings borne to the ears of the expectant people that the hour of the Christians' woe, the hour of the pagans' triumph had come.

Forth from walled mansion and squalid hovel, from shop and market-place, from government office and temple cloister, from the boats in the harbor and the farmers' huts in the neighboring fields, from the islands in the outer bay, and from the winding mountain passes poured the people, filling every street and alley leading to the place of execution. It was a motley multitude. Here a party of merry, laughing girls, brilliant in their many-colored attire and the bright flowers that adorned their hair, hurried forward by the side of a group of religious pilgrims whose once white robes were grimy with the dust of many a weary mile of mountain-road. Yonder a spruce tradesman, having carefully locked the door of his shop, strode on by the side of a number of tonsured Buddhist priests clad in their sacerdotal vestments, a smile of pleased triumph on their cleanly-shaven faces. There a gang of desperadoes from the hill country skulked along through the dimly lighted alleys, conversing in low tones as they cautiously pursued their way. Up that broad street came some haughty prince and his mounted body-guard, preceded by a troop of *bettos* that made clear the way before them. Close after these followed a detachment of troops, brilliant with their gay banners and gaudy trappings of war. The soldiers marched to the shrill, piercing music of shell and horn, and behind them rushed along a tumultuous throng of boys and half-grown youths, their voices, at times, rising in concert with the fierce cry: "Down with the Christians."

III.

ANDO THE HUNCHBACK.

In the seventeenth century, one of the principal highways leading into Nagasaki was the thoroughfare known as the Mogi road. This highway, at present little more than a bridle-path, upon leaving the city, skirts the base of Higashi-yama on its northern side, and then leads off in an easterly direction some three miles, to the now wretched little fishing village of Mogi on the opposite side of the cape. At the time of which we are writing, however, Mogi was a prosperous port, whither came the junks from Higo and Chikugo, laden with merchandize for the Nagasaki market. Here the goods were unshipped and borne to the city on the backs of horses and oxen, or on large carts drawn by men.

Just as the Suwa bell pealed forth its summons to victims and spectators alike to repair to the execution grounds, a traveller on the Mogi highway came descending the western slope of the range of hills that form a water-shed between the gulf of Shimabara that lay behind him and Nagasaki bay about a mile distant ahead. As the stranger passes under one of the lanterns that are hung at regular intervals along the road, we perceive that he is deformed. He is not over four feet in height. As for neck, he has none; and his head is so sunken, that the points of his misshapen shoulders reach his ears. His back is crooked, and a large protuberance stands out from between his shoulders; his legs are short and slender, his feet large; his arms, as long as an ordinary person's, with his low stature, bring his hands almost to the ground. In the passing glance we have had of him, our eyes very likely have rested too long upon his poor, deformed body, to have noticed his face. Had we done so, we would have been struck with a remarkable contrast. His features are as delicate and beautiful as those of a lovely woman; his mouth as sweetly smiling as an infant's; his eyes as keenly piercing as an eagle's; and his forehead as broad and full as that of a sage. Altogether a very strangely made-up individual is this dwarfish hunchback.

But while we have thus been dwelling upon his personal appearance, our little traveller has been hastening on his way, as fast as those short legs could carry his ninety odd pounds of misshapen flesh and bone. The bells of all the temples in the city filled the air with a heavy burden of sound, broken every now and then by the frenzied shouts of a great concourse of people. The hunchback's eyes were steadfastly fixed upon the tremulous column of light thrown upward from the countless lanterns, torches and lamps on the execution grounds, and he was not aware of a noiseless step by his side.

"I observe, friend, that thou art in as much haste as myself."

The hunchback started, and, glancing at the figure at his side, saw a tall, strongly-built man dressed in the garb of a *mushashugoja*, or warrior pilgrim. A *fuka-amigasa**

---

* A hat made of plaited work, and so shaped as to droop over and conceal the face of the wearer.

concealed the stranger's face, and a dark-colored robe flowed loosely to his feet.

"I am in somewhat of a hurry," answered the hunchback in a low, pleasant voice. "It seems also that we are going the same way."

"All roads, to-night, my friend, lead to Oura, and all faces are turned thither."

"Indeed!" responded the other. "What is it that draws everybody to Oura? I see the lights ahead and hear the shouting of men and the sound of the bells; something very unusual is surely happening. What is it?"

The speaker looked up questioningly at his tall companion, who, he perceived, was narrowly watching him. At length he heard him laugh.

"Do you mean to say," cried the warrior pilgrim, in an incredulous tone, "that you do not know what is taking place to-night over there?" pointing with his hand toward the broad, upright band of light before them.

"Even so. I have not the remotest idea of what is going on."

"So, so! Then must I inform thee, O thou ignorant one!"

And straightway the tall man proceeded to acquaint the hunchback of Lord Oda's entertainment.

"And now," he added, in conclusion, "thou art going, of course, to behold the misbelieving dogs die?"

"Oh, certainly!"

"I also am going thither; let us keep together! But, perchance, it may not be safe for me to be with thee."

"Then friend," returned the hunchback, with a musical laugh, "since thou art afraid that I may hurt thee, thou wouldst do well to permit me to go alone."

The other roared with merriment.

"So, so, *kekko!* Well said. But thou didst not understand me. I do not fear the matchless prowess that one can very well perceive thou possessest." And the pilgrim roared again; then, dropping his voice to a whisper: "But, friend, how about thy religion? It is that which nowadays gets men into trouble; methinks, thou art dangerous there. Eh, friend, how is it?"

The hunchback started violently, but instantly regaining his self-possession, said, with a laugh, that betrayed just a little nervousness withal:

"Perhaps thou art thinking me a disciple of the barbarian priests, but I assure thee I am not. Take me to the ordeal and thou shalt see me trample the cross. But," and his voice assumed a bantering tone, "it may be that thou art a Christian, and fearest I may discover it and betray thee to the officials, I warn thee, to beware! if such be the case."

The pilgrim cast a careful glance about them. There were other pedestrians, both before and behind, but at too great a distance to overhear anything they might say. Nevertheless, when he spoke he did so in a low whisper.

"I believe that thou speakest truly, friend, when thou sayest that thou art not a follower of the doctrines of the priests. And yet I charge thee with being a Christian; canst thou deny the accusation?"

Getting no reply, the pilgrim spoke again:

"Dare you, I say, deny that you are a Christian?"

"I deny your right to question me. If you suspect me, you have it in your power to make known those suspicions to the authorities. When I am brought before them, I shall confess, and deny not, if so it be that I am a Christian."

"Nay, nay, now!" cried the other, soothingly. "You

are evading my question. But, I pray thee, if it be possible for thee, let us step up a little more briskly. It cannot be lacking much of midnight, and I must be at the execution grounds before that."

"Do not allow me to detain you," returned the hunchback, coldly, and slackening his pace as he spoke. "I am walking too fast now, and must take the remainder of the road more easily. You say you are needed at the execution?"

The other laughed.

"Nay, I said not that; yet it is so, and moreover I shall endeavor to keep you company. Am I to take it, then, that you will not answer my questions?"

The hunchback grew hot with indignation.

"I shall reply to nothing you ask me," he cried, fiercely. "You are, doubtless, some government spy, striving to entangle me. I shall answer to the officials, but not to you."

"Thou art right again, friend," said the pilgrim, in a low voice. "I am a spy, and since thou dost so foolishly object to my questions, I shall tell thee what I know concerning thee, to make it plain that I need neither thy silence, nor yet any admission of thine to hold thee in my power. I have been following thee ever since thou left Mogi, an hour or more ago. Thy name is Ando, and thou art of the household of the old Lord Mori, of Unzen."

"Well!" retorted the hunchback, impatiently. "Your knowledge is the common property of the countryside—"

"Hold, friend; not so fast!" The pilgrim's tone was now severe. "That is not all. I know that for these many years thy master has been a Christian; not, it is true, of the sect of the missionaries but what the Western barbarians call Protestant. I know Lord Mori's history. Twenty-five years ago he visited Holland and England, and became a zealous adherent of the form of Christianity that is believed in those lands. When he returned to Japan, he brought with him an English wife. She died shortly, and Lord Mori, surrendering his title and estates to his cousin Nabeshima, retired to private life, and with his infant daughter sought a retreat from the world among the solitudes of Mount Unzen. That daughter, now a woman grown, is your mistress."

The pilgrim bent another keen look on the hunchback, but the latter remained silent. The stranger continued:

"You have been sent to Nagasaki by your mistress to get news of some foreign ship. She fears the persecution may reach them, and she wishes to flee from the country with her aged father, and to seek safety in the land of her mother's birth. Now, friend, what say you? Do I not know— But what is the matter?"

The hunchback was lying unconscious at the stranger's feet.

IV.

THE WARRIOR-PILGRIM RECOUNTS A FAMILY HISTORY.

The warrior-pilgrim stooped down and raised the prostrate hunchback in his arms.

"Fool that I was!" he muttered. "I went too far; and now, to reward my rashness, I have this fellow on my hands."

Darting quickly into a thick grove of pine adjoining the highway, that he might not be seen by the passers-by, he laid his burden down at the foot of a tree, and began chafing Ando's forehead and hands. In a few minutes the hunchback gave signs of returning consciousness, and, as a long-drawn, gasping sigh broke from his lips, he raised himself to a sitting posture, and, seizing the pilgrim's hand, sobbed forth in a voice tremulous with emotion :

"You indeed know all! I am in your hands. My beloved mistress and her aged parent are at your mercy. But I implore you to spare them. Take me to the officials, if you will; torture me, burn, crucify, or bury me alive. Let this poor, worthless body of mine feel the punishment that you would inflict upon them; but spare my mistress. If money will move you to be merciful, you shall be rich with the gold I shall gladly give thee."

"Hush! Not so loud," whispered the other. "The people passing by will hear you. Do not fear. I was but trying you. I, too, am a Christian."

"Nay, nay, that cannot be," said the other, his heart filled with the contending emotions of hope and fear, doubt and belief. "You told me but a moment ago that you were one of the executioners."

The pilgrim laughed.

"Thou hast, in very sooth, a nimble wit in making assumptions. Behold thy process of reasoning, my friend. I told you that I must be at the execution grounds before midnight. You thereupon concluded that I am needed at the execution. Your conclusion, I informed you, was correct; and consequently you now infer that I am an executioner. Again thy reasoning has served thee well. I am an executioner, friend, but not of Christians."

"I do not comprehend you."

"I am not surprised. But, friend, we must be on our way. You are strong enough now, I perceive, to get on your legs," he continued, as Ando rose to his feet, "and so I infer that you are able to walk. We can converse as we go."

The two travellers, issuing from the grove, resumed their journey toward the city. The highway now began to bear off to the northward, and the light, streaming upward from the execution grounds, instead of being in front of them, as before, was falling away to their left.

"Here," said the pilgrim, pausing in his walk, "methinks we had better leave the road, and make our way across the fields in a direct line to Oura. Hast thou ever heard, friend, of the family of Oyano, retainers of the Lords of Kai?"

"I have, indeed," exclaimed the other. "My master still frequently speaks of the Oyanos, and never unless it is to commend their faithfulness, or to praise their bravery."

"It is sweet to think that Lord Mori, though long ago he hid his face from the eyes of his vassals, has not forgotten them. Friend, I am an Oyano."

The hunchback could not restrain a cry of mingled surprise and gladness. "Thank God!" he cried, fervently. "Ah! friend, my fears were indeed groundless, but how was I to know that, when you spoke so roughly? But how is it that thou art here, in the dress of a *musha-shugoja?*"

"Because I prefer the perils of the faith to the luxury of the court of an infidel prince. Time was when the house of Kai was the glory of the church of Japan. The first of the nobility to embrace the doctrines of the missionary priests, its princes became the zealous defenders of the religion they professed. With your master, Ando, the change for the worse began. He went to England, and there became a zealous convert to the sect called Protestant. With his fair-faced English wife, he returned to Japan, with the resolve to introduce the new teachings into the church of his native land. A furious controversy arose between him and the missionaries led by the Jesuit, Paoli. Finding all his plans frustrated, Lord Mori renounced his title and estates, and sought quietness and safety in the solitudes of Mount Unzen. Since that retirement, you know his history better than I. The present prince, Lord Nabeshima, is noble, brave and chivalrous. He is beloved by all his retainers, and his name is honored throughout the land. In his boyhood, his constant companion was Will Adams, the Englishman whom the great Iyeyasu loved. Three years of his early manhood were also spent in England; but when he returned, alas! it was neither as Romanist nor Protestant. Our blessed Lord he makes but a great, good man, and says that God reveals himself in the consciences of men alone, and that, therefore, conscience is the only certain and sufficient guide. His views have been embraced by all his followers to the ruin of the faith in Kai. What was once a Christian chapel is now a lecture hall, where the Lord Nabeshima gives Sabbath-day discourses on Confucius, Buddha, Mahomet, Jesus, and the wise men of the West. My family remained true to the teachings of the missionaries, and finding our lives intolerable because of the scoffs and sneers of our comrades, my two brothers and myself donned the garb of *musha-shugoja*, and went forth from the home of our ancestors as wanderers upon the earth. One of these brothers has already fallen a martyr to the faith we love, and the other is among the number of those condemned to die to-night on yonder execution ground."

The hunchback had been listening with rapt attention to Oyano's words. He already knew much of his mas ter's history, but some of it he heard now for the first time.

"I have been deeply interested in what you have told me, good friend; but I would fain hear more. You spoke of being an executioner, though not of Christians; I do not understand you."

Then Oyano proceeded to tell Ando of Paoli's scheme to rescue the Christians, and added:

"We are nearing the crowd ahead, and must very soon drop our conversation. If I mistake not, you shall see some bloody work to-night. About one hundred of us are to mingle with the spectators; of these I am the leader. The good bishop, with two hundred and fifty well-armed men, is to be at hand awaiting my signal. A detachment of five hundred soldiers from our army at Arima is now lying concealed in the cemetery on that hill to our left. After I give the first signal, which is to be a blue rocket exploding in the form of a red dragon, both of the waiting re-inforcements are to rush up, and when the bishop's division is sufficiently close, he is to send up a red rocket exploding in the form of a white cross. This is the signal for us who are among the spectators to raise our battle cry, and to rush to the execution grounds, to set free the prisoners. But, hush, here we are!"

V.

A CLIMAX OF PERILS.

Oyano and the hunchback had now reached the crest of Higashi-yama, and the vast multitude of people covering its western slope and the execution grounds on the little plain below burst into view. The sports were in progress on the open space before the governor's yet unoccupied pavilion; and dancing girls, wrestlers, and musicians were vying with one another for the applause of the spectators. Oyano's tall form, towering above the crowd about him, enabled him to see an open space a short distance down the sloping hill-side.

"Let us move forward," he said to Ando. "I see a better position ahead. Follow close at my heels, and I shall elbow our way through the crowd."

Their progress through the densely packed throng was slow enough, but finally reaching the open space, they were delighted to find a large rock, that would serve the hunchback as a seat, where he could have the view his diminutive stature would otherwise render impossible. On one side the earth had been removed, forming a deep hollow beneath the rock, a depository prepared by some farmer for the reception of the produce of the field.

"See here!" said Oyano, in a whisper to Ando. "Here is a place of refuge for you during the battle. As soon as you see me give the signal, slip down from the top of the rock and hide yourself here. Arrows and bullets will fly thick and fast, I assure you, and should you escape them, you nevertheless, would certainly be trampled to death by the panic-stricken multitude."

The hunchback whispered back an assent to the words of his companion, and was in the act of climbing up to his seat, when a rough voice accosted him;

"Ho, there, crooked-back! Down off that rock, or, by the gods, I'll beat straight that misshappen carcass of thine!"

The speaker was a powerful-looking fellow, and, like Oyano, was dressed in the costume of a warrior-pilgrim. Oyano, hearing the fellow's threat, hastened to the other side of the rock where he was standing, and, bending a fierce look upon him, cried out, sternly:

"Hands off, stranger! He who harms this man quarrels with me."

The other *musha-shugoja* swept a keen look over Oyano, and then replied:

"No quarrel, then, shall there be between us. I am but guarding this rock for a friend, who shortly will have need of it. This hunchback is the one-hundredth person, at least, that has tried within the past hour to mount it."

"Then let me tell you that the one-hundredth person shall not only mount this rock, but shall also remain upon it. There is room enough for two. Is your friend likewise a dwarf?"

The stranger broke into a loud, harsh laugh.

"O, ye gods, hear him! A dwarf! Well, no, scarcely, methinks."

"Then why should he need the rock?" demanded Oyano, irritated at the other's manner.

"Wait, and thou shalt see," returned the stranger, his eyes closely scrutinizing Oyano's costume. "Methinks, friend," he continued, "that thy pilgrim garb as ill becomes thee as mine does me."

"Perchance it does," replied Oyano, coolly. "Thy name, friend?"

The stranger shrugged his shoulders. "For the nonce I choose to be nameless."

"I likewise," the other said, in a confidential tone. He knew, he thought, the man's character, and he began to suspect that some mischief was afoot which it behooved him to know. The stranger glanced toward the hunchback.

"Do not fear him!" Oyano said, in a low voice; "he

is one of us. I have travelled far to-day, and have just arrived here. Some work is to be done to-night, is there not? If so, I am ready; see, I have come prepared," and the speaker swept aside his flowing robe for an instant, disclosing his swords to his companion.

"Yes, there is work for us to-night. Our chieftain, Gonroku, has been set free by the governor."

"Indeed!" exclaimed Oyano, with an astonishment that was wholly unfeigned.

"Ha!" cried the other, "there they come!"

Oyano looked toward the pavilion, and beheld about twenty of the seamen from the *Spuyten Duyvil*, armed with muskets, pistols and cutlasses, file slowly into the execution grounds, and take up their position before the pavilion.

"What does that mean, those foreigners; why are they here, and armed?" cried Oyano to his companion.

Briefly the stranger told him Lord Oda's plot for the destruction of the officers and crew, and the capture of the *Spuyten Duyvil*.

"But, by all the gods!" cried he; "those fellows will give us a tough job of it! There are, however, but twenty of them, and we shall outnumber them ten to one. Ho!" he shouted, in stentorian tones; "down with the foreigners!"

Some other voices caught the cry, and then hundreds, scattered throughout the vast throng, took it up, until a mad roar burst forth—

"Down with the foreigners!"

"Ha!" cried the stranger, with a terrible laugh. "Well begun! We must get the people worked up to a fury against those fellows, then we shall be twenty to one."

"Well done indeed, Gohei!" exclaimed a gruff voice just behind them, and Oyano, turning, saw a villainous-looking ruffian, equipped with a heavy suit of armor, but lacking a helmet. As he perceived the two men looking at him, he laughed, disclosing a double row of yellow fangs from ear to ear. "Keep the mob shouting, Gohei; it will make the work easier for us later on. But who is this?" pointing to Oyano "A new recruit, eh?"

"Yes," replied Gohei. "He is to be one of us. But how fares it, Gonroku?"

"Ah! indeed," thought Oyano to himself. "That cut-throat is Gonroku, the robber-chieftain. Woe, then to that handful of foreigners! I would they could understand the meaning of these savage yells! How this plot of the blood-thirsty governor is to affect our enterprise, I know not, but we dare not retreat from our purpose."

"*Kekko, kekko*," responded Gonroku to Gonhei's question. "Tidings have just come that both Yamada, the *Ronin*, and the governor's deputy, Kanshin, are in the escort that conducts the barbarian captain and the Englishman hither from the Dutch trading-house. As soon as I mount this rock and give the signal for the riot to begin, they and their companions will take care of them. There, look! by the hand of Buddha! they are coming! Here, Gohei, move thou to that side, while I go this way. Our presence will stir our people up, and bring us new recruits. And do thou, friend," said the robber-chief, addressing Oyano, "stay by this rock and keep it clear."

The two outlaws now disappeared among the spectators, whose numbers, increased by hundreds of new-comers, presented the appearance of an unbroken sea of faces over the entire length and height of the two converging hill-sides. The little hunchback, pointing toward the pavilion, cried out to his companion:

"See, good friend, knowest thou that fair and noble-looking foreigner?"

"Ah, that is the Englishman, of whom thou hast just heard the robber-chieftain speak," said Oyano, his eyes resting upon Beaumont, Van Neist, and the two Dutch traders, Santvoort and Koeckebacker, who, escorted by their guards, had just arrived before the pavilion. "There, there, by the side of the Englishman," continued Oyano, excitedly. "Knowest thou him, man? He is thy master's cousin, Lord Nabeshima, Prince of Kai. And look yonder at the other side of the pavilion. Lord Oda and his train, the government officials, and the military officers! By my life Ando, do not thine eyes dazzle with all that display of gold and color?"

The appearance of the governor's party had hushed the spectators into a respectful silence, for Orientals never greet their state officials with the uproarious applause or the ringing cheers that salute the public appearance of a Western ruler; but as soon as Oda, the officials, and the invited guests, including the captain and the young Englishman, had taken their seats, the frenzied throng raised again the mad cry:

"Down with the foreigners!"

At that moment the head of a long double column of government troops appeared approaching the execution grounds. Between the two lines of soldiers came the Christian prisoners. At the first sight of these, the howling rabble screamed with savage delight, and as the long column passed over the open space before the pavilion, on its way to the inclosure at the farther end of the grounds, where the prisoners were to await each his turn to be led forth to torture and execution, the vast multitude, now one shrieking, cursing, frantic, and blood-thirsty mob, became threateningly insubordinate in its mad excitement. Cries of "No, no, don't put them in there, bring them out! Away with the sports! The Christians, the Christians! Begin their torture now! We will wait no longer!" rose amid the deafening uproar and confusion.

"Mother of mercy!" cried the alarmed Oyano. "The blood-thirsty pagans are breaking over the barriers into the execution grounds! See, see! they are driving the guards backward and our poor friends are left to the fury of the mob! Merciful God, hear the shrieks of the women!"

While Oyano was speaking, he was hurriedly preparing to give the signal; and scarcely had the last words left his lips, when, with a sharp, whirring sound, a rocket emitting a blue flame as it mounted aloft, rose high into the air, where it burst with a loud report and a red dragon fell circling above the governor's pavilion. In a minute more another sharp explosion above him caused the little hunchback to glance upward. There, enveloped in a halo of sparkling red flame, hovered the figure of a white cross, Paoli's signal of attack.

BOOK SIXTH.

THE HOUSEHOLD OF MORI.

I.

UNA THE EURASIAN.

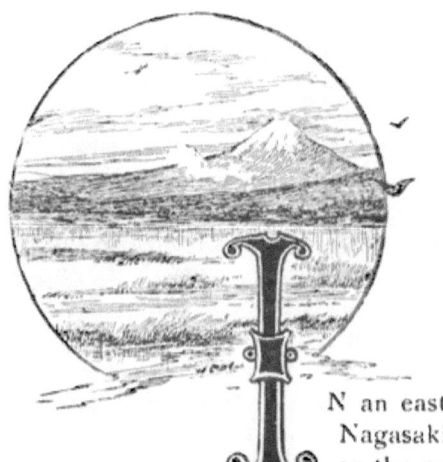

IN an easterly direction from Nagasaki, some twenty miles as the crow flies, towers the volcano of Unzen, its huge bulk lying athwart the narrow peninsula of Shimabara, between the northern and southern plains of which it renders communication impossible, except by boat along the rock-bound coast or through steep and winding mountain-passes. In our day Unzen is classed among the inactive volcanoes of Japan; but less than one hundred years ago, a terrific eruption occurred, occasioning the destruction of numerous villages and the greater part of the city of Shimabara, with the loss of many thousands of lives. At the time of which we are writing, it was active, though not dangerously so. Over its crater there hung by day a snow-white column of smoke and steam and at night the light from the red-hot rocks below shone upon this, transforming it into a pillar of fire that served through the darkest night as a beacon to the belated traveller in the plain below and the fishermen on either bay.

On the day succeeding the night of the execution at Nagasaki, as the afternoon sun was drawing near the western hills, and the deeper valleys and gorges that furrowed the scarred sides of Unzen were already full of twilight, two persons might have been seen seated upon a large, flat bowlder that crowned one of the lesser peaks which commands an extensive view of the southern plain. Of these, one was a man past fifty years of age; but his long beard and hair of snowy whiteness, his hollow cheeks and temples, and shrunken form gave him the appearance of a much more advanced age. At first glance, one would have recognized in him the scholar and the recluse; for, besides the student dress that he wore, there was that in his thoughtful face and massive forehead, his large, dreamy eyes and general figure and demeanor, which marked him as the retiring scholar who shunned the world and its busy whirl of labor and pleasure to court solitude and the pursuits of the intellectual life. In youth he must have been of a remarkably handsome and commanding presence; for even now in old age his wasted form was tall and erect, his step, though slow, was yet light and firm, the contour of his face was regular and well-formed, and an air of quiet dignity and thoughtfulness in his bearing betokened him to be of noble birth and accustomed to command.

Of his companion, a young woman of twenty years, how shall we speak? What exquisite loveliness of form and feature did she not possess? Were there ever eyes more softly lustrous than the dark blue ones of this maiden, or richer masses of glossy raven hair, or features more beautifully moulded, or lip and brow touched with a gentler dignity and tenderness, or hands more shapely and delicate, or form comelier than hers? And as she turned to speak to the old man at her side, no meadow brook was ever softer or more musical in its murmurs beneath the summer flowers than was the sound of this maiden's voice.

"My father, thou art weary; it was wrong in me to ask thee to climb this height."

"Nay, nay, dear child!" returned the other, faintly, yet soothingly withal. "Reproach not thyself! The ascent was, indeed, trying to one, who for the past month has not looked once on the face of the sky; yet a little rest, Una, a little rest, and I shall be myself again;" and the old man, pallid and exhausted with his late exertion, closing his eyes in his weariness, leaned back against the trunk of a small mountain pine that had found a cranny in the bowlder with soil enough therein to support its stunted growth.

For a time the girl's eyes rested on her father's thin, pinched face, and a shadow of sadness stole over her sweet countenance; but at the prompting of some happier train of thought, this disappeared, and in its place a bright smile irradiated her features. The old man, opening his eyes and perceiving his daughter's joyful face, said in tones of gentle reproof:

"Day dreams and visions again, O, my Una! Beware! Beware! Bitter, indeed, will be thy disappointment, if, haply, thou shouldst find thy expectation vain!"

The girl's face assumed a more sober expression.

"True, dear father ; but did I not hear some pilgrims yesternoon say that they beheld from yonder height across the bay the sails of a large foreign vessel approaching our coast ? Were there no ship in Nagasaki harbor, Ando would have returned before this."

"Pray God, my child, that you may be right ! Not for my sake, dear Una, but for thine own."

From these words of the father and daughter, the reader, who remembers the conversation between Oyano and the hunchback during their journey together on the Mogi highway, will have no difficulty in divining who they were. None other, indeed, was that old man than the Lord Mori of Oyano's story, and this fair young girl, no one else but Ando's mistress, the daughter of the English wife whom the Prince of Kai had brought to his ancestral home from her far-off native land, a maiden in whose veins flowed the blood of the Oriental and of the Westerner, of Asia and of Europe, Una the Eurasian.

Lord Mori, leaning back against the tree, again closed his eyes ; and Una's gaze wandered over the broad plain below, that sloped, at a gentle inclination, from the foothills to the shore of the bay. Far off to her left, the girl descried a rocky promontory extending some considerable distance into the sea, and on the extreme point of this rose the walls of Hara Castle, the stronghold of the Christians, who had taken up arms against their rulers. Across the narrow neck of land connecting the castle with the plain, fortifications had been thrown up, and a broad, deep *fosse* dug. Far out into the plain, the Christian lines extended, and up toward the mountains a number of rude defenses had been constructed ; and Una, looking down on one of the foot-hills at her feet, saw a body of insurgents busily engaged in fortifying its summit, that they might command the mountain pass directly opposite. In the open plain before the castle, what had been but a month before nothing more than a little village, was now the city of Arima, with nearly forty thousand inhabitants; for here had all the Christians of Amakusa and Shimabara assembled, and daily were their numbers augmented by new recruits from the surrounding provinces. The plain was alive with the bustle of preparation for war. Men and women, old and young labored, side by side, some digging deep and wide trenches, which, as soon as completed, were flooded with water from the mountain streams; others were busily engaged in transporting provisions from the country granaries to those within the castle; still others were employed in the manufacture of bows, arrows and catapults, and these in large quantities, together with huge piles of broken stones for the slingers, were collected and stored away in places prepared for them within the walls.

The sight that now met Una's eyes as she looked down on the plain of the Christians, and the confused murmur of sound that was borne to her ears from the busy multitude below were no new experience to the young girl. Day after day, for more than a month, she had gazed down from her lofty look-out upon just such an animated scene as the one now before her. It had not been, therefore, to watch the preparations for war that she and her father had this day come hither.

II.

THE PROTESTANT OF UNZEN.

With all her gentle tenderness and sweet disposition, Una Mori possessed great strength of mind and fortitude of spirit, that the peculiar conditions under which she had grown up from childhood had served to develop, making her, for one of her years, a wonderfully discerning and resolute woman.

Ever since her father had renounced his title and position as a prince and had retired to their present retreat, his mind had become more and more abstracted from the world and ever the more closely fixed upon his studies and his plans for the future of Christianity in Japan. For be it known that, like Bishop Paoli and Shiro, Lord Mori was also an enthusiast, yes, even a fanatic, if the reader so pleases; but his enthusiasm and fanaticism were of a type widely different from that of the other two. With them the church was first, the church last: with him, Christ was all in all, and the Bible the veritable Word of God, the one safe and sufficient guide for the conduct of life. It was for the advocacy of these doctrines that Lord Mori had incurred bitter opposition and persecution, nigh even to the taking of his life, at the hands of the missionaries. It was his still steadfast belief in them that led him, after the death of his wife, to seek an asylum from both his heathen and his Christian foes in the hermitage that he built for himself, his daughter, and the few faithful retainers who chose to follow their master's fortunes, high up among the mountain fastnesses of Unzen.

Here, in this quiet retreat, sixteen years had passed away—years of preparation, Lord Mori was accustomed to say. The little stock of English books that he and his wife had brought with them from Europe had been read and read again, until they were, in large part, memorized. Years of his time had been spent upon a translation of the Bible into his native language; and this labor he had come to regard as peculiarly his divinely appointed work. With his own hand, he had prepared hundreds of manuscript copies of the Scriptures. Binding these carefully, he would lay them away, saying, with a gentle smile: "Wait, dear Book, until, in the fullness of Heaven's own time, Japan is ready to receive the Word of God, instead of the word of the missionaries." Thus he toiled on unceasingly through long years, rising with the dawn and bending over his manuscripts until midnight; and as the number of his Bibles increased, the strength of the scribe failed.

Una, a name suggestive of one of the characters of the hermit's favorite English author, whose great work he knew by heart, from her early girlhood had assumed the management of the little household; and latterly in her father's growing feebleness, she had become his almost constant companion, ministering to his wants and assisting him in his labors.

But while the father heard with listless interest the tidings that their servants brought them, of a great uprising at their very doors, and of the resolve of the government to destroy all who bore the name of Christian, the daughter, with her keen, discerning foresight, read in these ominous reports a warning to them, too clear in its import to be mistaken. Sooner or later, some lurking spy would discover that, though no cross or figure of the Virgin was to be found in the Unzen hermitage, yet among its inmates the name of Christ was honored above every other name, and that there, morn and eve, prayer and praise went up from faithful hearts to the God of the Christians. Then Una, courageous and self-reliant as she was, would shudder as she reflected upon the terrible consequences which she well knew would inevitably follow the discovery that they were believers in any form of the proscribed religion. To her there was but one safe asylum—England, the land of her mother's birth. Could they but secure passage thither by some of the Dutch merchantmen, they would be safe. It required hours of patient reasoning and explanation to convince her father that danger really threatened them, and then days of entreaty, prayers and tears were spent in gaining his consent to leave his native shores again, this time forever. But finally the heart of the father prevailed over that of the scholar and the would-be reformer. For himself he cared not; but the prospect of certain dishonor, torture and death that awaited his darling child, should they be detected, terrified him at last not only into a consent to their leaving Japan, but also into a nervous apprehension of immediate peril and a feverish anxiety to get away.

"It was the desire of my manhood, and long has it been the dream of my old age to give the people of our Japan the Christianity of the Word of God," said Lord Mori to his daughter one evening, after they had been discussing their contemplated flight, "yet never in my lifetime shall this desire and this dream be fulfilled. My daughter, we shall go to the land whence came thy mother; but before we leave this hermitage, hallowed to my memory, O my child, by all the tender ties that bind this heart of mine to the beloved labor of long years, I shall hide safe and deep in the cave behind our house all these into which I have poured the strength of my life," and the old man laid his arms lovingly over the high stack of manuscript Bibles piled up in a corner of the room. "And then, when the doctrines of the missionaries are utterly extirpated in Japan, I shall write to my fellow princes that they have indeed destroyed a church but not the Christ. His caricature only have they beheld; but would they know Him and see Him as He is, let them go to Unzen and there, in the place which I shall designate, they will find Him awaiting, in His infinite patience, the fullness of the time when the people of my native land shall permit Him to speak in His own behalf."

It was shortly after this that Ando, going to Nagasaki, learned that the Dutch traders had been, for a month or more, expecting the arrival of a ship. Twice a week thereafter had the hunchback gone to the city, and on the evening of the execution of the Christian prisoners he was on his way thither once more when Oyano, disguised as a *musha-shugoja*, had overtaken him on the Mogi highway, and the conversation, narrated in a preceding chapter, ensued. The rumor that a foreign sail had been seen approaching the coast had reached Unzen the day before, and Una felt confident that this time Ando would bring back the report that the long-expected ship was lying in Nagasaki Bay, and she had persuaded her father to accompany her to her lookout station, from which, for a full league, the road by which the hunchback would return, lay in open view.

Looking down this highway, Una perceived a cloud of dust raised by some large company moving toward them over the mountain road.

"Look, father," said the girl, pointing toward the approaching troop. "Yonder comes a goodly throng of people! What may they be, thinkest thou?"

"Alas! my child," Lord Mori replied, as he turned his attention in the direction indicated by Una's outstretched hand, "I see but a cloud of dust. These dim old eyes of mine are too weak to distinguish more. But what say you they are?"

"Christians, methinks; ah, so they are, for just now I caught a glimpse of their banner with its red cross on a white field. And yonder chieftain riding ahead is Ashi-

"I BEHELD THE JESUIT'S TERRIBLE FORM TOWERING OVER LORD NABESHIMA."—*See Page* 217.

zuka, bravest and best, they say, of all the Christian warriors. By his side rides a tall and noble-looking man clad in—what? not, most surely, the armor of the *Samurai*, for his fits close to his body, and the fashion of his helmet is such as I never saw before. Behind these comes a body of mounted men, then foot-soldiers, and after these a large company of men and women, and these, in turn, are followed by another detachment of warriors."

"Some villagers, most probably," said her father. "They have risen in revolt, and are now on their way to join the insurgents at Arima."

"Yet I understand not Ashizuka's presence among them," responded the maiden. "I saw him yestereven, with a large company of armed men, hastening down this road in the direction of Obama. Perchance, however, he was on his way to escort these hither."

"So, perhaps," returned the old man; "but look again down the highway, dear child. See you aught yet of Ando?"

"Would *Sensei** behold his unworthy servant, he has but to look this way," said a low, musical voice at their side, and with a cry of joyful surprise, father and daughter turned to see at the other end of the bowlder, on which they were sitting, the childlike, smiling face and dwarfish figure of the hunchback.

---

* Master; a respectful form of address, used by students and others in addressing their teachers or superiors in learning.

III.

THE STORY OF THE RESCUE.

"Ando!" exclaimed Una, joyfully. "It is indeed you!"

"Ay, mistress, thy servant," said the hunchback, kneeling before the young girl, and pressing her hand to his lips, a custom he had learned, not from the manners of the East, but from the English books of chivalry in Lord Mori's library.

"And the ship, O Ando? Has the ship that is to bear us away to peace and safety come?"

"The long-expected merchantman, my mistress, is lying in Nagasaki harbor."

With a glad cry, the girl threw her arms about her father's neck.

"Dear father, the time has come. Let us hasten our departure. See!" she added, pointing to the plain of the Christians; "they are making ready for defense. Shortly the government troops will be here to attack them; these mountains will then be full of the enemies of our faith; escape will be no longer possible. Let us flee now while yet there is time."

"Nay, mistress," the hunchback broke in; "wait. I have much to tell thee. Escape, methinks, will be possible; but we cannot go as soon, perchance, as thou wouldst wish."

Then Ando told the story of his meeting with Oyano on the way to Nagasaki, of the fright the latter had given him, and of his subsequent disclosure that he, too, was a Christian and a former retainer of Lord Mori.

"Ah, well do I remember him," said the old man.

"He was a zealous disciple of the missionaries, yet withal a faithful vassal of mine. When Paoli was plotting to seize and transport me to some lonely place, where he could try me for heresy and put me to death, it was Oyano who played the spy upon his movements and disclosed to me his designs. And now you say, Ando, that he is one of the insurgent chiefs?"

"Even so, *Sensei*."

"Why ventured he, Ando, to go to Nagasaki, the stronghold of his foes?"

Briefly then the hunchback gave an account of Paoli's and Shiro's return to Japan, of the Takaboka massacre, of the governor's preparation for a wholesale execution of Christian prisoners, of Paoli's plan for their rescue, of the plot against the *Spuyten Duyvil*, and of Oyano's part in the proposed deliverance of the captives.

With breathless interest, Una and her father listened to the marvelous tale; and when Ando spoke of their arrival at Higashi-yama and his first sight of Marmion Beaumont, the Englishman, with his fair face and commanding figure, the girl clasped her father's arm.

"Hear him, my father! He has looked upon one of my kin beyond the sea, one of that goodly race of which you have so often spoken. Alas! alas! that I should hurt thy gentle heart! But I, who remember not my mother's face, I, who have never looked upon the countenance of one whose native speech was hers—forgive me, dear father, if half my being longs to behold those men and women to whom it is bound by the bond of a mother's blood."

Smiling sadly, the old man laid his hand with a caressing touch upon his daughter's bowed head.

"Nay, my dear Una, there is naught to forgive. It suffices me that thou lovest thy father. Dost thou not know, my daughter, that thou art the very image of thy mother? Neither in form nor feature art thou a child of Japan; and should I marvel that thy heart goes out in passionate yearning to look upon thy yet unseen kindred? But now let us attend Ando's story, child; how fared the enterprise of Paoli and Oyano?"

"Yes, go on, Ando," added the young girl eagerly, her mind still dwelling upon the Englishman, and her interest in the hunchback's narrative centering in him. Ando continued:

"I was seated on a rock, Oyano standing close by me; the two outlaws, Gonroku and Gohei, had disappeared among the spectators; then the Christian captives were brought up to the grounds by the soldiers. Immediately the mob raised such a savage outcry for their blood, that my heart grew faint at the sound. From where I sat I had an excellent view of both the spectators and the prisoners. I beheld a religious pilgrim leap over the barrier that had been raised along the edge of the execution grounds to keep back the populace. A soldier knocked the fellow down. Thereupon a fierce yell arose from the mob, and at once, more than a hundred sprang over among the guards and a fierce struggle ensued. It was then that Oyano sent up his signal. In the brief interval that elapsed before Paoli's answering rocket appeared, the encounter on the execution grounds developed into a desperate fight. The mob, pouring down upon the soldiers in overwhelming numbers, drove them back and began to bind some of the prisoners to the stakes, and was preparing to nail others to the crosses. Just then a stream of red flame shot upward into the sky, and a moment later a white cross was seen floating downward upon the heads of the people."

"A wild scream arose as the spectators beheld this

symbol of the hated religion above them ; and, among the terrified shrieks of thousands, arose the cry that the God of the Christians was Himself coming to deliver His followers. It was just at this juncture that I heard the roar of cannon, and, looking toward the bay, I beheld the flashing of guns in the direction of the foreign ship ; and I knew at once that a detachment of Gonroku's outlaws was making an attack upon the seamen still aboard."

An exclamation of horror from the two listeners interrupted the speaker.

"Heed us not, good Ando," Lord Mori cried anxiously. "Go on, go on ! What happened then ?"

"Then I turned my eyes from the ship to the foreigners on the grounds below me. I saw the young Englishman, followed by the two traders and the Dutch captain dash out of the pavilion, and, above all the hideous uproar around me, I heard the captain shouting out some command to his men, that were now gathered about him, and then the whole party, rushed off in the direction of the bay."

"And they made good their escape, did they not, Ando ?" interrupted Una, breathlessly. "They arrived at their ship in time to save it and their comrades from Gonroku and his murderers, was it not so ?"

"Nay, nay, now ! Patience, I pray thee, dear mistress ! I shall hasten on anon to tell thee," replied the hunchback, with a smile. "At the same instant that the foreigners dashed off into the darkness, the air was rent with the battle-cry of the Christians : ' *Yaso-Maria*, Takaboka and vengeance !" Oyano, shouting to me to hide myself beneath the rock rushed with drawn sword down the hill. In the thrilling excitement of the moment, I became heedless of the peril to which my conspicuous position exposed me ; and I was so fascinated by the terrors of the awful scene, that I seemed to lose both power and desire to conceal myself. The Christians, disguised among the spectators, now drew their weapons and made a furious assault upon the mob. At the same time, Ashizuka, with his force of insurgents from Arima, attacked the multitude from the crest of the hill, their merciless swords cutting down the guilty and, alas! I fear, the innocent alike. The terrified spectators fled shrieking from the place, as fast as they could extricate themselves from the whirling press of soldiers, citizens, prisoners and attacking Christians mixed together in the most indescrible confusion.

"Again another wild shout from the Christians: 'Yaso-Maria, Paoli to the rescue,' drew my attention to the execution grounds. The Jesuit, at the head of more than two hundred Christians, had burst into the open space before the pavilion. He was clad from head to foot in a suit of European mail, and carried no arms save a ponderous battle-ax. Never was such a terrible weapon pitted against Japanese sword and armor! The former was too short to cope with it, the latter afforded no protection against its descending edge. Little indeed, did that warrior-bishop resemble a servant of our gentle Saviour, as, with the fiery courage and prowess of some heroic crusader, he hewed his way up to the very entrance of the pavilion, and there, whirling his ax above his head, he thundered forth in tones that reached my ears above the shouts of the combatants, the screams of the terrified spectators, and the shrieks of the wounded: 'Ho, thou bloody destroyer of babes! Thou, who hast doubled the price set upon the head of Paoli, know that I am he!' Then, with a tremendous leap, he sprang upon the stage, and with another bound, was at the governor's side. I saw his ax rise and fall, and then I perceived that Lord Oda was lying prostrate at his feet. Cutting down all who dared to remain and oppose him in the pavilion, the bishop once again dashed into the fray that was raging around the prisoners. Thy cousin, *Sensei*, the Prince of Kai, with his little band of guardsmen, had thrown himself between the captives and Ashizuka's force, and was successfully resisting the latter's attempts to reach them. A great shout of 'Paoli! Paoli! Paoli to the rescue!' arose, and I beheld the Jesuit's terrible form towering over Lord Nabeshima, whose sword he had dashed from his hand. Methought, as I beheld that murderous ax swinging aloft, that the Prince was doomed; but one of his retainers, hurling his lord aside with his hands, received the fatal blow intended for him, and the faithful vassal, cloven to the teeth, sank to the earth.

"Just then, some one seizing me, dragged me from the rock and pushed me into the hollow beneath. It was Oyano, his face soiled and bleeding, and his sword stained with blood."

"Still the same brave heart as of old," murmured the old man, musingly. "Always thoughtful for the safety of others, reckless of the dangers to which he exposed himself!"

"Soon the battle was raging around my place of refuge," continued the little hunchback. "I could hear the deep breathing of the warriors, the horrible cutting thud of their blows, and, mingling with all other sounds, the incessant cry: 'Paoli! Paoli!' I lay in my retreat until the tumult of battle had rolled eastward beyond my hearing, and then, as I crawled forth, what a sight met my eyes! A late moon hung like a silver crescent in the eastern sky and its faint light was sufficient to disclose the heaps of slain that covered the hill-side. On the execution grounds, the dead lay thickest, for there the battle had been exceedingly bitter. The candles were burned out, but the gaily painted lanterns were swinging to and fro in the night wind. The stakes and the crosses had been torn from their places, and lay scattered about among the slain. The governor's pavilion was broken down, and the mats, upon which he and the officials of state and army had been seated, were soaked with blood. Here and there a wounded man was feebly calling for help. Climbing to the crest of the hill I looked off in the direction of Mogi, and as far as my eye could reach, the same heart-sickening evidences of carnage were to be seen. A disabled soldier was slowly and painfully making his way toward the city, and in reply to my inquiries, he said that the Christians had rescued the prisoners, made good their retreat, and were, probably by that time, crossing the bay to Arima."

"And the foreigners, Ando?" said Una, unable any longer to control her anxiety; "did they escape?"

"Ay, mistress. By dint of hard blows, Van Sylt, the officer in command of the ship, kept his assailants at bay until the captain with the seamen from the shore came to his assistance. Then, learning the defeat of their chieftain's plans, the outlaws hastily withdrew from the attack."

IV.

HOPES AND FEARS.

"When does the foreign ship set sail on her homeward voyage?" inquired Lord Mori, racked in soul between his eagerness to get his child beyond the reach of danger, and the bitterness of leaving his native shores to see them no more.

"Ah! that God alone knows, *Sensei*. Her captain, Van Neist, has engaged to bring his vessel to Arima to assist the government troops against the insurgents. Lord Oda is lying at the point of death from the wounds he received from Paoli last night, and Kanshin, his deputy, was killed in an attack he made upon the foreigners on their way to the shore from the execution grounds. Baba, the vice-governor, is now at the head of affairs, and we may be sure that he will not release Van Neist from his contract. The Dutch captain will, therefore, first take his vessel to Hirado, to discharge the cargo she has for the factory at that point, and then, as quickly as possible, will report for service at Arima."

"Patience, patience, dear child," said the old man, gently, as he perceived the look of bitter disappointment on his daughter's face, and added reverently: "Our lives, my Una, are in the hands of Him that careth for us."

The girl seemed not to hear his words.

"O my father," she cried, bursting into a storm of passionate sobs; "we are lost! In all Japan, outside of our own little household, there is no soul in whom we may trust! Robbers may make us their spoil; the now maddened heathen may persecute us even to death; and, in the hour of our peril, to whom can we flee? Not to thy kinsman, the Lord of Kai, for he, alas! hath no sympathy or shelter for those of any faith; we may not seek an asylum among yonder Christians, for, with Paoli among them, they would be as bitter against us as are their foes against them. O, my father, we are lost!"

"Dear mistress," said Ando, again bowing before the young girl, and imprinting a kiss upon her hand, "thou dost wrong Prince Nabeshima. He is brave and chivalrous, and, had he his will, all people would have liberty to follow the dictates of their own consciences in religious matters. He is our friend, and if need be, he will be our protector. He is to be here to-morrow. I saw him this morning aboard the merchantman—"

"Hast thou been aboard the foreign ship?" exclaimed both father and daughter, in one breath.

The little hunchback perceived that Lord Mori and Una were grevously disappointed over his report that the *Spuyten Duyvil* was to remain in Japan an indefinite length of time. With a view, therefore, to dispel their sadness and despondency, he assumed as gay and bantering a tone and manner as he could command:

"Ay, that I have," he returned in reply to their question, and using the English tongue; for in Lord Mori's household the native speech of Una's mother was as frequently employed as was the language of Japan: "And ye ought to have heard the prince, in speaking with the Englishman, laud his cousin, Lord Mori! Ay, and thou, too, mistress! Marry! but he extolled thee as the paragon of all excellences!"

A blush stole into Una's cheek, and a smile, all the brighter because it shone through tears, mounted from lip to eye.

"Prithee, enough of that, sirrah! How comes it that the Prince of Kai, was aboard the foreign ship?"

"Troth, mistress, he and Master Beaumont, the Englishman, have become such sudden and fast friends, that people say they seem like twin-brothers re-united after a long separation. The Lord Nebeshima has prevailed upon his new friend to accompany him overland to the government camp at Shimabara. The Englishman will, therefore, be with the prince when he passes this way to-morrow."

A cry of astonishment from the father greeted this announcement. Una was silent, and Ando continued:

"Ye have not heard all. Through the intercession of Master Beaumont and Lord Nabeshima, the Dutch captain has promised to take you with him on his return voyage to Amsterdam. In the meantime, your cousin will see to it that no harm befalls you."

V.

THE HERMITAGE.

The hermitage which Lord Mori had built for himself and daughter stood at the head of a small, secluded valley, directly beneath the main peak of Unzen. A little grassy plateau, not more than an acre in extent, lay before the door. On three sides of this rose the mountain, clothed with a heavy growth of pine. In front, the plateau terminated in a precipitous wall of rock that fell fully five hundred feet to the valley below. It was in this direction alone that the inmates of the hermitage caught any glimpse of the outside world. The valley bore away to the south, widening as it approached the plain, and from the little plateau at its head, the beholder looked out on Hara Castle and the village of Arima that lay in the immediate foreground. On the left stretched away the waters of the Gulf of Shimabara thickly set with clusters of little islands, and upon the right, the prospect closed in the gently sloping plain covered now with the camp of the Christians.

The hermitage itself consisted of a medium-sized Japanese house built against the face of the mountain, covering the mouth of a little grotto that extended a short distance into the rocks. The outer apartments of the dwelling proper constituted the living rooms of the family; the cavern chamber, fitted up with hanging-lamps and furnished with many conveniences, European in their pattern, served Lord Mori as a study, and here the greater part of his time was spent.

In addition to the father and the daughter and the little hunchback, the household consisted of two aged female servants and a youth, the son of one of his retainers who had followed Lord Mori into his retirement, and at his death, had besought his master to care for his motherless child. Sanji, as the youth was called, was now sixteen, and his part in the domestic economy of the hermitage was to make periodical visits to Shimabara or Ishihaya to purchase food and such other things as the simple wants of the hermit's family required.

In the early afternoon of the day following Ando's return from Nagasaki, Lord Mori, Una and the hunchback were seated on the little veranda of the hermitage. They were evidently expecting some one, for frequent glances were cast by one or other of the three toward the steep path that led up and around the heights to the left of the dwelling.

"You said you saw him half an hour ago, Ando? It is time that he was here." It was Una who spoke.

"You are all too impatient, mistress," responded the hunchback, smiling. "Sanji, I admit, is a nimble-footed lad, but remember that between yonder point, where I caught a glimpse of him, and us, a deep valley and a toilsome climb intervene. But there—doubt my eyes again, wilt thou? See, there he comes!" and Ando pointed up the path where the youth could be seen descending the mountain.

"Nay, I yield," Una returned, good-humoredly. "Thine eyes, Ando, are all thou mayest claim them to be."

"Where are the purchases thou wast sent to make, boy?" inquired the old man, as Sanji came up to the group.

"Alas, *Sensei*, in Shimabara, and no fault of mine that they are!"

"What meanest thou, saucy fellow?" demanded Una.

Sanji pretended not to hear his young mistress's question, nevertheless he answered it, addressing her father.

"The government troops, *Sensei*, fill all the space between the mountains and the city, and it was in vain that I sought a passage through them. General Itakura, early this morning, gave orders to transfer the camp to Arima to-day, and the princes and captains are mustering their forces and making ready for battle."

"A sudden move, is it not?"

"A soldier told me that the army was impatient to be led against the rebels. Prince Nabeshima's troops arrived early this morning, and their leader is expected to-day. To-morrow a battle will be fought."

"Are the troops now moving against the Christians?" inquired Una, rising to her feet.

"Ay, mistress," responded the boy. "A grand sight it is from yonder point to look down upon them, as they wind through the passes below."

"Sanji, do thou rest a bit, and have some food," the girl said. "Then haste thee to Obama. Thou canst purchase there the things we lack. And I, dear father," continued Una, pressing a kiss on her parent's brow, "I have not been out yet to-day; let me go to see the army on its march. I shall soon return."

The old man hesitated. "Una," he said gravely,

"thinkest thou, child, there is no danger? May not the mountains be full of spies, sent ahead by the princes to watch the movements of the Christians?"

"Saw you any?" the girl inquired, addressing Sanji.

"Nay, none, mistress; the only person I met was old Shibata, the charcoal burner."

"Thou hearest him, father," Una pleaded, putting her arm caressingly around Lord Mori's neck. "The government spies would scarcely have need to climb to such a height as this. Let me go, father, I shall not be molested."

"Go, then, dear child; yet, I think, Ando had better accompany you."

"Ay, mistress, do not refuse my companionship," said the hunchback, coming to Una's side, his eyes upturned appealingly to hers.

"As thou wilt, Ando," the girl replied. "I thought that you might still be weary from your journey to Nagasaki;" and then, looking down on the dwarf with a soft light in her beautiful eyes, Una added lovingly: "Thy company, dear Ando, is always welcome."

VI.

A DREAM AND A PORTRAIT.

As Ando and Una were hastening up the path, by which Sanji had returned to the hermitage, the little hunchback suddenly asked:

"Mistress, hast thou forgotten that thy father's cousin and the young Englishman are to visit the hermitage to-day. Perchance they may come in our absence; what if they should?"

"Not so, I think. They are coming, you have said, by

the Obama road. From the point whither we are going we can see their approach in time to return to the house before their arrival."

"Ah, mistress," said the hunchback, roguishly, "thy prompt response argues premeditation. Scarcely methinks, wouldst thou have begged thy father's leave to come hadst thou thought there was danger of missing the prince and the noble stranger."

The color mounted to the girl's temples. Perceiving this, Ando, with a mischievous chuckle, added, falling again into the English speech :

"Prithee, mistress, the truth now. Is it the army, marching over the Shimabara foot-hills, or thy father's guests on the Obama highway, that thou art going forth to see?"

The girl laughed merrily.

"Both, sweet rogue!" was her frank reply ; and then she added more gravely :

"Thinkest thou, Ando, that I would lose this first opportunity of mine to behold one of my mother's race? All last night my dreams were of the Englishman. I saw him, but something concealed his face that I could not look upon his features ; yet I noted his tall, commanding figure, and I heard his strong and pleasant voice. Methought that I was in peril and that he came to my rescue. I saw him as he stretched out his hand, bidding me come to him. I endeavored to obey, but it seemed that a horrible gulf suddenly yawned between us. In its awful depths I beheld the faces of fighting men, and some of these were wounded and others dead. Up from its seemingly fathomless depths came the clashing uproar of war ; and still all the time I beheld the stranger on the farther brink, his face ever concealed, **yet** his arms always outstretched toward me, and his voice calling upon my name. Then, in my dream, methought the day gave place to the night. A storm—the fiercest that ever swept land or sea—blotted out the stars above and, below, filled the earth with its fury. For long hours, it seemed, the pitiless tempest beat upon my uncovered head. In the gleaming lightning I still saw the awful, yawning chasm before me, and, lo! at last, as I looked upon it, I beheld it closing up, hiding the wild faces of the armies and stifling the voices of war. And even as it slowly closed, I felt something dragging me into its depths. Then a strong hand reached down to my rescue, and I felt myself drawn upward and laid at the feet of the Englishman. I turned to thank my preserver, but he was himself sinking into the horrible pit whence he had but rescued me. Then the chasm closed above him, the awful sounds were hushed into silence, the land became sea, and I heard the rush of angry waters about me. I seemed to be afloat, the English stranger still by my side, my hand in his. Then I would awaken only to fall asleep again, and in another dream to see the same faces and to hear the same sounds."

"God spake of old to his children in visions of the night-time," the hunchback said reverently, when Una had finished the account of her dream. "Perchance He has spoken to you to assure you that, though dangers and trials may await you, deliverance and safety are eventually sure to come. Would I were another Joseph, that I might say unto thee, dear mistress, as he said unto his companion in the Egyptian dungeon: 'This is the interpretation thereof.' Yet I can dispel the cloud which thou sayest hid the face of the stranger from thy sight. The morning I was aboard the Dutch ship, before I knew that you were to see the Englishman so soon, I made a sketch of his face, that I might give it to thee.

Neither last night nor this morning did I have an opportunity of seeing thee alone. But now are we together; and behold, mistress, here it is!"

As he spoke, Ando thrust his hand into the wide sleeve of his *haori** and drew forth the portrait. The hunchback must have had the artistic instinct strongly developed in him, for the picture was a life-like sketch of Marmion Beaumont. Eagerly Una seized it, and long and breathlessly did she gaze upon the face of the stranger, a smile wreathing her fair countenance and pleasure sparkling in her eyes.

"Ah, Ando!" she cried, "is this true to life? Has not your fancy, rogue, been busy here? I know well thy skill to transfer to paper the subtlest expressions and the finest lineaments of the face; but tell me, has your art here drawn upon your imagination, or has it faithfully followed nature?"

"Nay, now, mistress mine!" cried the hunchback, in playful indignation at the girl's insinuation. "What is there in that very common face before thee that would honor the imagination of a true artist? As the stranger is in the sketch, methinks, thou shalt see him to be."

Una bridled up in a sportive defense of the Englishman.

"What! Callest thou that a common face, Ando? Father says that England is a land of fair women and brave men; but, marry, a brave, fair man is this stranger, say I;" and with a merry peal of girlish laughter the maiden thrust the portrait into her bosom.

During the remainder of their walk up the mountain, the girl fell into a silent mood. Before her ardent young mind danced visions of coming peace and happiness

---

* An outer garment or tunic.

amid the beauties of an ideal world that her fancy had created and called England.

The path was rough and toilsome, and fully an hour was consumed in reaching the point whence the two could look down upon the eastern foot-hills. As they gained the crest of the heights, the hunchback sank down by the wayside, overcome with fatigue. Una, her step as airy and elastic as when she had set out from the hermitage, sprang upon a rock, and an exclamation of delighted surprise broke from her lips as she beheld all the country beneath her feet swarming with government troops. To the left, the roads leading from Shimabara were filled with long columns of soldiers marching around the mountain, while, upon the open foot-hills at her right, heavy masses of troops were drawn up, awaiting the arrival of the remainder of the army that was still pouring forth in a ceaseless stream of mounted warriors and footmen, mailed soldiers and camp-servants, from the cover of a heavy wood that flanked the eastern base of Unzen.

It was the first time that the young girl had looked upon so imposing a spectacle. Armor of every color, banners of every hue and form were there. From the gay trappings of war that covered them, the roads that wound among the lower heights appeared like brightly colored ribbons on a green field. Over the slowly moving columns on the open hills shone the bright afternoon sun; and above the heads of the gayly decorated warriors and the ensigns, that sparkled with jewels and gold, the air seemed tremulous with that semi-transparent shimmer of changing color that, in fine weather, is frequently observed to hover over marching armies.

For half an hour or more Una gazed down on the animated spectacle, and ever the hills became more densely crowded with men; and still, in unintermitted succession, column after column marched out of the wood. More than a hundred thousand veteran warriors, levied from among all the retainers of the Kiushiu princes, were going forth to crush a force of ill-armed and undisciplined farmers, fishermen and tradesmen one-fourth as large.

Turning her eyes from the foot-hills below, Una now looked toward the west, where the Obama highway lay in open view. A few pedestrians here and there were visible, but no such company as the Prince of Kai would be certain to have was in sight. Going to the place where the hunchback was still reclining by the wayside, the girl said:

"When you are rested, Ando, climb up on the rock where I have been standing. By my troth, it is a brave sight, and well worth the fatigue of coming hither. I have looked down the Obama road, and the prince is nowhere to be seen. Yesterday, my father left his book on my lookout yonder," pointing to the peak on the opposite side of a deep ravine, where Ando, the day before, on his return from Nagasaki, had found father and daughter. "I am going there to get it."

VII.

THE HOST OF THE KWASSUI-YA HAS A TALE TO TELL.

A short distance inland on the western coast of the Shimabara peninsula lies the village of Obama, celebrated throughout southern Japan for its hot-springs. The village consists of scarcely anything more than a collection of inns and bath-houses, frequented by sick folk from every quarter, attracted thither by the medicinal properties of the water. At the time of which we are speaking, the Kwassui-ya, or, as we would say in English, the Living Water Hotel, was the largest and most pretentious-appearing public house in Obama, and its baths had a wide celebrity among the nobility and the wealthier class of citizens.

On the day after the hunchback's return from Nagasaki, the host of the Kwassui-ya was seated on the mats before the open doors of his house, in the company of a few of his guests. They were discussing what had become within the past forty-eight hours, wherever it was known, the all-absorbing topic of conversation : the rescue of the Christian prisoners at Nagasaki. One of the guests, who was a new arrival, had been among the spectators on Higashi-yama, and he was giving the landlord a graphic account of the affair.

"Ah, ah!" sighed the host, as the guest finished his story. "Evil are the times in which we live, and evil, methinks, shall they remain until the foul doctrines of the *jashiu-mon* are stamped out of Japan."

A hearty murmur of assent showed that all present shared the same view. The host continued, addressing his remarks to the stranger:

"Yesterday noon that accursed Paoli, with the rebel chieftain Ashizuka at the head of about five hundred soldiers from the Christian camp at Arima, conducting the prisoners that they had rescued, had the boldness to pass through this village on their way over the mountains. They even dared to halt and demand food."

"Of course, you refused to feed the dogs!"

"In my heart, yes," replied the host, lugubriously. "Nevertheless, I made haste to set all I had in the house before them. I knew by the threatening look in the barbarian's eye that if I hesitated I would have my head laid open by that murderous ax of his."

"Humph!" returned the other, contemptuously. "Were there none here in Obama that dared to arm and attack the dogs?"

"The sick folk, such as were able to flee, made haste to seek the cover of the hills," returned the landlord, a little nettled at the guest's sneering tone. "The handful of innkeepers, with their servants, were kept too busily engaged in waiting upon their unwelcome visitors to have time to get together to plan any resistance."

The stranger laughed sarcastically.

"*Kekko*, by the gods! Then the Christians quartered themselves upon the village?"

"That they did," responded the other, mournfully. "My share was the leaders and about two hundred of those that had been prisoners. The other *yadoyas** were likewise filled to overflowing. For four hours they kept us sweating like slaves, cooking them food and preparing their baths."

"Methinks your larder, host, was well-nigh empty when they left you."

"Empty! Last night, friend, there was not food enough in all the *yadoyas* in Obama to feed ten men. We were compelled to await the return of our servants from Ishihaya this morning before we could breakfast. Ye gods! How those that had been prisoners ate! Governor Oda's dungeon, forsooth, had not been a palace of feasting to them! And as soon as the barbarian priest had finished his own meal he mounted his horse, and, riding up and down the street, shouted to his followers to eat, drink and be merry, for it was the idolators that banqueted them."

* Inns.

"Devil or no devil," cried the stranger; "that priest knows no fear. No one but a brave man would have ventured his life as did he at Nagasaki the other night, with such a price set upon his head."

The others made no reply. The name of Paoli had become anathema throughout the nation, and men were careful not to speak of him except in terms of the bitterest execration. Just then a traveller, dressed in the garb of a well-to-do tradesman, stopped before the door. The host and a troop of serving girls rushed to the street, uniting their voices in a noisy chorus of invitation for the stranger to enter their *yadoya* and to partake of their hospitality.

The new-comer was Yamada, the *Ronin*, who had assumed this disguise for purposes we shall permit himself, a little later on, to disclose. He was on the point of entering the inn, when a *betto*, wearing the livery of some nobleman, dashed up.

"Is the landlord of the Kwassui-ya present?" he demanded, gazing from one to another of the group before him.

"*Hai, hai!** I am he," responded the host, coming forward with a low bow.

"My Lord Nabeshima, Prince of Kai, is on his way hither," the *betto*, said. "He would rest for a time at the Kwassui-ya; prepare him room and bath."

At the mention of the name of Nabeshima, the landlord prostrated himself on the floor before the messenger.

"His worshipful highness confers a most distinguished honor upon me in gracing my wretched house with his presence. Convey my humblest thanks to your noble lord, and assure him that room, bath and refreshments shall await his pleasure. Is your master alone?"

* Yes, yes.

"Ah, I forgot. No; a foreigner is with him."
"Eh? a barbarian!" cried the host, aghast. "A prisoner, of course?"
"Not so! I warn thee, host, that thou be careful to show the foreigner all attention, if you would escape the wrath of the prince. Lord Nabeshima, and the Englishman are as brothers, and woe to him that shows disrespect to a friend of the Prince of Kai!"
"Ah, ah, pardon! I beseech you not to mention my foolish speech to your most excellent master," the frightened landlord implored, again bowing profoundly. "It's unusual to hear of a Japanese prince travelling with a foreigner, or making one his friend."
"Yet Iyeyasu loved an Englishman," remarked one of the guests.
"So, so, true, he did," the flustered landlord assented, eager to put himself right before Lord Nabeshima's servant; but the *betto* had disappeared down the street whence he had come. Having given orders to the servants to make ready to receive the prince, the host bethought himself of the traveller, who, a minute before, had stopped at his door. But Yamada was gone.

VIII.

OLD FOES IN NEW SURROUNDINGS.

Hearing the *betto's* announcement that Nabeshima and a foreigner were at hand, the *Ronin* at once knew that the latter could be none other than the Englishman who had worsted him in their encounter before the Suwa temple, and whose destruction he had twice plotted, only to have his plans each time defeated. Fearing, moreover, that Beaumont would recognize him, even though disguised, he concluded that the Kwassui-ya was not the place for him to remain. Therefore, it happened that, while the host was engaged in conversation with the *betto*, the *Ronin* crossed the street to another *yadoya* directly opposite. Entering this he called for a room that might command a view of the inn he had just left. Here he seated himself to await the arrival of the prince's party. The adjoining apartment was full of guests, and amid the loud bursts of drunken revelry, that reached his ears, he thought he recognized some of the voices. Pushing the sliding doors slightly apart, he peered in; and, sure enough, there were Gonroku, the robber-chief, and Gohei, with about a score of others, as desperate-looking characters as themselves. Yamada had made the acquaintance of Gonroku's gang in Nagasaki, and he knew a number of those present. Pushing the door open, he entered the room, and, as soon as he was recognized, an uproarious welcome greeted him.

"Ha! It is Yamada, the *Ronin* of Ishihaya!" the half-intoxicated Gonroku cried, the fellow's brutal features now still more repulsive from the effects of drink. "And so you, too, escaped the swords of the Christians and the ax of the priest, eh? Come, *gejo*,* sake,† sake* for the friend of Gonroku!" and the outlaw's arm encircled the waiting-maid's waist in a drunken caress.

"Yes, I escaped, thanks to a pair of nimble legs," Yamada replied to Gonroku's question. "We attacked the Dutch captain and his companions on their way to the bay, but Kanshin and five or six more were killed. I could do nothing," and here the *Ronin* held up his disabled hand, "and I relished not the idea of remaining

---

* Female servant.   † An intoxicating drink prepared from rice.

there and running my chances of being cut down by the dogs. But how fared it with your band?"

The outlaw-chief endeavored to look sorrowful, and his voice took on a maudlin whine.

"Ah! ah! Alas! Nigh a hundred of my brave fellows I left on Higashi-yama, and half as many more fell at the foreign ship. Ah, Yamada, shamefully did our gods betray us into the hands of the Christians and the barbarians."

"Heed it not," called out the voice of Gohei; "heed it not, say I. The less the number, the greater the share of the spoils we are yet to win. But ho, Yamada, what thinkest thou? Our sweet and gentle Gonroku is no sooner out of prison than he falls a captive once more, and is now on his way to surrender."

A coarse laugh from all present followed Gohei's words. The *Ronin* looked perplexed; he failed to perceive the point of the fellow's sally, and said as much.

"Thou art slow of mind, friend, or else thou knowest not Gonroku's impressionable nature. Dullard, our tender-hearted chief is in love."

"Ah, about to take a wife, is he?" inquired the *Ronin*, glancing at the robber, who answered his look with a hideous smile.

"Nay, scarcely a wife; yet call her what you will, the gentle Gonroku careth not! She'll serve a month or so until he tires of her. Gonroku, sad to say, is as fickle as he is susceptible. His love waxes and wanes with the moon; new moon, new maid!"

Gohei's speech was greeted by another roar of drunken revelry, in which Yamada joined lustily as any. Less brutal than the debased wretches about him, the *Ronin's* feelings respecting women, nevertheless, like those of his countrymen in general, felt not at all outraged at Gohei's horrible jests. Another of the company here bawled out:

"Yes; and, by the gods, the people are getting tired of his inconstancy! When a pretty maid suddenly disappears from some farmer's hut, and then as mysteriously returns, rather the worse for her month's sojourn among the mountains, a howl is raised along the whole countryside."

"This time, however," rejoined Gohei, "we shall be spared the inconvenience of having the officials dogging our footsteps in quest of the missing damsel. For once, Gonroku is considerate enough to cleave to a friendless maiden, and yet she is a nobleman's daughter with a dash of barbarian blood in her veins, withal."

"Gods!" exclaimed Yamada, with a laugh. "Your description fits but one woman in all Japan! You must have in mind the beautiful daughter of Lord Mori of Unzen!"

"*Kekko*, shrewd fellow! Thou hast guessed aright," broke in the outlaw-chief, with a horrible leer. "Una they call her; barbarous name, yet a dainty piece of flesh, methinks. To-night we go thither. They call me inconstant, do they? Ho, ho, ho!" and Gonroku roared with mirth. "By the hand of Buddha, comrades, I'll reform forthwith. Lord Mori's daughter shall not go home short of three months. Eh, comrades, call ye that inconstant?"

Another burst of laughter, with shouts of "No, no, *kekko*, Gonroku, *kekko!*" followed that worthy's speech.

"Will you join us, Yamada?" inquired Gohei.

"On one condition," the *Ronin* answered.

"Name it," exclaimed the chief.

Yamada informed the outlaws of what he had just heard at the Kwassui-ya.

"I shall join you," he added, "on condition that you

help me to avenge myself on that accursed Englishman. I have other and more important work on hand, and I wish my affair with him out of the way that I may attend to it."

"A bargain! We shall help you," Gonroku cried, clapping his hands together, thus signifying that the agreement was made. "But this other work, friend, what is it? We may serve you a good turn there, also."

The *Ronin* cast an apprehensive glance toward the *gejo*.

"Nay, nay, Yamada, don't fear the girl," the outlaw said, assuringly. "She is Gohei's sister, and she is our good right hand in Obama. All in this *yadoya* are friends; we would not be speaking so freely were it otherwise."

"Paoli, the barbarian priest, has escaped to Arima. I have sworn to get the reward set upon his capture, dead or alive, and thus to avenge my Lord Kaneko's death."

"Dangerous venture, that," Gonroku observed doubtfully. "You will have to go into the very midst of the Christians."

"I shall pretend to be one of the persecuted sect, fleeing from danger that threatened my life. As a supposed fellow-Christian they will receive me. I am no longer Yamada the *Ronin*, but Kuroda, a trader of Ishihaya, who for his adherence to the teachings of the priests, has had to fly to his brethren at Arima. Eh! how sounds the tale, my merry comrades?"

The outlaw was still fearful.

"I tell you, Yamada, you'll have to face that devil, Paoli the priest; and if he does not see through your pretentions, it will be the first time he has been deceived."

"You asked a minute ago if you could help me," said the *Ronin*, not replying to Gonroku's objection. "I think you can, but in what way I do not yet fully know. In the meantime, Gonroku, that Englishman—"

"Leave that to us whose trade is blood," the other said grimly. The prospect of work ahead had exerted a sobering effect upon the entire gang. Gonroku continued : "In a short time Nabeshima and the foreigner will be here. They will stop at the Kwassui-ya, for baths and refreshments, and then resume their journey over the mountains. We must leave the village before they enter it. Up, comrades ; rare, red sport ahead !"

The outlaws now arose, and descending into the back yard of the *yadoya*, passed through a narrow alley that joined the main road at the foot of the hills. In a few minutes they were toiling up the steep mountain pass. The shouting of men below caused them to look down on the village they had just left. A party of mounted warriors had halted before the Kwassui-ya.

"Lord Nabeshima and his train !" exclaimed the *Ronin*, and his face darkened with ferocious hatred as he perceived the tall form of the young Englishman at the prince's side. "Gonroku," he cried, savagely, " that accursed barbarian must die !"

"Ha, ha !" roared the outlaw. "By the gods, Yamada, thou lookest as if thou couldst devour the fellow alive ! Nay, fear not ! Ahead of us the road passes through a deep ravine, and there, from the shelter of the rocks above the highway, we shall fill your foreigner as full of arrows as thy revenge can wish. Ho, men, step up lively ! On to the ravine ! The Englishman this afternoon ; and Una of Unzen to-night !"

With uproarious mirth the outlaws hastened on their way. After an hour's sharp walking, they came to a footpath that diverged from the main road and led up over the mountain. It was a short cut across some rugged heights to their left, and joined the road on the other side. Gonroku's party turned into this path, and in a short time had reached the crest of the ridge To their right a sharp-pointed peak towered a hundred feet or more above them, and descending this with a light, springing step came the figure of a young girl. It was Una the Eurasian. Gonroku saw and recognized her.

"Ho, comrades, in luck!" he roared. "We've bagged half our game! It will be both man and maid before nightfall."

Fortunately, Una caught sight of her foes while they were still at some little distance from her, and their savage appearance warned her of danger. For a moment the girl stood regarding the outlaws with a terrified look, and then, as she heard the words of Gonroku, she turned, and, with a loud, piercing scream of fear, darted off around the mountain.

BOOK SEVENTH.

FRIENDS AND FOES STRANGELY MEET.

I.

AN INCIDENT BY THE WAY.

HAD Una Mori looked down on the Obama highway a little earlier than

she did, she would not have reported to the hunchback that the prince's party was not yet in sight. While she was gazing down upon the government troops marshaling on the eastern foot-hills, Nabeshima and Beaumont, with some score of the former's retainers—all that had come out of the battle on Higashi-yama alive—were galloping over the stretch of road visible from the point where she stood ; but when she turned her attention that way, they had just dashed under the cover of a small grove of camphor-trees that concealed the road, where it wound around the side of a hill, not far distant from the base of the mountain upon which she and Ando were then standing.

The cavalcade soon emerged from the shade of the camphor-grove, and while they were walking their horses up a steep ascent, two of the *bettos* in advance of the party were seen at the top of the hill dragging a youth out of a thicket by the wayside, and seeking to hasten his speed by the administration of not a few cuffs and kicks.

"Who have you there, fellows?" said the prince, riding up to the place where the struggle was going on. "Unhand that boy instantly, you rascals!" he shouted angrily, as he caught a glimpse of the terrified face of the youth, who, indeed, was none other than Sanji, whom, it will be remembered, Una had dispatched to Obama on an errand.

"Please you, most excellent master," whined one of the *bettos*, as both fell upon their knees before the prince, "we caught this fellow hiding himself away among the brush, and we thought that perhaps he might be a Christian and the bearer of important dispatches. Thy pardon, most august master, if we have offended," and the two prostrated themselves until their foreheads touched the earth.

"Seizing suspicious-looking persons is to be commended," their lord replied; "but needless violence such as I saw you employ with this youth, is cruel, and shall be punished. I forgive your present offense; see to it that you err not again!"

With profound bows, the *bettos* slunk away, glad to escape so easily. Nabeshima turned to Sanji, who had recovered somewhat from his fright, and who, as soon as he perceived the prince looking at him, dropped upon his knees.

'Well, lad," said Lord Nabeshima, addressing him, "what have you to say for yourself?"

"Great Lord, your servant's name is Sanji. He lives among these mountains, and is now on his way to Obama."

"Sanji, art thou a Christian?"

"Will the great Lord lay a cross before me that I may trample upon it?"

"Well said! But we do not carry crosses about the country, Sanji, to try old women and boys," Nabeshima returned, with a laugh. "I perceive by thy clothing that thou art some man's servant. Thy master's name—what is it, boy?"

"My master, excellent sir, is naught but a poor old man that dwells up among these hills."

"His name?"

Sanji was silent.

"Dost thou not hear me, fellow?" cried Nabeshima, sharply.

Sanji prostrated himself upon the earth, but remained dumb.

"Boy, stand up."

Sanji sprang to his feet.

"Now lad, I shall ask thee once more : what is thy master's name?"

At a sign from the prince, a score of swords flashed from their scabbards and the retainers formed a ring around the boy. Sanji's eyes swept the circle of mounted warriors, and his young heart swelled with indignation. Fear and courtesy were alike forgotten. His little figure, quivering with rage, was drawn up to its full height, and with head thrown back, he turned a scornful look on the prince.

"Thou thinkest, great sir, that twenty naked swords can frighten one defenseless boy into betraying to thee the name of his master? Thou art mistaken."

Nabeshima turned away his head to conceal the look of mingled merriment and admiration that passed over his face. In a moment he had controlled himself sufficiently to demand, with as great a show of anger as he could muster:

"Impudent boor! dost thou know to whom it is that thou art speaking?"

"I am not a boor, your highness," retorted Sanji, his face flushing at the insult. "I am a *Samurai*, and the son of a *Samurai* of renown. I know not thy name, great lord, and," he added, with a defiant flash in his eyes, "thou knowest not the name of my master."

"I am the Prince of Kai."

Instantly Sanji again prostrated himself before the feet of Nabeshima's horse.

"Great sir, my master is thy cousin, Lord Mori of Unzen. May it please thy highness to forgive thy servant's rudeness. My master has told me not to give his name to any—"

"Noble youth," cried the prince, interrupting him, "arise! It is needless for thee to say more. It is I who should ask forgiveness. The fidelity of a vassal to his lord can go no further than it has in thee."

The boy had arisen to his feet, and was now standing with bowed head, and hands crossed upon his breast. The prince again addressed him :

"And now, my lad, you perhaps know that we are on our way to your master's house. Be so kind, I pray you, to tell my *bettos* the quickest and easiest route thither."

With a low bow, Sanji went forward to the two men, who but a few minutes before had dragged him with kicks and blows out of the thicket, but who now received the information he gave them on their bended knees.

"A noble lad, that," Nabeshima said to the Englishman, who had been a deeply interested spectator of all that had passed, though understanding nothing of what had been said ; and the prince proceeded to inform him of the conversation between himself and Sanji.

II.

FORTUNE FAVORS YAMADA THE RONIN.

While Nabeshima was still speaking, a woman's scream, from the heights above them, fell upon their ears, and was followed by another and another in quick succession. It was Una, who, in her flight from Gonroku and his followers, had run wildly on around the mountain, not knowing whither her course was leading her. She could hear the heavy tread of her pursuers and their deep breathing close behind. She turned a sharp corner of the rocky bluffs, and the Obama highway burst into view. She saw the group of horsemen below, and instantly she divined who they were. While she sped on, her piercing

screams drew the attention of the warriors, and in the circle of upturned faces, she recognized one that was the original of the portrait that she had in her bosom. She stretched out her hands to him, and cried in English :
"Help! Help! Save me! O save me!"
The horsemen, mountains, valley and pursuers reeled in her eyes; she felt herself plunging forward. Another shriek pealed from her lips, and she knew no more.
"Merciful God!" exclaimed Beaumont, as Una's cry for help reached them. "She is an Englishwoman!"
"Dismount, men, and up these rocks to the rescue!" cried Nabeshima to his retainers.
But the Englishman was already off his horse and dashing up the steep mountain-side, the boy Sanji at his heels. Gonroku had been close upon the fleeing girl as she sank insensible upon the rocks. Raising her in his arms he shouted to his comrades to follow him, and the whole gang sped off around the mountain. They also had perceived the prince's party; but, with the start they had, they were confident of escape. The course they had taken was over a ledge of rocks that jutted out like a terrace along the face of the mountain, which at this point fell off in a precipice hundreds of feet in depth upon one side, and towered up an almost perpendicular wall of rock on the other.
"Comrades, who knows where this accursed ledge is leading us? By the gods, I like it not!" exclaimed the robber-chief, as they sped forward with the Englishman, who had just gained the summit, in swift pursuit. Nabeshima and his warriors, encumbered by their heavy armor, were struggling on at some distance behind.
A savage yell of rage from the outlaws caused Beaumont to pause for an instant. He perceived that their advance had been checked by a high cliff that formed the

termination of the ledge. They had run into a trap, and now, gathered in a little group, they were taking counsel together.

"Down with that girl, Gonroku!" cried Gohei. "We can get her another time. Unencumbered with her, we can scale the rocks ahead, and make our escape."

With curses, loud and deep, the chieftain dropped Una on the rocks, and, with his followers, began climbing the side of the sloping cliff before them. Yamada alone remained. Darting behind a huge bowlder, he awaited the Englishman's approach. In a short time, Beaumont dashed up, still far in advance of the others. Perceiving at once that the outlaws were beyond reach of his sword, he stooped over the still unconscious maiden to lift her up. As he did so, the *Ronin*, with a tiger-like spring from his hiding-place, dashed himself against the Englishman. There was a shout of startled surprise, a momentary struggle on the brink of the awful abyss, and the form of Beaumont disappeared over the precipice.

"*Kekko, kekko*, comrade!" roared Gonroku, who had witnessed the deed from the rocks above. "Lively, friend; thy hand! So, so; here you are!" as he assisted the *Ronin* up the steep face of the cliff to a little plateau. Now we are safe, and thou hast had thy revenge, though I did lose my bird. May the gods prosper your plot against the barbarian priest, and my further wooing of the fair maid of Unzen?"

III.

BACK TO LIFE.

A momentary glimpse of his foe; an effort, as he hung over the edge of the cliff, to save himself; then the sense of falling down, down; the awful shock of being dashed against some opposing object; a roar in his ears, a flash of fire before his eyes; then silence and darkness. Such were Marmion Beaumont's sensations when he felt himself hurled off the edge of the rocks, as he bent over the prostrate form of the unconscious Una, whom Gonroku had dropped perilously near the brink of the precipice. Though stunned by his fall, the Englishman was not rendered entirely insensible. He was powerless to move his body, yet his mind was active. He had a sensation of extreme cold, and of excruciating pains in his right arm and leg. He was dimly conscious of the sound of voices far above him. Then, after a time, he felt himself lifted up. The voices seemed to be at his side, and he felt the touch of gentle hands. Then followed the sensation of being borne somewhere on a litter supported on men's shoulders. He could hear the breathing of his bearers, and the trampling of horses' feet behind him. The rythmical motion of his carriage, as it rose and fell and swayed from side to side with the echoless tread of the bearers, soothed him into restfulness, and he slept. But his sleep soon lapsed into unconsciousness.

After a long interval, he again recovered

"See, dear father, he revives! He will get well again, will he not?" said a low, sweet voice at his side.

"Ay, child, the young man is strong; do not fear for him, he will recover," said the deeper voice of a man. "Una," the speaker continued, "do thou, my daughter, go into the outer apartment and tell thy cousin that his friend is reviving. And remain there thyself, dear child; it is not seemly that thou shouldst be here when the stranger awakes."

Beaumont heard the rustle of the girl's garments as

she left the room. He now tried to move, but his limbs felt stiff and of the weight of lead.

"Nay, friend, move not, I pray thee! Thy right arm and leg are broken and thy whole body is sorely bruised," said the same voice that had just been speaking to the girl. The young Englishman opened his eyes to see the face of Lord Mori bending over him.

"Where am I?" he asked in a whisper.

"Among friends, Master Beaumont, and at the house whither you were going when you so bravely rescued my child."

"Thank God, she was saved!" Beaumont exclaimed, faintly; and then, fixing his eyes on his attendant, he said, with a wan smile: "Then thou art Lord Mori of Unzen, I take it, and the maiden whom those villains were bearing off is thy daughter."

"Thou speakest truly; my child has just left the room."

Beaumont turned his head and cast a glance about upon his surroundings. He was lying on a bed in the scholar's cave-study. A number of lamps, suspended from the roof of the cavern, shed a soft light throughout the apartment. A few paintings—the work of the little hunchback—hung from the walls. A student's table occupied the center of the room. In one corner stood a small book-case, and in another was the huge pile of manuscript Bibles. From the cursory glance at his surroundings, the Englishman's eyes turned to rest again upon the gentle face of the old man.

"How long have I been here?" he inquired.

"They brought you here about sunset; it is now nearly midnight."

As Lord Mori was speaking, Beaumont saw the sliding doors at the other end of the room open, and the Prince of Kai enter the apartment. Coming to the side of the wounded man, Nabeshima laid his hand on the sufferer's brow, saying softly:

"It is like beholding the sun after the *niu-bai** to look upon the light of thine eyes again, Master Beaumont. Ah, it was a terrible fall thou hadst, but a far more terrible one didst thou narrowly escape!"

"I dimly remember someone dashing himself against me and hurling me over the cliff."

"It was that accursed *Ronin*, Yamada."

"And I was saved from death," said Beaumont, feebly. "But how, or by whom?"

"Speak no more, friend, I pray you. You are weak, and the effort may do you harm. I shall tell you the story. When the *Ronin* pushed you off the ledge of rocks along which you were pursuing my cousin's captors, I was still a considerable distance behind you and but a little in advance of my own men. I hurried up to the place; but the cowardly would-be assassin, by the assistance of his comrades, was already far up the cliff beyond my reach. I at once peered over the brink of the precipice, and my heart leaped into my throat at the sight. About twenty-five feet below where I stood, I beheld a dwarfish mountain pine projecting almost horizontally from a cleft in the perpendicular face of the rocks. You had fallen into the top of this tree, and were lying firmly lodged among its gnarled and twisted branches. More than three hundred feet below you, was a grove of large camphor-trees, that appeared from the summit nothing more than a thicket of shrubs. Into this you would have fallen had not the pine-tree caught you in its boughs. By means of a rope, one of the men descended and brought you up safely to the top. A rude litter was has-

* The rainy season, occurring in June, during which for days together the sun is hidden by heavy clouds.

tily constructed, and on that the *bettos* bore you to this place. We found both your right arm and leg to be broken, and your body otherwise bruised and wounded. The broken bones have been set, and all it requires now is rest and patient waiting to effect a cure."

The Englishman turned his face to the wall with a heavy sigh.

"It will be weeks before I am myself again. And yet," he added, after a pause, "I ought to be thankful that I escaped with my life. By heaven, Prince, if I ever again meet that dastardly *Ronin*, methinks he will not escape with so slight a token of the encounter as a disabled hand."

Lord Nabeshima smiled. "I trust that you will be forestalled in your vengeance, Master Beaumont. It is more fitting that a Japanese sword should wipe out the disgrace with which Yamada's cowardly assault has tainted the honor of the *Samurai* caste. All of my bodyguard I at once dispatched in pursuit of the *Ronin* and his confederates, who I understand are none other than the notorious Gonroku and a number of his outlaws. I trust that before daylight we may hear that they have paid the penalty of their crimes."

IV.

UNA MEETS HER HERO.

While Beaumont and Nabeshima were speaking, Lord Mori had passed out of the room, and he now returned accompanied by Una. Timidly and with downcast face the girl approached the wounded man.

"Master Beaumont," said the scholar, in his softly

quiet voice, "my daughter has come to thank you for rescuing her from such terrible peril to-day."

With a smile, the young Englishman raised his eyes to the fair face of the maiden. "Nay, lady, it was little, indeed, that I did! Thy captors ran themselves into a trap, and were obliged, perforce, to leave thee."

"Gentle sir," Una replied earnestly, fixing her calm, truthful eyes on Beaumont's face, "thou dost unduly belittle thine own work. My cousin, the prince, and all who were there say it was thy close pursuit that compelled the robbers to drop me on the rocks that they might make good their own escape. Hadst thou not been so near, they could have carried me with them up the side of the mountain. Ah, good sir," she continued falteringly, "alas! sorely have you suffered—"

"Nay, fair maiden, speak not of that! I was but doing my duty."

The words died away in a half articulate murmur upon his lips. He had fallen into a semi-unconscious slumber.

"What thinkest thou, cousin?" Nabeshima asked anxiously, as the two moved off together to the other end of the room; "thou art skilled in the science of healing; will my friend live?"

"He will if he be patient and prudent," the old man returned slowly. "I think he has suffered no serious internal injury. He is young and strong."

"Yes, and that will, of course, be in his favor. If I can be of assistance to thee, cousin, do not fail to command me. I shall protect thy household until the foreign ship arrives at Arima. Then it will be well for you all to go aboard at once. And may you find, cousin, in the land of the stranger, the peace and safety that can, it seems, no longer be yours in our Japan!"

"It is for Una's sake, cousin; it is for Una's sake," the scholar said brokenly, his eyes misty with tears. "It is for the sake of my child that I go. Danger and death in the land of my fathers have no terrors for me. A little longer, and my life work will be finished, and then I care not by what path I reach the grave. But, my daughter," he cried, as he perceived Una, who had stolen noiselessly to her father's side, "the image of her departed mother, O, my child! it is for thee, for thee, that thy old father makes himself an exile forever from the sunrise land of his birth!" And Lord Mori gathered his daughter to his breast in a long, affectionate embrace.

"Hark!" said Nabeshima, "I thought I heard some one calling before the house."

"Surely, it cannot be," the scholar said. "The lights are extinguished in the outer dwelling, and how could any one be drawn hither?"

"Perhaps it is my retainers, returning from the hunt after the outlaws," the other replied, moving toward the door. "I shall see."

"I shall go with you," said Una, taking a lighted lamp from her father's table, and accompanying her cousin. "Occasionally travellers lose their way in passing over the mountains, and, finding our path, they follow it up until they come here. It may be some such folk to-night. Who is there?" she called, as she and Nabeshima reached the door.

"Belated travellers, who have lost their way," came the reply, in a man's voice, from without. "We have a sick woman here, and crave shelter for her until the morning."

"Never did my father turn a deaf ear to such an appeal," said Una, addressing the prince. "Open the door, I pray thee, cousin, and let them in."

V.

EXULTATION.

We must now return to Shiro and Ine Tanaka, who, it will not be forgotten, were left at Kayaki upon the night of the rescue. In accordance with the Jesuit's instructions, Shiro had assisted the women and children in their embarkation ; and when they had sailed away, and the bishop and his armed band had also taken their departure, the young man, in company with Obata, repaired to the hut of one of the latter's servants, which was hidden away in a thick grove on the mountain-side. Hither for greater safety, the wounded woman had been borne, and here she and the two men were to remain until they set out on their overland journey to Arima. Entering the dimly lighted room where she lay, Shira and Obata seated themselves by her couch, and, in anxious, prayerful suspense, the three waited. Neither of them spoke, for, in the thrilling excitement of the hour, their hearts were too full for words.

Then, as the uproar of battle following Paoli's attack upon the execution grounds rolled wildly echoing down the bay, the three silent listeners knew that the onslaught had been made, and that the fate of hundreds depended upon the issue of the terrific conflict that was then raging along the sides of Higashi-yama. And they could, indeed, only wait and pray ! It was a time in which hearts beat like drums and every shuddering breath seems to measure an hour. The struggle at Oura, the rescue of the prisoners, and the retreat over the crest of the hill to the Mogi road did not occupy more than forty minutes, but to the anxious watchers at Kayaki it seemed to be as many hours. At last one of the servants, that had been detailed by Obata to stand on the hill opposite the execution grounds, and to watch and report the progress and final outcome of the attack, dashed into the house, breathless from the speed with which he had come.

"The bishop and Ashizuka are attacking the heathen, front and rear," he exclaimed, as soon as he sufficiently recovered himself so that he could speak. "The surprise was complete. A gang of outlaws, it is said, are assailing the foreign ship;" and with these words, the messenger darted out of the house and away into the darkness again on his return to his post of observation. At regular intervals, tidings now came in of the progress of the rescue and escape. Morning had come and the sun was already high in the sky, when the last messenger arrived.

"I followed our friends in their retreat to Mogi," he reported, "keeping myself concealed among the trees by the side of the highway. I saw them safely embarked, and, pushing off into the bay, head their boats for Obama."

"And the fight at the foreign ship; what about that?" Shiro asked.

"The assailants were beaten off."

"Have you heard of the losses in the battle at the execution grounds?" inquired Obata, anxiously. "Did our friends suffer severely?"

"I returned by way of Oura," replied the messenger. "The battle-field presents a terrible spectacle; yet, I believe that not more than a hundred Christians were killed. How many were wounded I do not know, as our friends carried these away with them. But the loss of the government troops must have been very heavy, as the execution grounds are piled high with the dead. Scores of the citizens, and of the mob who opposed our men,

THE BOND, WITH A TIGER-LIKE SPRING FROM HIS HIDING-PLACE, DASHED HIMSELF AGAINST THE ENGLISHMAN.—*See Page 249.*

likewise fell; their bodies are thickly strewn over the entire hill-side."

"So let all Thine enemies perish, O Lord!" cried Shiro fervently, when the man had finished his report.

But Ine, weak as she was, had sprung to her feet. Her arms were outspread, her face upturned, and the light of triumphant joy lit up her countenance and flashed from her large, lustrous eyes. She, who but two days before had seen her friends massacred by the brutal agents of a merciless governor, she, who had stood on the summit of Takaboka and, with anguish unspeakable, had beheld her brother sink down lifeless by her side, she, whose soul had been pierced by the death-shrieks of the helpless women and children whom the ruthless soldiery had cast off the cliffs into the sea, was now untouched by pity for the sudden destruction that had fallen upon these same red-handed murderers, and she felt no thrill of horror as she pictured to herself those ghastly heaps of slain, lying upon the bloody slopes of Higashi-yama. Nay, she exulted in their destruction! In their fury, they had cursed her Lord and had insulted the sacred symbol of her faith; they had hardened their hearts against mercy and had made themselves drunken with innocent blood; and now she rejoiced to know that upon many of them had fallen, even in the midst of their orgies of torture and slaughter, a sudden and terrible punishment, and that, on the self-same grounds, which they had set apart as the death-place of others, lay their own lifeless bodies, their blaspheming lips cold and silent, their pitiless hearts stilled forever.

She looked beyond the human agencies that had wrought this great work of retributive justice to the spiritual and unseen. It was God, the All-terrible Avenger, who had made bare His omnipotent arm, and had launched upon the destroyers of His people the swift thunderbolts of His wrath. She remembered the deliverance which the same Divine Power had of old wrought for another people, and from their song of triumphant gladness there rose to her lips the impassioned words of praise :

" Thy right hand, O Lord, is become glorious ' ι power ; Thy right hand, O Lord, has dashed in pieces the enemy. And in the greatness of Thine excellency, Thou hast overthrown them that rose up against Thee."

VI.

HIM WHOM WE WOULD SHUN WE MEET.

The day passed quietly. The government officials were too much exercised over the crushing defeat they had sustained the night before, to pay any attention to the reports of their spies that the Christians of Kayaki had fled to Arima. Lord Oda was dying, and the Vice-Governor Baba had assumed his office ; but it required time to reorganize the demoralized forces of the city, to fill the places of officials that had been killed, and once again to take up the work of persecution.

All this Obata's servants reported to their master, and he and Shiro decided that on the following day they would set out on their overland journey to Arima. Early the next morning, therefore, the household was astir, making ready for their departure. Ine was to be borne in a *nori-mono* by four servants, Shiro and Obata keeping slightly in advance while passing through the city. A great number of women had been trampled down in the panic among the populace on the night of the rescue, and the sight of *nori-monos* bearing away the injured to their homes in the surrounding villages had become too frequent to attract any attention.

Thus it happened that Ine and her bearers passed through the streets unnoticed. Once out of Nagasaki, and on the highway that led up the valley to the northeast of the city and over a range of high hills in the direction of Ishihaya and Shimabara, the little party felt that the greatest danger was past. At noon they halted in Ishihaya. Tidings of Paoli's return to Japan and of his rescue of the Christian prisoners had preceded them, and the village was agog to hear still further accounts of the awful doings of the accursed barbarian. As soon, therefore, as it was discovered that Shiro's party was from Nagasaki, the *yadoya* in which they were resting was beset by an excited throng of villagers eager to hear their story. It required all the dexterity of the three to satisfy the people's curiosity and yet not to imperil themselves; for it was evident that their listeners were mad with hatred against the Christians, and had the little party, either by word or action, excited their suspicions, ill would it have fared with them.

Finally, they succeeded in getting away from the village. Their course now lay through the little isthmus that connects the Shimabara peninsula with the mainland. Before them towered the peaks of Unzen, from the highest of which heavy volumes of smoke and steam rolled up lazily into the cloudless sky. A few hours brought them to a small hamlet, and here the road to Obama and Arima branched off from the main highway. It was sunset when they had surmounted the foot-hills and entered upon the pass that led over the mountains. From travellers that they met, they learned that Nabeshima had arrived at noon in Obama, and, not knowing how long he might remain, they did not dare to enter that village, lest the prince, if still there, might recognize Ine. The little party, therefore, struck off over the mountain by an unbeaten route, hoping to reach the highway beyond Obama before it became too dark for them to distinguish the way.

In this they were disappointed. Night came upon them, and the road was yet far distant. Still they wandered on, the servants, wearied with the long journey, stumbling over rocks and plunging into pitfalls. At last they struck a path that seemed to lead in the direction of the road they were in quest of. This they followed for an hour or more, now descending into deep ravines, and now clambering up steep and stony slopes. Suddenly they emerged on a little plateau. On their left rose the black mass of the mountain, its summit now surmounted with a pillar of fiery cloud. Far away to their right they beheld the gleam from countless camp-fires on the open plains below. But just before them rose the dark shadow of a dwelling. No light shone from it, nor did there come any sounds of life from within. All was dark and silent.

As the reader has doubtless already surmised, they were standing before the hermitage of Lord Mori of Unzen, and it was Shiro's request for shelter for Ine that had led Una to ask her cousin to admit them.

VII.

NABESHIMA MEETS A FAIR FOE AND IS CONQUERED.

Neither Shiro nor Obata perceived the tall form of the Prince of Kai, when, in response to Una's invitation, the two men entered the hermitage.

"The lady that is ill—where is she?" the girl asked in alarm, beginning to fear that in opening the door they had fallen into some trap.

"She is in the *norimono* without," said Shiro. "Is there some place at hand where she may rest?"

Between the outer room and the scholar's cave-study was a large apartment, and, in answer to Shiro's question, Una pointed to this.

"You may have the use of that room to-night. While you are bringing in the woman, I shall call the servants to prepare her couch."

The prince came forward out of the shadow in which he had been standing. Shiro and Obata were visibly agitated as they looked upon him; and a swift glance, that did not escape Nabeshima's keen eyes, passed between them.

"With your permission, friends," he said to the two men, "I shall assist the lady into the house. Do you both remain here;" and before they could interpose an objection, the prince had passed out of the door and was standing by the side of the palanquin. Ine had already alighted and was wearily awaiting the result of Shiro's solicitation.

"Thou art ill, lady, they tell me," said Nabeshima, approaching the young woman with a profound obeisance. "A couch is being made ready for thee within—"

A low cry of surprise and terror interrupted him. The young woman leaned heavily against the *norimono* for support. She had recognized Nabeshima's voice. The very one she had most dreaded to meet, and, in their efforts to escape whom they had left the highway and had become lost among the mountains, was before her. Then, as a sudden impulse flashed into her mind, she raised her eyes to the prince's face, which she could dimly discern from the light that streamed through the open door. She would throw herself and her companions on his mercy. It was their only hope; escape was impossible.

"Prince Nabeshima," she said in a low, rapid, tremulous whisper, and he started at the sound of his name, "throughout all the proud empire of our Japan thou art honored as a pattern of noble generosity and courteous chivalry toward friend and foe. Thou hast never sullied, they say, the honor of thy manhood with treachery or by taking a cowardly advantage of an ememy whom misfortune has thrown into thy power. Thou art brave and good. My Lord, there is one woman whom thou hast professed to love, whose heart thou hast sought to win—a heart long ago given to another. That woman, who believes thee to be all that common fame reports of thee, stands before thee."

Nabeshima sprang to the girl's side.

"Ine Tanaka! is it thou?" he cried, in a voice that betrayed the deepest emotion.

The woman waved him back. "It is I, my lord, and lo, I am in thy hands! It was in our efforts to avoid thee that we left the highway and went astray upon the mountains. But, noble Prince, it is not for myself that I speak, for I know that I am safe in the presence of the Lord of Kai."

Nabeshima would have spoken but Ine raised her hand entreating his silence.

"Thou knowest me, my lord, to be a Christian. I am on my way to Arima, in the company of my betrothed husband."

"What!" exclaimed her companion, no longer able to control himself; "Nirado Shiro! He, whom thy people believe to be their heaven-appointed leader! Has he, too, returned to add his presence to the woes that already afflict our unhappy country?"

"Our leader he is, my lord; our deliverer he shall be. He has come back to our Japan that the woes you lament may come to an end in the triumph of the truth," replied the woman with an awful earnestness. "But enough of this; I may not hope to convert you to our side at this late hour. Nevertheless, you perceive, great sir, that I am trusting the honor and chivalry that have thrown such a halo of glory about the name of Nabeshima, Prince of Kai, in thus commending my companion to thy mercy. My lord, is that trust misplaced? Have I spoken in vain?"

The man at her side bowed his head in silence. Ine could hear his labored breathing, but she knew nothing of the fierce struggle that was rending his soul; she was only conscious of her own heart's loud throbbings. What if he should refuse to be merciful? Her brain reeled at the thought. Slowly the prince raised his head; slowly his eyes sought the face of the woman by his side; slowly, and with a terrible solemnity, came his answer.

"Ine Tanaka, because it is thou that hast spoken, Nirado Shiro is safe until he enters the Christian camp on the morrow! Think not that I hesitated because I coveted the honor of being the slayer of the arch-rebel! It was the heart of the lover and not that of the warrior, that made pause. Nirado Shiro stands between me and the woman that is dearer to me than my own life. But no more of this, else I am unmanned," and the bitterness of a love that was vain made harsh the young nobleman's voice and darkened his handsome face.

The heart of man is exceedingly mighty; the fair foe had conquered. Yet from her attitude, one would have thought otherwise; she was kneeling at the prince's feet.

"Nay, Ine Taneka, arise!" said Nabeshima, tenderly, and as he gazed down upon the woman he loved, suddenly she seemed to be wrapped about in mist, for he looked upon her through tears. "Thou hast my pledge, O maiden!" he continued brokenly, "that thou and thine shall suffer no harm from Nabeshima of Kai."

But she to whom he spoke, heard not his words. Still weak and suffering from her wounds, the fatigue of the long journey from Nagasaki, together with her recognition of the prince, had proved too heavy a strain upon her, and she had swooned.

VIII.

ENEMIES AND RIVALS.

Gathering up her slight form in his arms, Nabeshima bore her into the house. The two women servants had made ready a couch in the room, which Una had pointed out to Shiro. The latter was holding a whispered conversation with Obata in the outer apartment, when Nabeshima entered, bearing the unconscious Ine in his arms. Resigning her to the care of Una and her women, the prince returned to the outer room, and, approaching the two men, said, in a coldly courteous tone:

"Strangers, you appear disturbed and anxious. Let me assure you that there is no cause for fear this side of the Christian lines. Yonder noble woman has told me all, and I have pledged my word that she and her friends shall suffer no harm."

Shiro's face wore a look of defiant disdain, as he replied hotly:

"If Ine Tanaka thought it necessary to supplicate thy mercy, magnanimous sir, she grievously erred. I fear thee not," and the young man's hand sought the hilt of his sword. "Thou art, I understand, but a guest here, like ourselves," he continued; "I would see the master of the house, and treat with him."

Nabeshima bit his lips in anger. The insolent tone of the speaker, and the manner in which he spoke of the noble act of the woman whom the prince loved, but whose plighted troth the other held, stung the chivalrous nobleman to the quick. Curbing the resentful words that rose to his lips, Nabeshima replied, with a cold stateliness that rebuked Shiro's passionate outburst more effectually than any words could have done:

"Nirado Shiro, thy boyish bravado is lost on Nabeshima of Kai. I repeat—thou art safe until thou reachest the camp of thy friends at Arima; thenceforward, beware! I shall expect thee to make good thy boast, that thou dost not fear me, upon the field of battle!"

The sound of approaching footsteps without drew the attention of the three men to the door. Then a voice called Nabeshima's name.

"It is my body-guard returning," said the prince to his companions who, upon hearing the name of the person whom Shiro had so insolently defied, had stood abashed and humbled before him. "It will be well for you to retire to the inner room. Even my presence might be powerless to save you, did my retainers know who you are."

Thereupon Shiro and Obata entered the apartment where Ine was reclining upon the couch that had been spread for her on the mats. She had recovered from her swoon, and her large bright eyes turned with an affectionate look upon Shiro, as he went to her side. She felt that he was doubly hers now, for had she not saved his life and secured him a safe conduct to the very ranks of his waiting army? Una had been seated by the injured woman's couch, but at the entrance of the two men, she arose, welcoming them with a gracious smile.

"Thy lady, gentle sir," she said, addressing Shiro, "has been telling me of your wanderings on the mountains. You must be wearied and a-hungered. Rest you, I pray; the women will bring in meat and drink presently."

The young man's eyes met those of the maiden; then, with a low bow, he replied, in his most courteous manner:

"We were happy indeed, fair lady, in losing our way, since chance has conducted us to so gracious a hostess."

The girl's fair face colored and her eyes fell before the speaker's ardent gaze. Yet none of the displeasure and confusion she felt did she suffer her guests to see, as with a calm and quiet dignity she replied:

"Nay, good sir, were thanks at all called for, it is to my father that they belong. Many a night have lost travellers sought shelter at this door, and never once has their request gone unheard."

"Thy father, good hostess," said Ine, rising to a sitting posture, "is he within to-night? I would thank him for this unlooked-for shelter."

"Heed it not, I pray thee," Una responded gently. "He is indeed within, but—Ah, he comes," she added, as Lord Mori came noiselessly through the sliding-doors between them and the room wherein lay the wounded Englishman.

"Our guests, dear father," his daughter said, with a slight wave of the hand in the direction of Shiro's party. "They lost their way upon the mountains."

With low bows, Ine, Shiro and Obata saluted their host, thanking him for the hospitality of his roof.

While they were still speaking, the prince entered the apartment. Going to his side, Una asked eagerly:

"Did I not hear your retainers returning, cousin? What success?"

"Alas! Una, they utterly failed to get any trace of the outlaws," the other replied moodily.

The girl's face showed the anxious foreboding of peril that she felt. While Gonroku lived she knew that she would be in danger. Nabeshima, perceiving the troubled look in her face, took her hands and said, assuringly:

"Fear not, fair cousin. The hunt has not yet ceased; to-morrow these mountains shall be thoroughly searched. Until the foreign ship comes to Arima and you are safely aboard, a guard of my bravest and most trustworthy retainers shall keep constant watch over you. Again I say, dear cousin, do not fear."

IX.

THE VERY WONDERFUL EXPLOIT OF BISHOP PAOLI.

Great was the rejoicing among the Christian multitudes at Arima when the triumphant Paoli, at the head of the long line of prisoners, whom he had rescued from the cross and the stake at Nagasaki the night before, rode into the camp. The women and children, who had left Kayaki by boat, had already arrived, and the general jubilation over the great victory was marred only by the sight of the sorrow-stricken widows and orphans whose husbands and fathers had fallen in the terrific conflict on the slopes of Higashi-yama.

Wearied as he was with the toils of war and of travel, Bishop Paoli stopped not to rest until he had visited the castle, carefully inspected its walls, ridden through the camp and examined the outer defenses even to the rude fortifications that had been thrown up upon the summits of the foot-hills. It was long after nightfall when he returned to the village. As he was passing through the camp, a vast concourse of Christian warriors poured out to meet him. Halting on a slight eminence, his gaze swept over the sea of faces before him, and into his eyes, heavy with weariness, there flashed a look of triumphant exultation.

"The army of the living God!" he exclaimed aloud; "strong in His name for the overthrow of the infidel, and for the salvation of the Church of Japan!" And blessing the dense throngs that bowed their knees as he rode by, he entered the village.

The forenoon of the next day Paoli spent busily engaged in his duties as bishop. He laid aside his armor and the battle-ax, still stained with blood, and in the rich vestments of his office he received the native priests, hearing their reports, and consulting with them upon the measures to be adopted for the spiritual welfare of the army during the coming campaign.

At noon, intelligence was brought in by the spies that the government forces were moving over the hills between Arima and Shimabara; and for the remainder of the day Paoli was again a warrior, riding in full armor here and there through the camp, his terrible weapon hanging at his saddle-bow. Everywhere the insurgent forces felt the inspiration of his presence.

Toward evening some Christians brought in a man, whom they said they had discovered among the foot-hills, closely pursued by enemies, who had already disabled his right hand, and inflicted other wounds upon him. They had rescued him, and, learning that he was a Christian, who had been fleeing to Arima, when he had been beset by his foes, they had, at his own request, brought him before the leaders. This man, it need scarcely be said, was Yamada, the *Ronin*, who, with the assistance of Gonroku and his gang, acting the part of pretended pursuers, had been able to deceive the spies, and to gain an entrance into the Christian camp. And thus the wily avenger's first step in his plot was completely successful.

That night Bishop Paoli did not retire to rest. The soldiers slept with their armor on and their weapons lying by their sides. It was not known at what hour the foe might begin the attack, and the Christians employed the utmost vigilance to prevent a surprise. All night long detachments of men and women labored upon the defenses, strengthening them wherever, in the bishop's opinion, they were weak. Paoli moved among the workers, superintending their labors and encouraging them by his word and presence. Suddenly, about midnight, as he was passing like a shadow among them, they heard a hollow groan break from his lips, and saw him stagger to a tree to support himself, his face blanching to a death-like pallor.

Some of the women hastened to him, thinking that he had been taken suddenly ill. But Paoli waved them aside, and with a tremendous bound sprang upon the breast-work upon which they were laboring. In another instant he had leaped down on the outer side, and, to the consternation of the beholders, who quickly gave the alarm to the camp, the bishop hurried off in the direction of the mountains. On and on he went through the thick darkness, his tall form stiffly erect and his eyes fixed and staring; his breath came in quick, sharp gasps, low moans burst now and then from his lips, and the perspiration stood out on his forehead in heavy drops and rolled down his face.

Bishop Paoli was in a trance.

In his rapid course, the Jesuit reached the Obama highway; and up this he sped. A path branched off from the main road, leading over a mountain to his right; he took this, and hastened on and on. Above him, the fires in Unzen's crater cast up a lurid gleam on the smoky pillar that swayed to and fro in the night wind, and in this dim, tremulous light the bishop's swiftly moving figure shone out tall and ghostly. The path he was following led to Lord Mori's hermitage, and soon Paoli had gained the little plateau upon which it stood, and in another minute, he had reached the house. The door was slightly open, and, noiselessly as a shadow, he passed through. Around him lay a score of sleeping soldiers, and from a room beyond came the glimmer of a light and the sound of voices. Without a moment's pause, the bishop strode forward, and sweeping the sliding door of this further apartment aside, he glided like a specter into the room and into the presence of Una, Nabeshima, and Shiro's party.

The sudden and startling appearance of Paoli and his wildly staring eyes seemed to paralyze the beholders, and to strike a strange awe into their hearts, but of this, or even their presence the Jesuit appeared to be unconscious. Straight to the place where Shiro was sitting he strode, until his form towered above the head of the young leader. The bishop spoke not; for a short time he moved not; but his terrible eyes burned down into those of the younger man.

Mechanically Shiro arose, his own face becoming as

"STRAIGHT TO THE PLACE WHERE BIRBO WAS SITTING HE STRODE.—*See Page 272.*

pallid as that of the strange being bending over him. His lips moved, but no sound save a hollow groan escaped them. The mesmeric spell of Paoli's eyes had fallen upon him, and he was powerless to resist its subtle influence. Speechless and with bated breath, the little group of spectators watched the movements of the two men. They saw Paoli turn and glide toward the door, with the same swift and noiseless tread with which he had entered; they saw him pass through the midst of the sleeping guards in the outer room, and they watched him as he gained the open air and disappeared in the darkness. But he went not alone. Behind him, with a step as quick and as echoless as his own, sped the slender figure of Nirado Shiro.

It was not until the two had vanished from sight in the thick darkness without, that the spell, which seemed to bind every soul in the room into a motionless silence, was broken.

And then Obata, groaning aloud, bowed his face to the floor.

And Una gave utterance to a low cry of surprise and terror.

And Lord Nabeshima sprang forward to rouse his retainers to the pursuit.

And Ine Tanaka flung herself upon the breast of the prince, whispering the words: "For my sake, forbear!"

And the guard slept on.

X.

HER FOE AND LOVER.

"As I stood by your *norimono* last night, you said that you could not hope to convert me to your side at this late hour."

The speaker was Nabeshima, and the person to whom his words were addressed was Ine Tanaka. The two were riding side by side through the semi-tropical brightness of the autumn morning down the mountain road that wound through the Unzen passes in its descent to the plain of the Christians. At some little distance in advance, rode the prince's body-guard, while behind them Obata and his servants were following on foot. In fulfillment of his promise of the night before, Nabeshima was conducting Ine and her friends to the Christian camp. As the young nobleman uttered the words we have just given, he looked questioningly into his companion's face. The woman understood the motive of his remark, and her earnest, truthful eyes met his as she answered :

"You would know, my Lord, whether I ever entertained hope of your conversion to our faith. Time was when I did, but I do so no longer. Your name is now enrolled among our foes ; the retainers of Kai, at the bidding of their prince, are even now encamped on the plain below to do battle against the Christians. Yet, my Lord," and the woman's sad voice grew touchingly tender in the childlike confidence it evinced, "yet I believe you do not hate us with such a merciless hatred as do some of your fellow-princes."

The pathos of Ine's words and the simplicity of her manner stirred the man's soul.

"Nay, Ine Tanaka," he cried, his voice unsteady with the emotions that agitated him, "believe me, I do not hate your friends, much less the religion they profess. It were impossible, indeed, for me to do so. Was not the House of Kai the first of our nobility to embrace Christianity? Were not my father, and his father, and his grandfather as well, zealous adherents of the foreign faith? And are not a goodly number of my kindred still its believers?"

"Then, O my Lord, why—?"

Nabeshima threw up his hand in a deprecatory gesture.

"You would ask, Ine Tanaka, why it is, then, that I have taken up arms against your people. I could not do otherwise. My duty as the prince of Japan, is to uphold the laws which I have helped to make. What matters it that the edict, commanding the utter extirpation of the Christian religion, is not to my liking, or that this dreadful work of torturing the condemned and murdering helpless women and children is abhorrent to me? All the other princes advocate the severest measures against the proscribed faith, and, when they summon me to their assistance, I must go."

"But, my Lord," the woman eagerly rejoined, "you are popular aud influential, your house is one of the most powerful in the nation. Even late as it is now, were you disposed to make the effort, this cruel persecution might be stopped, the suffering Christians might yet be granted freedom of worship, and, thus, would the impending conflict be averted."

Never could Ine Tanaka forget the look upon Nabeshima's face, as he listened to her words. Respect and love for her strove with the resolution forming in his mind to tell her plainly the character of the cause with which she was heart and soul identified. Her appeal for his intercession left him no alternative. He must either justify his course in her eyes, or permit her to believe that he and his fellow-princes were engaged,—not in the honorable work of suppressing a dangerous revolt, but in a persecution, ruthless as unprovoked.

"Ine Tanaka, you compel me to say what I would choose, in your presence, to leave unspoken. It is not freedom of worship for their converts that the foreign priests have most desired; it is authority for their church over our rulers. Freedom of worship they did enjoy for many years, and most grievously did they abuse their privilege. What intrigues did they not engage in, what conspiracies did they not form, what treasonable doctrines did they not teach their followers, what overtures for the armed intervention of foreign nations did they not make that they might establish the power of their Pope in Japan? Need we be surprised that our people, through their fear for the safety of our country, have been maddened into unnecessary cruelty? or that our princes, anathematized by the missionaries and openly defied by their Christian subjects, have declared that a religion which so alienates the hearts of its disciples and calls for national subjection to an European lord must be extirpated from the soil of Japan?"

In vain had Nabeshima spoken; his words were lost upon the woman who rode by his side.

From her childhood, Ine Tanaka had been taught to believe that as there was but one God, so He had but one vice-regent on earth,—the head of His infallible church, who was, by divine appointment, a king over the kings of all nations, a lord over every earthly lord. It was, therefore, impossible for her to appreciate the feeling that inspired the heathen princes of her land. This liberty, of which they were so proud and for the safety of which they had become alarmed, was, to her, nothing more than the lawless freedom which a pirate or a brigand might enjoy in defiance of the justly established government. Earthly rulers had no power save that which they received from God through his representative among men. And that representative abode in Rome. Such were the teachings that Ine Tanaka had heard again and again from the lips of Francesco Paoli, and so complete had been her acceptance of them that the principles they inculcated had become interwoven with the inmost fibre of her being, controlling even the powers of her reason and will.

"My Lord, my Lord! These arguments of yours have been in the mouths of God's enemies ever since angels sinned and fell; by such pleas have they hardened their wicked hearts against both warning and repentance. It was so with the rebellious nations in the days of Noah, and the waters of an offended God swept them from the face of the earth; it was so with the sinners of Sodom and Gomorrah, and brimstone and fire from the Lord out of Heaven destroyed them and their evil works. So, O my Lord, shall it be with the enemies of the Church of Japan! It is the promise of Heaven that we shall triumph over those who have risen up against us. The little Christian army in yonder castle, however feeble and contemptible it may seem to its foes, is no less invincible than the Omnipotence that stands behind it and will, in the day of battle, clothe it with victory."

The woman's conscientious earnestness, her lofty faith and devotion thrilled Nabeshima's soul with an admiration for her such as his passionate love had hitherto failed to evoke; her utter inability to perceive the hopelessness of the cause with which she had indissolubly linked her own destiny, her blindness to the destruction awaiting her appalled him.

The heart of the lover prevailed over the chivalrous honor of the prince. Spurring his horse close to the side of his companion's, he seized both the woman's hands, and, as her startled gaze was raised to his wild, anguished face, he cried out, all his passionate longing and anxiety ringing in his voice :

" Madness, madness, Ine Tanaka ! Like Nirado Shiro, thou, too, art under the baneful spell of Francesco Paoli, who, insanely fanatical himself, is luring all who trust him to ruin."

Ine attempted to speak, but the man's grasp tightened upon her hands.

" Nay, woman, thou shalt hear me !" he continued wildly. "Thou hast long known Nabeshima to be a suitor for thy love, but thou hast preferred another before him,—another, Ine, whose heart will never be thine. Nay, start not ! it is the truth which I speak. Saw you not last night his indifference to yourself, his admiration for my cousin, Una Mori ? Mark me ! he will forsake you for her."

The two had now gained the summit of the last foothill, and the camp of the government army, stretching far away to the left, the village of Arima, and, a little beyond this, the fortress of the Christians burst into view. Just before them the road that they had been following divided, one branch leading to the camp, the other to the village. Here the prince reined in his own steed and that of his companion.

" It is not yet too late, Ine Tanaka, to save thyself," he pleaded, with touching earnestness, " or to make me happy in the choice that makes thee Princess of Kai. O Ine, cast no longer aside the love with which Nabeshima would crown thee! This road leads to the camp of my waiting army; come, then, with me, and life and love and honor are thine; the other, believe me, O believe me! will bring thee to faithlessness, suffering, and death."

The woman's face had grown very pale, but it had lost none of its queenly calmness and dignity. Her eyes, full of gentle compassion, met, for a moment, the passionate, yearning gaze of the man before her, and then, looking away in the direction of the Christian camp, she spoke, as if communing with herself, and in so low a tone that the prince had to bend forward to catch her words:

"What I said last night, my Lord, I say again,—thou art brave and noble and good, and Ine Tanaka is highly honored in the proffer of thy love. Yet what thou wishest cannot be. Faithlessness, suffering, and death, thou sayest, await me; impossible, my lord! And yet, were it so to be, faithlessness, suffering, and death must Ine Tanaka choose."

And the Lord of Kai bowed his princely head.

"Thou hast spoken, O woman, and Nabeshima hath no more to say. Hereafter, when thou seest him in the forefront of battle against thy people, know, then, Ine Tanaka, that he is there, not for the honor of being the first to plant his standard upon the walls of the captured castle, but, if it be within his power to do so, to save from the hands of those who would slay her, the woman he loves."

And, with these words, the prince conducted Ine Tanaka down the hill-side by the road that led to the camp of the Christians.

At daybreak consternation and excitement had prevailed throughout the village of Arima and Hara Castle.

"Bishop Paoli is gone; he was seen hastening off about midnight in the direction of the mountains!" were the tidings that carried astonishment and dismay to thousands of hearts. What could it mean? Where did he go? Would they ever look upon his face again? As the sun rose, there went through camp and village and castle the joyful cry: "The bishop is returning, and a stranger is in his company!" Then, as Paoli and Shiro, side by side and without looking to either right or left, moved swiftly through the camp of the army and past the throngs of wondering women and children in the village until they disappeared within the house set apart for Paoli's quarters, the people gazed into one another's faces in mute bewilderment. Had their beloved bishop gone mad?

Another report sped over the Christian plain in the early hours of this memorable day. Nabeshima, Prince of Kai, with about a score of horsemen, was approaching the outer defenses. Thousands rushed to the hill-tops to behold the far-famed chieftain, whose prowess they must soon encounter in the field of war. There, sure enough, was the little cavalcade bearing straight down upon the Christian lines. Slightly in the rear of the horsemen and seated on a gayly caparisoned steed, came a woman and by her side rode the redoubted warrior. At a short distance from the line of fortifications the cavalcade stopped. The woman dismounted, and, accompanied by five men, came on toward the Christians; the prince and his horsemen in the meantime galloping off in the direction of the government troops. Soon it was heralded abroad, through camp and village, that the Lord of Kai had escorted Ine Tanaka, the betrothed wife of their commander-in-chief, from Unzen to Arima; and the astonished multitudes wondered what strange thing would happen next.

BOOK EIGHTH

HOW THEY KEPT CHRISTMAS AT ARIMA.

I.

A SURPRISE THAT WAS NO SURPRISE.

IN former times, Hara Castle, which had now become the stronghold of the insurgent Christians, had been the fortress of the Shimabara princes, but about the close of the sixteenth century it had been deserted for a new stronghold in the city of Shimabara, and the old castle had fallen into neglect and ruin. Situated on a high and narrow tongue of land running out into the gulf, its position was well-nigh impregnable. To the seaward, the towering perpendicular cliffs made access from that quarter impossible; while landward, on either side, were abrupt bluffs falling off into almost impassable marshes. The only possible way of approach to the fortress was over a fan-shaped ridge of land having its narrowest part resting against the castle walls. Across this neck of land, that gradually widened until it opened out into the plain, the Christians, when they repaired the castle for their own occupancy, had constructed an outer line of defense. This consisted of a deep *fosse* that cut across the ridge from side to side, having on the brink nearest the castle a strong wall of earth and stone. The open space between this outer fortification and the walls of the castle proper was occupied by the camp of the Christian army, the women and children having been already removed, for greater safety, to the interior of the fortress.

During the first few weeks following the events narrated in the last book, a number of engagements occurred between the Christians and the government troops, in which the insurgents invariably succeeded in repulsing the assaults of their foes. Nevertheless, they found it necessary to gradually abandon their outposts upon the summits of the foot-hills and also on the adjacent islands, so that, by the middle of December, their entire force was stationed in Hara Castle and the outer fortifications, already mentioned. Shiro, as commander-in-chief of the Christian forces, had general supervision of their movements, Paoli acting as his adviser. The army was divided into four divisions. Of one of these Oyano had command

and the others were placed under the leadership of three chiefs—Ashizuka, Chijiwa, and Komekine—all of them veteran warriors, who, in their youth, had fought in Korea under the standard of Konishi, the famous Christian general, and, later, had seen him overthrown in the bloody battle of Sekigahara.

Upon the part of the government troops, no efforts were spared to suppress the insurrection. A fleet of war-junks was prepared to cut off the enemy's retreat by sea, and a permanent camp for the large land force was constructed on the heights commanding the plain of the Christians. The *Spuyten Duyvil*, after discharging her cargo at Hirado, had set sail for Arima, but a furious storm had driven her far out to sea, and when she put back, it was in such a shattered condition that Van Neist was compelled to run into Nagasaki harbor for repairs. The Dutch factory at Hirado had loaned a dozen or more foreign cannon, and these Itakura had mounted on rude carts to serve as field-pieces. The army was constantly receiving re-inforcements, and by the middle of December, all the princes of Kiushiu, either in person or by deputy, had reported themselves at Arima; and the number of the troops encamped along the base of Unzen was, it is said, fully one hundred and twenty-five thousand fighting men.

In a council of war, called by General Itakura on the twenty-fourth of December, it was decided to storm the Christian stronghold the coming night, and the day was spent in preparation for the assault. Alone among the leaders, Nabeshima opposed the plan of a night attack on the ground of the impossibility of surprising so vigilant a foe as the Christians had proved themselves to be; but when the other generals unanimously favored an attempt, none labored with more tireless energy for the success of the undertaking than did he. Riding out of the camp in the early afternoon, he approached as near to the hostile defenses as was possible, and made a careful reconnaissance of the ground. Upon his return, he summoned his captains, and gave orders for the preparation of a portable bridge. Night came, and with it a storm of freezing rain, mingled with snow and hail.

"Have the soldiers bind *waraji** upon their feet," he commanded, as he forecast the icy condition in which they would likely find the hill-sides leading to the defenses of the foe.

Shortly after midnight the orders came for the storming army to move upon the Christians. Kuroda, Arima, Ogasawara, Nabeshima, Tachibana, Hosokawa—such was the order in which the chieftains were told off,—and in that order they led forth their several divisions to the attack.

"Strong and steady, men of Kai! Spears first and swords when I draw mine?" cried the prince to his followers, as, with unhelmed brow, he passed along the line, and in a minute more they were in motion.

Down the hill-side, under trees dripping from the storm, across the plain of the Christians and over their deserted fortifications, Nabeshima and the eighteen hundred fearless souls behind him marched on. Before them, the van of the long black line had already reached the ridge leading to the outer defenses of the foe. Behind them, Hosokawa was but issuing from the camp.

Then sharp and shrill, above the roar of the wind and the sea and the rattle of the hail upon their armor, rose a human voice. Then another and another, until the sound broke into one loud and constant scream, pealing from

---

* Straw sandals.

hundreds of throats. A cry of surprise and anger burst from the whole army, and far away upon the heights, the tens of thousands still in camp strained their eyes through the darkness in breathless amazement at the sound. Itakura, grinding his teeth in fury, cursed, in the name of Buddha and all the gods of Japan, the unhappy wretches whose terrified shrieks had betrayed the approach of his troops to those within the castle.

Along the line of the storming army confusion soon ensued. "The Christians are out and are attacking Kuroda! Forward to the rescue!" came the cry, and the rear divisions dashed madly forward on those ahead, rendering more hopeless and terrible the disorder in front. At last the truth became known: "Beware! The ridge is covered with ice; the men are falling down into the marshes by the score!"

The warning sped from mouth to mouth back along the entire line. But it came too late to save hundreds. Of Kuroda's division, more than half were struggling in the miry marshes that flanked the ridge on either side. The remainder—a demoralized rout—were now dashed into the moat before the Christians' defenses by such of Arima's panic-stricken troops as had effected the passage in safety.

Those that followed came on in a more soldier-like order. Ogasawara, at the head of three thousand Satsuma men, the flower of the entire army, reached the fatal ridge, but with proud and stately step the veteran troops marched steadily on, and, as man after man lost his footing and plunged down the treacherous slope, no sound, save a muffled groan, escaped his lips as he disappeared in the black depths below.

And after Ogasawara followed the Prince of Kai; none more brave and daring than he, none more considerate of the dangers to which he exposed the lives of faithful followers.

"Lean upon your spear-points, my heroes, slow and steady!" rang out his manly voice, in command to his retainers. The men thrust their spears into the ice-covered ground, and this precaution, with the help of the straw sandals they wore, kept their feet from slipping. They had not, however, reached the narrowest and most dangerous part of the ridge, when a number of fires flamed up on the fortifications ahead, and Paoli's form, huge and shadowy, was seen standing erect on the summit of the wall. Nabeshima was unable to hear his words, but he saw his ax circling about his head and he could easily imagine the meaning of his address to the Christians below.

"That Jesuit again, curse him! Oh, that I may be brought face to face with him to-night!" muttered the young leader through his clenched teeth. "Men of Kai!" he shouted to the dusky line behind him; "behold the slayer of your comrades at Higashi-yama! Let him not escape our vengeance—ye gods!"

The last exclamation was called forth by the cloud of arrows which the Christians discharged against their foes and which for an instant darkened the light of the fires. In the present storm of mingled rain and hail, firearms were useless. Bow and spear, and, above all, the terrible two-handled sword must be this night the weapons of defense and slaughter.

II.

TAKABOKA IS AVENGED

Paoli was still upon the wall, and, as he perceived the havoc the Christian bowmen's first discharge had wrought among the foe, he called for another.

"Nobly done, Sons of the Church! Down before your death-shafts like grain before the reaper sink the enemies of our faith! Again, stout archers! Strong arms, steady hands, let fly!" And once more came the shrill hiss of arrows, and through breastplate and helmet pierced the merciless iron bolts. A muffled groan of dying men, like the hollow boom of the surf on the rocks, came across the moat to the ears of the Christians.

"Down with bow and spear, throw wide open the gates, and upon the infidel with the edge of the sword!" shouted the warrior-bishop, himself the first one to leap down upon the causeway that led across the moat from the great gate of the fort.

The few surviving soldiers of Kuroda's division, as they beheld the dreaded Jesuit dashing upon them, fled right and left. Their leader finding himself deserted by his followers, sprang forward to meet Paoli, his long spear leveled at the throat of the oncoming foe. One swift, sweeping blow, and the spear was hewn in twain; a fierce cry of "*Yaso-Maria!*" another terrible stroke, and the ax that splintered the spear cleaved the infidel, helm and head.

At that moment the gates flew wide open, and with their thrilling war-cry, "*Yaso-Maria*, Takaboka and vengence!" the Christians poured forth. Deep into the midst of Arima's men, Paoli plunged, and close after him followed the dauntless Ashizuka. As quickly as room could be made in the level space before the walls, it was filled with Christian warriors. Arima, at whose suggestion the ill-starred attack had been made, strove nobly to stay the tide of disaster, and to drive the insurgents to the shelter of their walls. Around him rallied his devoted clansmen, and before the fury of their assault, the insurgents were hurled back almost to the brink of the moat.

"Arima! Arima!" rose the shout of the infidel; "Paoli! Paoli!" the rallying cry of the Christians.

For an instant the Jesuit's blazing eye swept the dismal scene of storm and carnage; then, with a loud call to Ashizuka to follow with his warriors where he led, he threw himself into the thickest of the fray. High in air wheeled the bloody ax; each time it fell, a foeman sank to the earth. Against the stout cuirass of Spanish steel clanged hostile spear and arrow; but vain was the thrust of the one, vain the quick, hurtling blow of the other. On, on to Arima's side, Paoli hewed his way, paving his path with the slain. The Japanese general looked up in time to see his chief captain sink beneath that invincible ax. Then the fierce laugh and the defying voice of the haughty *Samurai* rang out above the thunder of the conflict:

"Ho, barbarian! thinkest thou Arima quails before thee? Dog of a Christian! mine shall be the price set on thy accursed head!" and swinging with both hands his long, ponderous sword, he rushed upon the Jesuit. Calm and terrible stood Paoli, his ax poised aloft, his left foot planted firmly forward, ready for advance or retreat; his blazing eyes watchful; every muscle nerved to the utmost. Forward bounded Arima; high in the air flashed his sword; down with lightening speed it swept, down to be buried deep—in the earth! For swifter than Arima's stroke was Paoli's leap aside, and, as his enemy bowed forward from the force of his own blow, down flashed the ax upon his neck, and the headless trunk fell at the feet of the victor.

The death of the chief created a panic among his followers. Backward they surged, with feeble efforts at defense; then broke and fled. Behind them, Ogasawara had drawn up his veterans in battle array, and was calmly awaiting the onset of the Christians. Right into these motionless columns dashed the terrified fugitives from the front. The ranks were disordered and broken; wide gaps yawned along the line. Into one of these plunged the ax of Paoli; into others, the merciless swords of Ashizuka and his followers. What availed then the dauntless valor of the veteran, or the prestige of the name of Satsuma! With incredible swiftness the disordered columns were hurled back upon the fatal ridge. Ice beneath their feet, the foemen's weapons above their heads; down plunged hundreds into the dark and miry marshes.

"My arm grows weary!" roared Paoli to Ashizuka. "The handle of my ax is slippery with blood. *Yaso-Maria!* Down with the infidel!"

"*Yaso-Maria!* Takaboka and vengeance!" rose afresh the fierce chorus of the Christians above the howling of the storm and the sickening sound of blows and groans.

Swept back finally over the ridge and out upon the plain, the Satsuma men turned and fled. Tachibana and Hosokawa ordered their troops to open their ranks to let the retreating warriors escape to the rear; then again they closed and presented a firm front to the victorious foe that, mad with the fury of battle, was rushing upon them.

"Ho, avengers of Takaboka!" shouted Paoli. "Behold the dragon banner of Hosokawa, the pitiless murderer of our brethren at the foreign ship, and of the women and children on Takaboka!" and the bishop pointed with his ax in the direction of that leader's forces that loomed up dimly in the light shed through the storm from the distant fires. "Ho, swords of the church, warriors of the cross! Upon them and spare not! Forward! I see the fleshless hands of our murdered brethren beckoning us onward. The spirits of the women slaughtered on Takaboka wheel in the air above their butchers. Forward! Saints and angels are our shields in this holy war. On! on!"

The effect of Paoli's words was indescribable. A mad roar went up from the Christian host about him. Back across the ridge, through the gate of the fort, and even into the castle sped the tidings: "The Takaboka murderers are on the plain!" Forth rushed Chijiwa and his warriors; forth poured the followers of Oyano. Over the ridge, with scores plunging down on either side, for the ice was as treacherous to Christian foot as it had been to infidel, into the open plain they dashed. How it happened no one knew, but before he was aware, Hosokawa found himself entrapped. Between him and the camp, the soldiers of Oyano; between him and Tachibana, Chijiwa's warriors; on his left, the marsh and the sea; before him, the ax of Paoli.

Grim and terrible was the struggle that ensued. Around the devoted *Samurai* closed the dense circle of infuriated Christians. Awful to the bravest ear rose the mingled chorus of their cries: "Fight for your lives! Remember Takaboka and perish! Vengeance! Vengeance!" More furiously than ever they threw themselves upon the enemy. The carnage was frightful. The infidel fell with a curse of defiance; the Christian with a prayer to his saints. In equal numbers they seemed to go down; but for every avenger that fell, another rose in his place. Alas! for the doomed *Samurai!* As the heap of their dead grew higher, the gaps in their ranks remained unfilled. At the foot of his dragon standard stood the heroic Hosokawa, and around him his warriors, giving thrust for thrust and blow for blow. They fell where they stood, their chieftain the last of all, and his dragon streamer, flapping and shrieking in the storm, sank down on the ghastly ring of the dead.

Terribly indeed had Takaboka been avenged.

III.

THE RIVALS MEET.

Where were Nabeshima and the men of Kai?

While Ogasawara's forces were yet drawn up and awaiting the coming of the Christians, a dusky line stole past them and disappeared in the darkness that concealed the extreme southern end of the fortifications. Here it paused and waited.

From the shadow of the defenses that covered them, the men of Kai looked out on the conflict raging before the gates of the fort. They saw Ogasawara's troops driven back over the ridge, and beheld the Christians, in heavy columns, pouring out from behind their walls. Ashizuka's division was already on the plain, and now came Chijiwa, and now Oyano. Nabeshima's eagle eye had been watching for his opportunity; it had come. Only a few thousands had remained within the fortress. A quick dash, and the fort, nay, even the castle itself might be his. And then, with the prisoners, for a time at least, in the keeping of his own retainers, the dearest object of all these tireless labors of his—the salvation of Ine Tanaka—would be attained. Nabeshima's heart beat tumultuously at the thought. With the rattle of the hail upon his armor, the roar of wind and war in his ears, and the prospect of a conflict, fierce and bloody, before him, the time and place seemed unsuitable for sentimental musings; yet the warrior's pulse quickened at the thought that there, in the castle before him, was the woman he loved. But there, too, was the man who stood between him and her, and then his handsome face darkened, and a terrible look came into his eyes. War was now in his heart, and out-rang his princely voice to the men about him:

"Forward with the bridge! Honor and promotion to the man who is the first to follow me over the defenses!"

Upon the shoulders of stout warriors, the bridge was rapidly borne to the front and flung across the moat. A minute more, and the prince stood on the top of the wall; another, and he had bounded into the fort; another, and he was surrounded by his warriors, while over the wall poured a steady line of shadowy forms. Unsuspecting an attack from that quarter, the Christians were unconscious of their danger. Not until all the men of Kai were within the fort, not until they had fired some sheds filled with straw and charcoal, did the Christians perceive the foe. High up on the castle walls, a woman's voice rose above the tumult and gave the alarm. Nabeshima heard the warning cry; he recognized the voice, and, in the light from the now blazing buildings, he swept the sea of faces on the ramparts above him in the hope that he might see her face; but the rain beat into his eyes and blinded him.

"Forward, men of Kai!" he shouted to his retainers, his voice thrilling with the vision of victory just before him. "Nabeshima to the onslaught! *Yaso-taiji!*"*

With a dash they were upon the insurgents, who, some three thousand strong, under the leadership of Shiro, now heroically threw themselves between the men of Kai and the gates of the main castle. Fast and furious fell the blows of the opposing swords as Christian and infidel clashed together. "*Yaso-Maria!*" rose the battle-shout of the one; "*Yaso-taiji!*" the war cry of the other.

In the van of his warriors, Nabeshima led the way to the castle gates, and despite their most gallant resistance, Shiro and his soldiers were slowly driven back. The young Christian leader's gaze, too, turned to the frowning battlements above him, and eyes, that recked not for the longing look of the prince, beheld the upturned face of Nirado Shiro. A white flag was waved from the top of the wall, and the face of Ine Tanaka shone out on the man she loved. But another eye saw her, another eye beheld Shiro, in answer to her salute, wave his mailed hand to the maiden. The Prince of Kai leaped through the press, cutting down all who opposed him until he reached the Christian chief.

"Nirado Shiro!" he cried "again we meet; this time on the field of honorable battle! In the presence of the woman who loves you and in the sight of both armies, make good thy boast that thou fearest not the Prince of Kai!"

In obedience to a gesture of their leader's hand, the men of Kai fell back from the furious onset that had borne them almost to the castle gates. A cry for the cessation of hostilities ran along the line; and the Chris-

---

* Down with the Christians.

tian soldiers in amazement involuntarily followed the example of their foes, and likewise retreated a few paces from the place where they had been standing. An open space was thus formed between the infidel and the Christians, and here stood Shiro and Nabeshima.

The young chief of the insurgents was no mean match for the prince. Shorter in stature and slighter in figure than Lord Nabeshima, he, nevertheless, was quick of movement and well trained. During his long residence at Manila, the best instructors in both Western and Oriental military tactics had been procured for him; but in nothing did he prove himself a true son of Japan more than in his love for the keen-edged, two-handed sword of his nation, and he became exceedingly skillful in its use. Thus, while in physical prowess the advantage was on the side of the prince, Shiro's greater adroitness in the management of his weapon made the two combatants about equal.

"Thou speakest, Prince Nabeshima, as if it were necessary to urge me to fight," said the Christian chief with a haughty dignity. "That night on Unzen I told thee to thy face I feared thee not. Again we meet, and once again I say: I fear thee not. As I was ready then to cross swords in mortal combat, so stand I ready now. Guard for thy life, Prince! God and Holy Cross!"

With his last words, Shiro swung up his sword and poised it above his head. Nabeshima's blade also flashed aloft, but as he raised it, the prince's eyes were lifted to the wall on which he had seen Ine Tanaka. As he did so, there came the sharp hiss of a flying arrow, and full on the upturned forehead of the Lord of Kai fell the descending bolt. The sword dropped from the hand of the stricken prince; he reeled for a moment, as if in an effort to recover himself, then, tossing up his arms wildly, he fell heavily at the feet of his foe.

A cry of rage broke from the ranks of Nabeshima's men, and with drawn swords, they rushed forward to rescue the body of their lord, and to avenge his fall. But Shiro, dropping his own weapon stretched out his arms:

"Hold, men of Kai!" he shouted. "Stay your hands! We fear your swords less than your scorn. Know ye that whoever shot that dastard shaft shall be punished! I swear it in the name of the God in whom I trust. Man to man and sword to sword, your leader and I stood here ready for honorable combat. Accursed be the treacherous hand that smote down my noble foe! Hear ye, followers of this chivalrous lord! Once my friends and I were in your master's power. With the generosity that has made the name of Nabeshima illustrious throughout our nation, he forebore to do us harm, though I, ignorant of who he was, insultingly defied him. My friends he conducted in safety to our lines. Men of Kai! permit me to-night to repay that courtesy! Take your lord, and, unmolested, bear him to his camp."

A confused murmur arose among Nabeshima's followers. Some were in favor of accepting Shiro's offer, others, it was clear to see, were for a bloody reprisal upon the Christians. While they were discussing the matter, the young man knelt by the side of his prostrate foe, and, unlacing his armor, thrust his hand into his breast The heart was still feebly beating, and, even as he looked, he saw the color beginning to return to the pallid face. By the side of the fallen man lay the treacherous arrow. The point had been entirely cut away with a knife, so that the head was but a broad disk; a shape well calculated to stun without inflicting a mortal wound, and this evidently, had been the purpose of the one who shot the bolt. Thrusting the shaft into his sword belt, Shiro rose to his feet.

"Your master lives, he is even now recovering;" he cried to the still debating men. "What say ye? Is it peace, or is it war? Hear ye that sound? The forces in the field are returning. Ye may avenge your master; ye may sell your lives dearly, but his life and the lives of yourselves shall pay the forfeit. Stay here and ye are doomed! Again do I tell you, the hand that struck down the Lord of Kai shall know my vengeance!"

As he spoke, Shiro glanced upward, and his eyes rested on Ine. She had arisen to her feet; her face was deathly pale, and, as she saw the upturned countenance of her lover, she stretched forth her arms wildly toward him with a look of unspeakable anguish and piteous pleading. Then, even as he gazed, she fell back swooning into the arms of the women about her, and with a horror-stricken face the young man bowed his proud head.

He knew whose hand had sped the bolt.

"We accept thy generous offer," said the captain of Nabeshima's body-guard, approaching the Christian chief. "The life of our prince is dearer to us than our own, dearer to us than even our thirst for revenge for that cowardly blow. We trust you to punish the wrong-doer, even as you have sworn."

"You had your choice, peace or war," Shiro responded, and his voice sounded hollow and strange to his own ears. "On another day, may the God of battles again bring Nabeshima and me face to face! Go, Obata," he continued, addressing that warrior, "and in my name give the men of Kai a safe conduct through our lines."

And thus the courtesy that Nabeshima had shown six weeks before at the hermitage of Unzen was repaid.

Out upon the plain the conflict was still raging. Itakura, upon hearing of the disaster that had befallen the storming army, had promptly sent down heavy re-inforcements, and the Christians were slowly driven back to the castle. The retreat, however, was made in perfectly good order, the ridge was crossed, and, while Paoli and Ashizuka held the government troops in check, the other divisions of the army filed through the gates into the fort, amid the tumultuous applause of the thousands on the walls and within the castle. Finally Ashizuka's warriors also retired to the shelter of the defenses, their leader and the bishop being the last to disappear within the gates, which closed with a heavy clang in the face of the foe, whom a tempest of stones and arrows from the top of the defenses swept back in confusion. Another dash upon the Christians' fortifications, another repulse, and the government troops sullenly withdrew. Paoli mounted the wall at the place where he had stood to give the signal for attack; and he gazed with a long and triumphant look upon the dusky columns of the foe sweeping across the plain in the direction of the heights.

The storm had broken away. The rain and hail no longer fell, but the wind still blew in fierce and frequent blasts. The clouds had lifted from the eastern horizon, and above the tossing waters of the gulf and over the distant range of the Higo mountains, the first faint beams of Christmas morn mounted into the cold and wintry sky. Over the field of blood, before the walls of Hara Castle, stole the morning's timid light, as if fearing to reveal to the eyes of men the ghastly wreck of war.

"Never before in the history of our Japan," say the native historians, "had the *Samurai* suffered so terrible a defeat at the hands of yeomen." And verily the Christians had cause to exult over their victory. Three generals, seventy-eight captains, and fourteen thousand soldiers had perished. No report of the loss of the Christians has come down to us, but it could have been nothing more than a mere fraction of that of the government army, because, after innumerable skirmishes, two months later, they still could muster twenty thousand fighting men.

IV.

YAMADA THE RONIN AGAIN.

After the great battle of the twenty-fifth of December, little of note occurred for nearly a month in the prosecution of the siege. A few sorties were made by the Christians, and about an equal number of assaults were made by the government troops on the outer defenses; but nothing was accomplished by either side, and the loss of life was but trifling.

News came from Yedo that the Shogun was dissatisfied with Itakura's conduct of affairs at Arima, and that he had severely censured him in making the fatal night attack. Still later came the report that Matsudaira, a veteran general who had served under Iyeyasu at Sekigahara, had received the Shogun's appointment as general-in-chief of the government forces, and that he was then on his way to Kiushiu to supersede Itakura in the command of the army. The latter, therefore, determined to exert himself to the utmost to subdue the insurgents before the arrival of the new leader.

Just at this junction of affairs, occurred an event that promised to give the commander-in-chief success in his undertaking. One evening a scout returned to the camp bearing an arrow, around which was wound a letter addressed to General Itakura. The scout said that it had been shot from within the Christians' walls and had fallen at his feet. The letter was as follows:

"My name is Uyemon Yamada, and I am a native of Ishihaya. I was a retainer of Prince Kaneko, whom the barbarian priest Paoli sank with a party of his followers in the entrance to Nagasaki Bay, on the night following the battle at the foreign ship. I learned this from one of the *sendos*, who recognized the Jesuit, and who, after the capsizing of the *sampan*, managed to swim ashore. I therefore became a *Ronin*, and swore to avenge my lord's death upon the barbarian. For this purpose, I pretended to be a Christian tradesman of Ishihaya, compelled to flee for my faith to my brethren at Arima. Among the rebels, my name is Kuroda. Since coming here, I have found no opportunity for carrying out the purpose that brought me hither, for the Jesuit is ever upon his guard. But I have been appointed captain of the gate-keepers, and it is in my power to betray the castle into your hands. This I shall do on the condition that mine be the office of executioner of the foreign priest, should he be captured alive, and that the reward offered for his head be given to me. If there be any Ishihaya men in your camp, question them concerning me. The Prince of Kai knows me as the one from whose vengeance he rescued the Englishman on the night of the cross ordeal, and whom I hurled from the Unzen cliffs above the Obama road some weeks ago. When you have well considered this matter, let an answer, tied to an arrow, be shot over the wall into the quarter where Lord Nabeshima burned the store-houses on the night of the attack, and I shall receive it. I shall give directions as to the time and the place for making the attack, in my reply."

Here followed the date and the seal. The news that such a letter had been received spread like wildfire through the camp, and caused the greatest excitement. A few Ishihaya men that were in the army knew Yamada, and were aware of his becoming a *Ronin*, and vowing the death of Paoli. Nabeshima was questioned, and he corroborated the statements in the letter respecting the Englishman. Having thus satisfied himself that this was no stratagem of the Christians to draw on an attack, in order to lead him into a trap, Itakura, the next morning, ordered a reply to be sent to the *Ronin*, in the manner in which he had directed, agreeing to grant his requests. The same day an answer was returned, naming the coming midnight as the time of betrayal. With this letter was sent a plan of the castle, and directions how best to make the assault.

The remainder of the day was spent in preparation for what Itakura and his generals were convinced was to be the final battle in the siege of Hara Castle.

"Great Lord," said the captain of Nabeshima's body-guard to his master, who had been busily engaged in giving orders to his officers, "thou wast ever a shrewd guesser of the future. What sayest thou shall be our fortunes to-night?"

The young nobleman's face was grave as he replied:

"To conquer a brave enemy through the treachery of a spy is not the honor a chivalrous soldier covets."

The captain was not certain of the meaning of the enigmatical reply. He turned a keen look upon the prince. "Then thou sayest that we shall conquer?"

"How can we fail with the gates wide open and the Christians not suspecting our approach?"

The captain cast a quick glance around, and perceived that the officers were all at a distance. "My Lord," he said in a low voice, "we are alone. I would speak with thee." He waited for permission to go on.

"Speak, then!" said the Lord of Kai, a faint smile lighting up his somber face. Since that terrible night before the walls of Hara Castle, the prince had seemed a changed man. His old-time vivacity was gone, and in its place had come an abstracted and melancholy air that with his haggard face, told of some secret sorrow preying upon his mind.

Of all the men of Kai, the captain of the Prince's bodyguard was the one on the most intimate terms with the young lord; and on subjects concerning which others would not presume to speak to the master, he could freely talk.

"To-night, my liege," said the officer, speaking in a low, rapid voice, "the castle falls into our hands; to-night the Christians perish by the sword. Such are General Itakura's orders. My Lord, what of the one who struck you down with her arrow that night when you and the rebel chieftain stood ready for conflict?"

Prince Nabeshima started violently, and then shudderingly averted his face. After a pause, he said:

"Heardst not thou the words of Shiro: that the hand that drew that bow should be punished?"

"My Lord, but that hand was the hand of his betrothed wife, Ine Tanaka, the woman whom you long ago would have made Princess of Kai, the woman you saved on Unzen and safely conducted to her fellow-rebels. O Lord, be no more in the snare of that sorceress, lest this time a worse fate befall thee. Away with this passion of thine for one who would have slain thee. For her crime of being a Christian and for her treachery to thee, let her die the death!" And the captain rushed away, leaving his master alone.

With a stifled groan, Prince Nabeshima staggered into his tent, and, sinking upon the floor, buried his face in his hands.

"Alas! it is true, then. My eyes did not deceive me

when my upward glance saw the bow in her hands. Would that thine arrow, O woman! had slain me! Woe! Woe!"

Alas! indeed, for a love so noble, so devoted and so hopeless as was Nabeshima's for Ine Tanaka.

FULL ON THE UPTURNED FOREHEAD OF THE LORD OF KAI FELL THE DESCENDING BOLT.—
See Page 296.

BOOK NINTH.

HOW NIRADO SHIRO KEPT HIS VOW.

I.

GATHERING SHADOWS.

TO the increasingly large number of women in Hara Castle, who from day to day were called upon to mourn the loss of dear ones who went out to battle and never again returned, Ine Tanaka had become an angel of consolation. In the hospital where the wounded lay tossing in feverish pain, no hand was so gentle and soothing, no voice so tenderly sympathetic as hers. Wherever she went,—and she was a frequent visitor to every part of the castle,—her presence was like a heavenly benediction.

And no one called forth so much affectionate esteem as she. The people loved their bishop, it was true, but in these dark days, when they beheld him in his suit of mail, with the terrible battle-ax by his side, stalking like a messenger of death among them, his burning eyes flaming with a baleful light, and his countenance fierce and fearful, the little children hushed their voices as he passed by, and the women shook their heads sadly.

"Ah, the good bishop is not what he used to be!" they would say. "Alas, that so great a change should come."

The soldiers, likewise, looked upon him with awe, as well they might; for no score of warriors among them had carried such destruction into the midst of the foe as had his single arm. But all classes alike had come to regard him less as a religious teacher and more as a military leader.

And in some such way did Paoli now consider himself. The public devotional services fell more and more into the hands of the native priests; less and less did the bishop appear in the chapel, and more constantly was he to be found either in conference with the generals or moodily pacing back and forth in the solitude of his own quarters. All this tended to make both old and young look upon him with an overwhelming sense of awe not unmixed with fear.

Shiro failed to gain the affections of the people. Just why, no one was able to say. Ever since his birth, the Church of Japan had been taught that he was the divinely appointed leader that was to bring God's people out of the Egypt of their oppression into the promised land of peace and freedom. For their unflinching faith in him, they had steadfastly endured hardships and persecutions that otherwise would have led them to renounce their faith, or at least its open profession. Now their leader had come, the die had been cast that must result either in the triumph of their cause or its irretrievable overthrow; and in this, their supreme crisis, the struggling Christians slowly awoke to the fact that Nirado Shiro did not fill their expectations. The young leader was unconscious of this feeling among his followers; but the other generals perceived it, as did also the bishop, and to all of them it was a source of poignant sorrow. But to none was this disappointment of the people more plainly manifest than to Ine Tanaka, and to no other heart did it bring such bitterness as to hers.

Thus, while the distressed people regarded Paoli with feelings of mingled love and fear, and looked upon Shiro with an ever-growing sense of distrust, their hearts went out to his betrothed wife with an amount of affectionate veneration that it is seldom the good fortune of either man or woman to inspire in those about them. She became their comforter and friend. To her they went in their sorrows, and she was the first to hear of their successes in the field and their plans and hopes for the future. Her fair face always smiled a welcome upon them, and her sweet voice never failed in the balm of its consolation nor in the inspiration of its encouragement and praise. Exquisitely tender and pathetic were this beautiful and queenly woman's relations to the sorrowing women and the stern, half-hopeful, half-despairing soldiers about her.

In the midst of all these ministrations to others, Ine Tanaka bore about in her own bosom a heart that was heavy and aching. The loving people saw her sweet face increase its pallor day by day, her features become thinner, and the light in her eyes wane and her gentle smile grow sadder as she welcomed them. They, poor folk, thought that it was her sympathy for their troubles that was telling upon her strength, and, out of their great love for her, they finally forebore to speak at all of their own sorrows, and brought her only such tidings as might cheer her drooping spirits. And so, in their simple way, they strove to comfort her, who so long had been a comforter to them.

II.

A WOMAN'S BATTLE AND VICTORY.

All in vain were their efforts. Ine's troubles had springs they knew not of. Hers was the sorrow of a woman who has loved long and faithfully, and finds that her love is unreturned. Nabeshima's prophecy, uttered during their ride together from Unzen to Arima, was having its fulfillment. Her fidelity to the man to whom her parents had betrothed her, was receiving only faithlessness and suffering as its reward. The conference between herself and Shiro and the bishop at Kayaki, which had there been broken off, was never resumed; and the woman instinctively felt that the reason for this was Shiro's opposition to discussing a subject, in which, from the first, he had taken only a languid interest, and for which he now entertained a growing dislike. Paoli, she well knew, was constantly urging upon the young Christian leader the duty of fulfilling the obligation his parents had laid upon him; but Ine quickly discovered that the Jesuit's mysterious influence over Shiro, absolute as it was in all other matters, was here baffled and set at nought.

The night that she and her lover had been the guests of Lord Mori, Ine very plainly perceived that the fair Eurasian girl had awakened in Nirado Shiro a feeling deeper than mere admiration for her beauty. She had seen a light in his eyes and a warmth in his manner toward Una that she had never evoked. And the knowledge that other eyes had noted this infatuation made the pain it caused her all the harder to bear, and Nabeshima's warning words: "Mark me! he will forsake you for her!" still rang in her ears and rankled her soul.

With all this came the bitterness of the discovery that the people were disappointed in their leader, and that their distrust of him was increasing as the weeks passed by. With what tender, compassionate pity did not this loving woman's heart go out to the man, who was, slowly but surely, losing the love of all others! How she longed to warn him of his peril, to comfort him with her own devoted faithfulness and, by her influence with the people and through their affection for her, to win back to him their respect and love! Then a great fear took possession of her. A presentiment that Nirado Shiro was destined to fall by the hand of the Prince of Kai haunted her mind. She, who, at Kayaki had believed him, by reason of a Heavenly appointment, to be invulnerable against the weapons of his foes, felt now, despite her earnest efforts to fight it down, a growing disbelief in both call and protection. And as this feeling strengthened in her mind, her anxious solicitude for his safety increased, her love for him deepened.

Then followed that never-to-be-forgotten Christmas morning, when she beheld Nabeshima cut his way to Shiro's side and challenge the Christian chief to a mortal combat. She knew the deep love the young nobleman bore her, and the feelings with which he consequently regarded her betrothed husband. She felt certain that if the two men were allowed to join battle, Shiro would be killed. Hastily seizing a bow and quiver that had been dropped by some soldier when Paoli's orders had come to sally forth with swords, she struck off the point of an arrow, that she might stun but not slay the prince, and, fitting the shaft to the bow, she shot the bolt with what effect we already know.

When she heard Shiro's vow to Nabeshima's retainers to punish whoever it was that had struck down their leader, a terrible horror seized upon her. Was this to be her reward? While Shiro was kneeling by the prostrate body of his foe, she sat there stunned, and unconscious to everything about her. Again, like the sound of the death-bell to the condemned prisoner, Shiro's renewed vow to avenge the blow that had saved his life fell upon her ear.

She saw him look up. She sprang to her feet and, stretching out her arms toward him, she endeavored to call upon him to retract his oath; but her tongue refused its office. For a moment, mute and anguished, she looked down upon him in piteous appeal, and then, with a low moan, she sank back insensible into the arms of the women who sprang forward as they saw her swooning away.

The young Christian leader, as the reader will remember, had seen her, and with a horror, second only to Ine's, did he feel now the full significance of the oath that he had made. Days passed by, and he brooded over the matter with increasing bitterness toward himself. If he did not love Ine, his frank, generous nature appreciated her motive, and rather would he have perjured himself a thousand times than, by word or act, rebuke the woman who so hopelessly loved him.

And yet he was fulfilling his vow to Nabeshima's retainers, and was visiting upon her, who sped the fateful shaft, a punishment more terrible than any the men of Kai could have enjoined. For what Ine intuitively felt to be Shiro's feelings toward her was the truth. He did not love her, and the prospect of making her his wife was growing more and more repugnant to him. He had been deeply smitten by the beautiful face of Una Mori, and what had at first been mere admiration rapidly deepened into a passionate love. In the early days of the seige, before the government troops had cut off all communications between Arima and the mountains, Shiro had made a number of secret visits to Unzen, disguised as a travelling *komamonoya*,* and had succeeded in seeing Una; and now, though it seemed no longer possible to make these clandestine expeditions, his thoughts dwelt upon her continually.

Toward Ine he was always courteous and respectful; but since that Christmas morn, a nervous discomfort had characterized his demeanor in her presence. No allusion to the shooting was made by either, though it was constantly in the minds of both. Upon the same day that the *Ronin's* letter was creating such a sensation in Itakura's camp, the two had met in the reception-room of the women's quarters, but the young leader's manner had been colder and more constrained than ever before, and it was with an audible sigh of relief that he left the apartment. The woman listened to his retreating footsteps in the corridor without, and, when they had died away, she fled wildly to her own room and threw herself on the floor, in a passion of sobs and tears. All the pent-up anguish, that had for so long a time been preying upon her spirits, at last burst through the control of her powerful will, and the fair and queenly Ine Tanaka, who so often had stood serene and composed amid perils that terrified all others about her, was now but a weak woman, bowed down beneath a weight of grief and woe that was breaking her heart.

* A dealer in toilet articles.

Was Nirado Shiro conscious of having so faithfully fulfilled his vow to the men of Kai?

When, a few hours later, Ine came out of her room, the supreme crisis in her life had been met and passed. She was again the sweetly smiling woman, whose gentle presence had so often brought fortitude and hope to many a fainting soul. Nor would any one have suspected that, beneath that calm and regal exterior, there was hidden away, from the sight of even her dearest friends, a crushed and broken heart. A battle, fiercer than the one which Christian and infidel had waged that Christmas morn before the gates of Hara Castle, had been fought in the solitude of the maiden's room, and forth from the struggle now came the victor who had conquered by the sacrifice of self.

Ine traversed a part of the main castle until she came to the quarters of the generals and the officers of the army. Here Paoli had his room, and to this the woman hastened. Approaching the sliding-doors, she softly called his name, and in response to an invitation from within, she entered. It was a long, narrow apartment, at the one end of which a rude wooden crucifix had been set up beneath a picture of the Virgin. At the other end stood the bishop's bed. From a wooden peg hung his armor, and under this, with its pole resting against the wall, stood his battle-ax. Paoli was pacing back and forth the length of the room when the woman opened the door, his hands clasped behind his back and his head bowed forward. Though he had bidden her to enter, he appeared to have forgotten the fact, so deeply absorbed was he in his meditations. Approaching the bishop, Ine knelt at his feet, bowing her head to the floor in a humble obeisance. It was then that Paoli first seemed to be aware of her presence.

"Ah, it is thou, daughter!" he said, gently. "Rise, I pray thee!"

"Nay, good father," replied the woman; "I come as a suppliant, and a suppliant's attitude best befits me."

"A suppliant, daughter?" the other questioned, mildly. "Thou knowest before asking that anything which I can do to help thee, it is thine but to speak and it shall be done."

"But, father, what if it were a matter of most momentous import, one that touched the interests of our cause?"

The bishop looked down at the kneeling woman a moment in silence, then he replied, softly:

"Nothing that would injure the cause, which she holds dearer than her own happiness or her life, would Ine Tanaka seek."

The woman shuddered. Her happiness! Alas, she would ever henceforth be a stranger to that word! Her life! Were it not for the good she might still do to others, that, too, would be unsupportable! Yet the bishop was right. She would not have bought back happiness, were that possible, had the price been the endangering of the deliverance of the church; her life she would not have permitted for a single instant to stand in the way of the accomplishment of that great work.

"I shall speak, then," she said, rising to a sitting posture, and facing the bishop, who had seated himself on the mats before her. Her voice was steady, and her countenance as calm and regal as ever, but she felt her heart beating tumultuously, and her brain reeled at the thought of what she was about to say.

"Speak on, daughter," Paoli said, encouragingly, as Ine hesitated. "Thou hast my promise."

"Good father, in a word I shall tell thee. I shall never

consent to marry Nirado Shiro. My petition is to thee, as head of the Church of Japan, to absolve me from the betrothal by which my parents bound me to this man."

Ine had expected to hear protests against the canceling of the betrothal; objections based upon grounds of present expediency, and urgent appeals to remain faithful to the covenant of her parents; but she met none of these. Paoli spoke never a word. He looked at her a minute or so in silence, then arose and walked slowly back and forth in the room, and then, still without a word to the woman, he opened the sliding-doors and passed out. Ine waited. Five, ten, twenty minutes passed, and he did not return. She determined to remain where she was until he did come back. Half an hour, an hour, two hours, and Bishop Paoli's step was heard outside, and then he entered the room. The woman raised her eyes to his face; it was careworn and haggard. He came and knelt by Ine's side.

"Thou hast thy petition, daughter," he said, and his voice trembled with emotion. "I absolve thee from thy betrothal to Nirado Shiro. I have seen him, Ine. These two hours have I pleaded, reasoned, threatened. In vain. O my poor child!"

Ine was silently weeping. This was a revelation to her. Paoli had looked into her heart and read its secret; a secret she would have hidden away from the world, and would have concealed even from herself. He had gone to her faithless lover, and pleaded with him in her behalf. Her pride and self-respect would have resented this in another; toward the bishop she felt only a pained gratitude. She bowed her head to the floor to thank him, but her voice broke down in a storm of sobs and tears. And Paoli, the fanatical Jesuit, the stern, uncompromising foe of both heathen and heretic, the dreaded warrior-bishop, whose fierce battle-shout had struck terror to the hearts of the infidel, now, with a sympathy as tender as that of a woman's, bowed his head over the sorrowing Ine and wept.

That afternoon Ashizuka and the other generals called upon Shiro to consult with him respecting some contemplated movement against the enemy. The young commander-in-chief was not in his room. Diligent inquiry was made throughout the soldiers' quarters, but he was not to be found; the entire castle was thoroughly searched, he was not within the walls. Nirado Shiro had mysteriously disappeared.

III.

AT THE HERMITAGE.

During these weeks filled with stirring events within and without the Christian castle at Arima, Marmion Beaumont was slowly recovering from his injuries in the restful quiet of Lord Mori's hermitage on Unzen. It was not long before he was able to be borne out to the front room of the dwelling proper, and here he could lie and look down upon the plain of the Christians. Day after day he saw the government troops slowly pushing the insurgents back upon the village, and extending their own lines toward Arima and the mountains.

Some one of the inmates of the hermitage was always at his side, and as the old scholar was anxious to improve the few remaining weeks left him before he should leave forever the scene of his long labors, his days and the greater part of his nights also were spent in his study. Una, Ando, and Sanji therefore alternated with one another in being the Englishman's companion, and one of the servants was detailed to wait upon him.

Between Beaumont and Una there soon grew up an intimate friendship that gradually ripened into love. To the young man, Una's sweetness and innocence, her ignorance of the world, her simplicity, and her lovable disposition had an irresistible attraction. Never before had he met a fairer maiden, never before one that so thoroughly charmed him. As for Una, even before she met Beaumont, her fancy had made a hero of him, such as those of whom she read in her father's English books of chivalry. It was, therefore, the most natural thing in the world for these two, brought together under such romantic circumstances, to love each other. Lord Mori, when Beaumont had asked his permission to wed his daughter, had readily given his consent, for he felt that he was safe in intrusting his child's happiness to the keeping of the manly and noble-natured young Englishman. And thus the days flew swiftly by at the mountain hermitage in preparations for flight and in love-dreams of the future.

Upon the evening of the same day during which the government troops were making ready for their second night attack upon the Christians, and Ine and Paoli had held that momentous conversation in the latter's room, Beaumont and Lord Mori were seated in the cave-study of the hermitage. The two men had been speaking of the approaching voyage to England.

"And yet, Master Beaumont," said the old man, sadly, "though we plan our journey and make ready, what assurance have we that we shall be permitted to go?"

The younger man looked up in surprise.

"You have been laboring too hard of late, I fear, Lord Mori, and the strain upon your strength has depressed your spirits. Why, it was only yesterday that I received Captain Van Neist's letter, informing us that within three weeks the repairs upon the *Spuyten Duyvil* would be completed, and that she would immediately thereafter set sail for Arima."

"I know, I know," returned the other, moodily. "We have my cousin's protection as long as we remain here ; the consent of the Dutch captain has been secured, you say, to take us away ; yet I feel anxious. What if this Van Neist should, after all, refuse to give us passage?"

Beaumont became thoughtful. There might, indeed, be danger here. He knew Van Neist's impulsive nature too well to deny the possibility of his changing his mind. Influences, also, might be brought to bear upon him, should his promise concerning Lord Mori become known, that would lead him to withdraw his offer. After a few minutes of careful reflection, the Englishman answered his companion's inquiry.

"I shall be frank with you, Lord Mori, and admit that there is a chance of Captain Van Neist's refusing to take us. Yet, I know his kind heart too well to believe that he is at all likely to do so. He and I are intimate friends, and," added the young man, modestly, "I know that I have influence enough over Jansen Van Neist to hold him to his promise under any circumstances, were I only with him."

The old man's face brightened.

"Then, why not go to Nagasaki, Master Beaumont?" he said, eagerly, "and remain with your friend until he brings his ship to Arima?"

"I shall do so," replied Beaumont, promptly. "And when I am once aboard the *Spuyten Duyvil*, depend upon it, Lord Mori, the question of our going to England with Captain Van Neist is settled beyond recall."

The Englishman spoke with such earnest confidence that the scholar felt inspired with a more hopeful view of their situation.

"I shall go to-morrow," Beaumont continued. "The Prince of Kai will, I am sure, give me an escort, and, in the meantime, you and Una will be safe under his protection."

"Are you strong enough?" asked the old man, a shade of anxiety again overspreading his countenance. "In my eagerness to make certain our flight, I forgot your wounds."

"Nay, now!" and Beaumont laughed heartily. "A cripple or an invalid would scarcely, methinks, be able to climb about these mountains in the way that I have been doing the past week. Thanks to your skillful treatment and the care of the others, I am as well and strong now as I ever was."

The old scholar rose and slowly walked back and forth in the room, his head bowed upon his breast.

"Master Beaumont," he at length said, "you leave us, then, on the morrow, to be gone three weeks and perhaps longer. What may happen in that time we know not. I doubt not my cousin's purpose to protect us, nor yet his ability to do so. Yet I have a presentiment that the sun of my life is rapidly setting, and that my eyes shall never look upon the green fields of thine and Una's England. And if such is to be my lot, I hope that my latest breath may be drawn in the air of my native land. Since thy coming, and the results that have followed it, such has been my prayer. Formerly it pained me to think that it might be my daughter's fate to find herself in the land of her mother's birth a friendless stranger. In thy strong and faithful love, that fear has been dispelled. I have your solemn word and promise, as a man of honor, that you will always tenderly love and cherish the woman

"IN HEAVEN'S NAME, WHAT MEANS THIS! NIRAJO SHIRO!"—See Page 327.

whose heart is so wholly yours, and whose future happiness or wretchedness is in your hands. And because I trust you as fully as does she, I am satisfied. When you reach England, search out her mother's friends. Some of them must still be living, and Una longs to look upon the faces of her English kinsfolk."

Marmion Beaumont had arisen while Lord Mori was speaking, and coming now to his side, he took his hand.

"Lord Mori," he said, with deep earnestness, "I appreciate your desire to have your last resting-place among the tombs of your ancestors, but let us trust that, though that wish will be finally fulfilled, many intervening years may be spent with us, your children."

The old man shook his head, sadly. "Nay, no more! When I consign these precious volumes," and he pointed to the pile of manuscript Bibles in the corner of the room, "to the receptacle which I have prepared for them, and have written to all my fellow-princes of Japan, that, in the secret hiding-place which I shall point out to them, they shall find the religion of my Lord, uncorrupted by priestly intrigue or by superstition, and shall be able to know what it really is—then my life-work shall have been accomplished, and I wish to live no longer."

The young man saw it was useless to say anything more, and, as the aged scholar, going to the pile of books, knelt down with his outspread arms and his face resting upon them, Beaumont quietly withdrew from the room.

IV.

THE KOMAMONOYA'S WOOING MEETS WITH AN INTERRUPTION.

While her father and the Englishman were conversing in the study, Una, with one of the serving-women was seated in a little summer-house that stood on the edge of the plateau before the hermitage, and from which an excellent view could be had of the plain below. Since the day upon which she and Ando had gone up to the mountain-side to see the government troops marching over the foot-hills, the girl had not dared to visit any of her favorite haunts, lest Gonroku and his band might be lurking in the neighborhood, awaiting an opportunity to seize her again.

So long as she remained at home, she had nothing to fear. In accordance with his promise, Nabeshima had placed a strong guard over his cousin's family. The only possible access to the hermitage was by two paths that led to it over the mountains, one on either side. The prince had two strong guard-houses built over these roads, so that no one could approach Lord Mori's residence or leave it without passing through one or the other of these. To each of the guard-houses he had assigned ten men that were to watch night and day. A system of signals was agreed upon; so that, in case of an attack, the prince could be quickly notified in his camp on the plain below.

Travelling venders of various articles of food or of clothing were permitted to visit the hermitage, after being carefully searched for concealed weapons. On the evening of which we are speaking, as Una looked up the path that wound down the mountain-side, she saw a *komamonoya* coming toward them. A square basket, folded in a large, black cloth and slung over his shoulder, contained his wares. His face was almost entirely concealed by his drooping hat and the dark-blue kerchief that was drawn over his ears and loosely knotted under his chin.

As the girl perceived the vender approaching, she turned to her companion with a merry laugh.

"As I live, Oban, if there is not my courtly peddler! Full long has it been since last he favored us with a visit. But I'll miss my guess if that box is not full of nice things and his head crammed with gallant speeches! And that reminds me, Oban," the laughing maiden went on, "my chivalrous knight of the pack is chary of his pretty sayings if a third person is within ear-shot. So go within, and if my Master Beaumont would venture forth, forbid him, I pray thee, under the pain of this valiant unknown's vengeance."

"Child, child!" exclaimed the old woman, reprovingly, "thou reckest not, dost thou, if that silly fellow falls in love with thee and cuts his throat in consequence? I have heard of such cases before. Encourage him not, I beg of thee; listen not to his foolish flatteries." And the old woman hobbled away.

The *komamonoya* had now reached the summer-house, and, laying his burden down, he made a profound obeisance to the maiden.

"How is this, sir?" demanded Una, as the man began spreading out an assortment of mirrors, combs, brushes, ornaments for the hair and such like articles. "It has been three, four, yes, five or six weeks since my ears last drank in those courtly speeches of thine!"

The *komamonoya* shot a furtive glance at the girl's face

and Una perceived that his hand was unsteady, and when he spoke, his voice was tremulous with emotion.

"It is not given us, fair lady, to always do as we would, else would the life of thy servant be spent at thy feet."

"*Kekko!*" cried the girl, gayly, " I told Oban when I saw you coming that your head would be full of fair speeeches, and, lo! you have but to open your mouth and set them free! Go on!"

The man was in no mood to appreciate this frolicsome banter.

"Nay, nay, lady, you mistake me! You would make me the sport of an idle hour. To you I am but a wandering vender of these trinkets," and, as he pointed toward his basket, Una detected a scornful ring in his voice. "But, lady, I am not what I seem. To those soldiers in yonder guard-house—your foes and mine—let me be the despised *komamonoya*, since in their contempt there is safety."

Una was serious enough now. She looked down at the man in silent surprise and wonder. He continued:

"Six times, lady, have I already been here. I have come once more that I might see you, hear you speak, know that you were yet safe."

Still the girl was silent; a growing fear at her heart, that some new danger was threatening her father and herself, chilled her and made her dumb. The man went on :

"I know that you are Christians, and, in these days of persecution and bloodshed, it were needless to say what that means when once the suspicion of the government officials is aroused. You and your father, with all those about you, will be lost. Dangers even now threaten you. You cannot any longer escape detection. And whither can you flee for safety? Go where you will, the heathen will slay you because you are believers in the proscribed religion. If you fly to yonder Christian camp, thy father's old-time foe, Paoli the Jesuit, is there, and he likewise will put you to death. Whichever way you turn, therefore, you are lost. Of all persons, I am the only one that can save you, and for this purpose have I come hither. Yea, more than this. Not only shall I save your friends, but I can exalt you to a position of the highest honor and dignity."

"And you, sir, who are you that speak thus?" Una faltered forth, her face deathly pale, her heart still with terror. "Tell me, O tell me how you can save my father, if danger, such as you mention, there really be!"

The *komamonoya* dashed aside hat and kerchief.

"Thou wouldst know who I am, Una Mori. Behold, then! Thou hast seen my face ere now. You know me, do you not?"

Before the girl had time to reply, Marmion Beaumont appeared on the veranda of the hermitage. With quick, noiseless steps, he crossed the grassy lawn to the summer-house. As the stranger removed his head-covering, the Englishman, though unperceived by him, was at his side.

"In Heaven's name!" he cried, in the utmost astonishment. "What means this? Nirado Shiro!"

The young Christian chief staggered to his feet and stared at Beaumont in speechless amazement. Una, freed by her lover's presence from the paralyzing terror which the *komamonoya's* words had caused, fled to the house, leaving the two men alone. Half-an-hour afterward, the Englishman rejoined her, his face wearing an amused expression. The girl, in her deep anxiety lest some new peril threatened them, saw nothing of this, however, as she breathlessly inquired:

"What is it, Marmion? What did the man mean? Did he tell you?"

"Oh, yes. I presume he told me nearly all that he did you, perhaps though with a little less dash of the frightful," the young man returned humorously. "The matter is a very simple one, dearest Una," Beaumont continued, seating himself by the girl's side. "Nirado Shiro has fallen desperately in love with you, and perceiving this, probably, the beautiful Ine Tanaka has had Paoli absolve her from her obligation to marry him. Your ardent suitor sees nothing but danger and destruction awaiting all your household. Only as his wife does he believe that you will be safe from the heathen as well as the heretic-hating Jesuit; and it was to offer you marriage that he to-day came to the hermitage. If in his pleading he painted your situation in rather gloomy colors, it was only to make you the more readily consent to marry him."

"He told *you* all this?"

"Yes. You remember I informed you some time ago how he confided in me on shipboard, so that during the voyage from Manila to Nagasaki we became very intimate friends. I told him just now of the circumstances that have made me an inmate of the hermitage, but, of course, I said nothing of our relations to each other, so that his placing confidence in me again is nothing remarkable. Fear no more trouble from him, dearest! A word to the guards and strangers of no sort shall be allowed to pass them. And yet, methinks, Nirado Shiro can be courteous enough; how is it, Una?"

The girl's vivacious spirits had returned to her, now that she had discovered that no serious peril threatened them.

"Courteous, do you say, sirrah?" she cried, with a

merry, ringing peal of laughter. "Marry! had your tongue been as glib of gallant speeches as was his, you know not how much faster you might have sped in your wooing!"

V.

A DISCOVERY THAT CAME NOT TOO SOON.

Up the mountain-side, down into the valley, then over the foot-hills in the direction of Arima went Nirado Shiro; his mind full of the fair maid of Unzen, and how he might win her for his own. In his rapid walk through the gathering darkness, he gained the crest of one of the higher foot-hills, and far below him burst into view the myriad camp-fires of the government army. Shiro paused, and for a time stood gazing down on the animated scene. The whole camp seemed to be astir. In the bright light cast from the blazing fires, groups of soldiers could be seen polishing their armor and weapons, and figures, whom he knew from their gorgeous trappings to be officers, were hurrying back and forth among the men.

"There is something on hand," the young man muttered, as he watched the proceedings below. "The bloodthirsty idolaters are preparing for another attack."

The sound of voices behind him caused him to turn and look down the path by which he had but a few minutes before ascended the hill. Very soon he could distinguish two objects moving towards him, and as they came nearer, he perceived they were huge piles of brushwood, and that beneath each staggered a coolie, bent nearly double with the weight of his burden. As the two men reached the place where Shiro was standing, they stopped, and rested their loads upon the staves that they bore in their hands.

"Heavy burdens, friends," said the Christian chief, addressing them, pleasantly. "Ah, alas! this cruel war brings heavy things! To the soldier, heavy blows; to many a good wife and her little ones, heavy hearts; and to such as you and me, heavy loads to bear."

"So it does, stranger, so it does," the foremost coolie responded, keenly eying the bundle on Shiro's back "But thou canst scarcely call that box of gewgaws, which thou hast there, heavy. If thou wouldst know what a burden is, try now this load of mine."

"Nay, nay, thy word for it!" Shiro returned good-naturedly. "Thou sayest, truly, my box is not heavy, and alack! it grows not any lighter. Time was when in three days I could have sold all my trifles to the maids and matrons of Shimabara, but alas! now their hearts are too full of mourning and anxiety to care ought for adorning themselves. Woe me! Would that this grievous war were over!"

"Too true, too true!" the other coolie broke in, with a mournful shake of the head. "But the gods be praised! to-night shall end the war! Hereafter may we have peace!"

It was well that the darkness concealed Shiro's face, as he heard these words. It was some time before he could trust his voice to speak; but finally he said:

"Well spoken, friend! May peace return to our Japan! Ah, but will not the slaughter be terrible to-night!"

"I should think, indeed, it might be, friend," the first coolie remarked, with a laugh, not at all suspecting but that the person whom he was addressing knew as much of the proposed attack as himself; "yes," he added, "something of a slaughter it is very likely to be, seeing that General Itakura has given orders to spare neither man, woman nor child of the accursed *jashui mon*. Gods! I am glad that I renounced the abhorred doctrine long ago," and the fellow, placing his two palms together, raised them to his forehead, repeating a Buddhist prayer.

"That Yamada, or Kuroda, as he now calls himself, is a shrewd fellow, isn't he?" the other coolie broke in. "Finely, indeed, has he duped those Christians! Ah, they'll repent that they ever made him captain of their gate-guard, when they see the enemy swarming into their castle to-night!"

"That they will!" exclaimed Shiro, breathlessly. "I perceive the troops are making preparations; I presume they will be soon forming into line."

"Scarcely, I think," one of the coolies replied. "The attack, as you of course have heard, is not to be made until midnight."

Shiro had learned all that he cared to know. He had need to make haste if he arrived at Hara Castle in time to give warning.

"It grows late, friends," he said. "Your wood, methinks, will soon be needed down at those fires; and I, too, must be on my way." And, with a parting bow to the two coolies, he hastened off in the darkness.

VI.

THE RETURN OF THE CHIEF.

In the officers' quarter of Hara Castle, Paoli and the four leaders, Ashizuka, Chijiwa, Oyano and Komekine were seated together in a small room, discussing Shiro's disappearance; and their hearts were sorrowful, as they forecast the disastrous effect it would have upon the army. For, although the soldiers were sorely disappointed in their young commander-in-chief, they had faith in the prophecy concerning a divinely appointed leader, and this, they were still hoping, might even yet find its fulfillment in him.

While they were talking, some one without called for admission. Chijiwa threw open the sliding doors, and a soldier entered. After a low bow of salutation to the occupants of the room, he said :

"A *komamonoya* is without, who craves an immediate interview. A short time ago, he appeared at the outer gate, calling for admittance. Kuroda, the captain, was opposed to granting his request, but the fellow pleaded so piteously, saying that he was a Christian fleeing for his life, that he was permitted to enter. Once within the main castle, he requested to be conducted to you. What is your pleasure respecting his wish?"

"Let him come in at once," Paoli said, promptly, speaking for the others as well as for himself. "It may happen that he has important tidings to impart, or, possibly, he is a spy. In either case, it behooves us to see him immediately."

Thereupon, Shiro, still disguised as a *komamonya*, and with his basket of wares yet upon his back, entered the apartment. The soldier withdrew, closing the door behind him, and the eyes of the five men were closely fixed upon the new-comer.

Putting down his burden, Shiro removed his hat and kerchief, and then followed exclamations of glad surprise as he was recognized. The stern, rugged Chijiwa and Ashizuka shed tears of joy, and even the bishop could scarcely control his emotions. Paoli was the first to recover himself sufficiently to ask :

"But what does all this mean, Shiro ! Where have you been?"

The young chieftain had no intention of telling the men before him of his visit to Unzen. He informed them, however, of his discovery of Yamada's plot to betray the castle that night into the hands of the foe. The men listened to his story in breathless amazement. Nothing, that evening, had been further from their minds than the thought of an attack, and the possibility of their castle being betrayed to the enemy had never occurred to them. Had it not been for Shiro's discovery, the surprise would have been as complete as Itakura could have desired, and the destruction he had planned for them might have been easily accomplished. At last Shiro had done something that would commend him to the hearts of his people. He was, indeed, their saviour; in a certain sense, the prophecy of the great deliverer was that night fulfilled in him.

When Shiro had finished what he had to say, Bishop Paoli sprang to his feet.

"Brethren," he exclaimed, "God has been good to us in returning us our leader, who has now become our preserver. We would be glad to rouse the army and to present to them their chief and their deliverer anew; but in a few more hours the foe will be upon us. It behooves us therefore to make haste. Let the men be made ready with all dispatch, for, behold! the God of battles has again delivered our enemies into our hands!"

After a hurried consultation, the leaders separated. Chijiwa was to hasten to the gate and to seize the captain of the guardsmen and to bring him before Shiro and Paoli; Komekine was to get his guns in readiness on the top of the walls; while Ashizuka and Oyano were to arouse the men and to place them in the most advantageous positions. It was decided to withdraw the force stationed in the outer fort into the main castle, and to allow the enemy to come within the first inclosure. They would there be exposed to the artillery and musketry fire from the walls, while the catapults and large bow-guns mounted on the higher ramparts could also be brought to bear upon them. Slingers and archers stationed in the interior of the castle could rain a veritable tempest of stones and arrows upon the heads of the foe, who would be penned up in the narrow confines of the outer inclosure, their retreat being retarded by the height of the fortifications and the impassable character of the moat.

BOOK TENTH.
FRIENDS BECOME FOES.

I.

ANOTHER MIDNIGHT CONFLICT.

GRIM and dark rose the walls of Hara Castle before the eyes of the government army, when, shortly after midnight, it came in heavy columns descending the hill-sides into the plain of the Christians. In the van was General Itakura himself at the head of a strong body-guard, and by his side rode his youthful son, who was this night to have his first experience of war. After the advance came Ogasawara's veteran warriors. Then followed Tachibana, Nabeshima, and various other leaders, each at the head of a large detachment. Orders had been given to use only the sword in the coming battle and massacre, and the men, unimpeded with their long spears and heavy match-locks, marched forward with swift and silent tread. So noiseless, indeed, was their approach, that the Christians, though ever on a sharp lookout, were not aware of their coming until, in the dim, uncertain light of the few lamps that had been allowed to remain on the top of the outer defenses, they perceived the dense ranks of their foes crowded close up to the edge of the moat.

It was here that General Itakura had halted his forces, to await the opening of the gates. Soon he and his guards were aware of the approach of some one in the darkness, and then the stranger said in a low, clear voice :

" The Christians no longer occupy these outer fortifications at night ; file into the fort, therefore, as rapidly and with as little noise as possible, and be ready to rush through the gates of the main castle as soon as you perceive a blue light flash out three times ;" and when he had spoken, the stranger turned and disappeared within the gate.

Itakura, thinking that the speaker was Yamada, did as he was directed, and drew up his body-guard before the gates of the castle. Ogasawara and Tachibana also crowded into the inclosure and took up their stations in the rear of the advance. For lack of room, the other leaders were compelled to wait outside of the moat. Be-

WHEN HE HAD SPOKEN, THE STRANGER TURNED AND DISAPPEARED WITHIN THE GATE.—*See Page 336.*

fore them towered the black wall of the castle from the top of which a few dimly burning lamps cast a feeble light through the blackness of the night. All was silent, as if the fortress had been deserted, and Itakura congratulated himself on the success of the plot, and he and the entire army were jubilantly confident over the prospect of a speedy victory.

Had the commander-in-chief of the government troops been able to have looked over into the interior of the stronghold before him, widely different would have been his feelings! There, behind their defenses, crouched thousands of determined warriors, their weapons lying by their sides, awaiting the signal to fire. Komekine's gunners lay behind their pieces, their matches in their hands. The musketeers covered the lower walls; archers, slingers and the catapults and heavy bow-guns occupied the higher ramparts.

To the waiting Itakura at last came the signal. A bright blue flame flashed out thrice from the castle gates, and the eager troops rushed swiftly but noiselessly toward them, only to find them still shut. At that moment, the area before the walls was flooded with light from thousands of torches, and a voice rang out on the night air:

"The plot of Uyemon Yamada was discovered, and he has suffered in his prison the death of a spy. Once again has the God of the Christians brought confusion into the councils of His foes! Hear, ye idolaters, and tremble and perish! *Yaso-Maria!* Woe to the infidel!"

As the voice ceased, the Christian flag—a red cross on a white field—was unfurled from the walls. As it fluttered out to the breeze, from within the castle arose a wild shout that was drowned in the roar of cannon and the crash of musketry. Every embrasure vomited forth its volley of death, while from along the entire length of the upper walls there burst upon the heads of the devoted troops a storm of arrows, stones and heavy rocks. In the closely packed ranks of Itakura's army the slaughter was frightful. To render their position still more terrible, Chijiwa, at the head of his division of the insurgents, dashed out of the castle by another gate, and hastily gaining the rear of Ogasawara's and Tachibana's men, he threw his force across the entrance by which these had gained admission to the inclosure, preventing their escape through the gates and also repulsing the attempts of the other leaders to cross over to their rescue.

The scenes of the night attack of the twenty-fifth of December were repeated, but with additional horrors; for, on the former occasion, the troops had a comparatively free field for flight, whereas they now found themselves imprisoned between the walls of the castle and the outer line of defenses, with the way of their retreat cut off.

Tachibana's men, not so experienced in warfare as those of Ogasawara, were soon thrown into a panic by the incessant and murderous fire that was poured into their ranks by an unseen foe, and, after a few ineffectual attempts to dislodge Chijiwa and to make their escape by the way they had entered, they began scaling the breastworks and throwing themselves into the moat in the vain hope of being able to cross it in safety. The *fosse*, at this particular place, was about fifty feet wide and twenty in depth, and was partially filled with mud and water. It now became the grave of hundreds who plunged into it until a very bridge of bodies made a passage possible for the few survivors, who escaping across the moat, fled past the other divisions of the government army into the plain and through the darkness in the direction of their camp.

Ogasawara succeeded in keeping order among his men, and, perceiving the impossibility of making any effectual attack upon the castle, he ordered a charge upon Chijiwa's force, with a view to driving them back from the gates. The well-trained and gallant soldiers, nearly a fourth of whose numbers were already stretched out in the silence of death, or writhing in pain in this terrible blood-pit, responded to their leader's command with a shout. Chijiwa, knowing the character of the men who now crossed weapons with his yeomen, prudently withdrew, and Ogasawara and his troops passing through, rejoined the other leaders outside of the defenses.

II.

DEATH BEFORE DISGRACE.

In the surprise and confusion attending the discovery that his plans had miscarried, General Itakura and his body-guard had fallen back into the southern part of the fort, where on Christmas morning Nabeshima had fired the store-houses. In an incredibly short time, the government commander-in-chief beheld Tachibana's division plunging over the breastworks into the moat and the Satsuma men retreating out of the fort. The second attack upon Hara Castle had proved as bootless and disastrous as had the first, and Itakura, disheartened beyond measure, decided rather than to face the reproaches of the Shogun and the disgrace of being superseded in the chief command, to die the death of a warrior before the walls of the foe. Calling his body-guard about him, he told them his decision, and the faithful retainers, upon hearing his words, begged the privilege of dying with their lord and asked to be led against the enemy. At that moment, the gates of the main castle was thrown open to admit Chijiwa's men, and, perceiving this, Itakura gave the order to advance ; and straight down upon the open gates, in a solid column, they charged with a fury that swept aside all resistance. The next moment, they were at the gate ; then, before it could be closed, they had dashed through into the castle, where they at once began a fierce onslaught upon Ashizuka's men, who had just descended from the walls. In the furious dash made upon the gates, Chijiwa's force had been driven away from the entrance, but quickly recovering themselves, a few of them followed the government soldiers into the castle and made fast the gates; the others, with their leader at their head, hastily returned to the outer defenses to repel any possible attack from the main army.

The struggle in the castle between Itakura's bodyguard, who had come there to die, and Ashizuka's soldiers, who knew that defeat meant the fall of their stronghold and the destruction of themselves, was one of indescribable fury. The Christians out-numbered their foes fully three to one, yet despite this advantage and their unflinching bravery alike, they found themselves no match for the disciplined and desperate warriors opposed to them, and they fell in such numbers that the ground upon which they fought was soon thickly cumbered with their dead. Finally, Ashizuka, seeing General Itakura mounted on his horse, dashing hither and thither in the fray, and with his heavy sword dealing death wherever he went, pointed him out to a group of musketeers, saying :

"Yonder is the commander-in-chief of the government troops ; if he should fall, this slaughter of our brethren would soon cease."

At that moment, Komekine raised his match-lock, and, taking careful aim, fired. Itakura, pierced through the breast, threw up his arms wildly, and, with a loud cry, fell from his horse.

"Fight on, brave hearts, fight on!" gasped the dying chief to his retainers, who had closed over him, eager to mingle their blood with his. "Ah, ye gods! A little more and the castle would have been mine!"

With a mighty effort, the fallen general rallied himself, sprang to his feet, and, rushing with uplifted sword in the direction of the enemy, he flung his weapon among them and with the effort fell lifeless upon his face.

The victory was now won for the Christians. The infidel gathered around the dead body of their lord that they might fall beside him. This movement changed their tactics from attack to defense. An encircling wall of foes soon gathered around the devoted little band, and their ranks were torn and broken by the heavy volleys poured into them from all sides. Stubbornly they stood and fought, neither receiving nor desiring mercy from an enemy they hated and, with their latest breath, scorned and defied. In a short time, the sound of battle lessened, and, before long, it subsided into silence. The luckless son of the fallen general, sinking down among the slain, with an expiring effort, sought his father's feet, and there, prostrating himself as if in humble obeisance, with his forehead on the bloody ground and his hands on his parent's knees, groaned and died.

III.

BEARDING THE FOE

Three days after the death of Itakura, Matsudaira, the new general-in-chief, arrived at the camp and assumed the command of the army. His policy was closely to invest the Christian stronghold both by land and sea, cutting off all possibility of the garrison receiving supplies from without, and then quietly to wait and let famine do its work. In accordance with this plan, which the new leader at once proceeded to put into execution, the fleet of war-junks was increased and the camp of the land forces was removed from the heights and placed upon the plain of the Christians, where it extended in a semi-circle from the shore of the bay on the north around the beleaguered fortress to the sea again on the south.

It was now mid-winter, and, though in southern Japan this season is unattended with severe cold, yet the winds of February and March are exceedingly raw and chilly. Tents of cloth were, therefore, scarcely adequate to protect the army from the inclement weather, and the soldiers, having nothing to do, were commanded to build small houses for the accommodation of their officers, and booths, constructed of bushes and brush, covered with cotton canvas roofs or thatched with straw, for their own quarters. In a short time the new camp took on the appearance of a large city, with regular streets, which at night were illuminated by huge oil-lamps set on the tops of high posts.

The Christians, as they perceived their enemies settling down around them with the evident determination of remaining until the castle was surrendered or captured, grew more daring as their situation became the more critical. Scarcely a day passed but they sallied out of their gates and attacked some part of the government camp, and after a spirited engagement with the enemy, they would fall back within their fortress. Small foraging parties would steal out at night, and by a sudden dash penetrate, not infrequently, into the centre of the camp, and before their retreat could be intercepted, they would cut their way out again, and return in safety to the shelter of their own walls, having left bloody tokens of their visit in the foemen's slain and wounded that marked their course.

These vigorous sallies and assaults defeated Matsudaira's plan for a bloodless siege and victory, and enraged the proud *Samurai*. They chafed, and grew more and more restive under the new commander-in-chief's policy, until finally they broke out into open mutiny. They were sent to Arima to fight, they urged, and not to lie in camp like foxes in their holes, and to endure the ignominy of being bearded day after day by a handful of rebel-peasants. Their swords were rusting in their sheaths; the Christians were becoming more and more insolent, their attacks more frequent and daring. A long petition, bearing the seals of thousands of the soldiers, and not a few of the princes, was sent to Matsudaira, begging him to order an attack upon the castle. The haughty general returned a point-blank refusal. Then followed a complaint and petition to the Shogun, asking him to dispatch at once to Arima the representative he had promised to take charge of the campaign against the insurgents.

This document was sent to Yedo, and in due time an answer was returned that the Shogun would soon send an able general to represent him at the seat of war, and that since Yorinobu, his regular deputy, was unable to go, he had decided to intrust the mission to Hojo, the Prince of Awa, upon whom he would confer full plenipotentiary powers as his representative in Kiushiu. These tidings created the wildest enthusiasm in the camp of the government army. Hojo, it was well known, was one of the bravest and most experienced military leaders of the nation, and the soldiers were convinced that upon his arrival more vigorous measures in the prosecution of the siege would be adopted.

The Christians kept themselves informed of affairs in the hostile camp through the agency of spies, and by carrying off prisoners whom they captured in their sallies and torturing these until they disclosed the plans of their leaders. The report that Prince Hojo was coming down to take charge of the siege filled them with alarm. They knew the determined character of the man, and were well aware that when he had come they would no longer be permitted to make the government troops the victims of their unrebuked scorn and defiance. Besides, their provisions and munitions of war were becoming exhausted. Various devices had already been resorted to to supplement their failing stores. Some of their horses were killed and served out as meat to the garrison; small quantities of fish were caught by dropping lines over the seaward wall of the fortress; and roots and leaves, seaweed and moss were used as articles of food. Their stock of lead becoming low, small round pebbles were covered with that metal and made to serve as musket bullets, and stones of various sizes were cut and polished for cannon-balls. The old men and the women and children busied themselves in making arrows and javelins and in breaking stones and heaping them up in huge piles along the outer walls for the use of slingers and the catapults.

IV.

SWORD OR FAMINE, WHICH?

Early in March, a conference of the Christian leaders was held, and it was unanimously agreed that something must be done to raise the siege. So closely were they invested by the foe, that re-inforcements from the outside could no longer reach them, and they feared that those throughout Kiushiu, who were friendly disposed toward them, would be deterred from joining their cause when they perceived the main army of the Christians to be hopelessly shut up in their castle. The officers, therefore, decided to assemble all within the fortress, and to have one of the generals address them. Ashizuka, being the oldest of the leaders, was appointed to this office. The same day the entire population of Hara Castle was called together in the first or largest division of the stronghold, and here the veteran chieftain, taking his stand on one of the lower ramparts, thus spoke:

"A wise man, when he is in imminent danger, will confess freely the peril of his situation and take counsel with his friends as to what methods will be the most efficacious for his salvation. Only a fool is wilfully blind to the harm that may be on the very point of assailing him, and he would be worse than a fool who cries he is safe, when he is encompassed by the most deadly foes. Let us be wise men to-day, and, like wise men, admit at once that our lives and the lives of our wives and children, and of all identified with us and our religion, are in the utmost jeopardy—admit the almost hopeless condition we are in, in order that we may at once proceed to devise, if possible, some desperate measures for escape. Were there no lack of provisions and munitions of war, our capture would be practically impossible ; but as it is, our present condition is such that even the stoutest-hearted among us may well be pardoned if he be cast down and full of despair. With the greatest possible economy, our provisions cannot last us more than half a month, and our supply of gunpowder is so low that three or four more engagements, at the most, will exhaust it. Such is our situation ; and what is to be done ? Shall we remain in the castle ? Do this, and our destruction is only a question of time : for, should our food fail us before our ammunition, we shall not have the strength to stand by our guns ; or if, on the other hand, our ammunition be the first to be exhausted, our guns will become useless and all other means and weapons of defense will be inadequate before a resolute attack of our foes. Therefore, to remain in the castle is to court death and to insure destruction."

A hollow groan broke from the multitude before the speaker. Ashizuka had not exaggerated the perils of their situation. In their own hearts, they had each reasoned in a similar way but they had not given voice to their anxious forebodings. Now for the first time in the history of the siege had such alarming language found utterance.

"Thanks be to God !" exclaimed a sorrowful-looking woman, devoutly crossing herself ; "the end is near, and I rejoice. Husband, brother, sister, son, all have won their martyr crown, and I long to pluck on mine. Dear Jesu ! be merciful and keep me away no longer from my loved ones ! I would be with them and Thee."

"Alack the day in which we raised our hands in rebellion against our rulers !" mournfully lamented a despondent man among a group of weeping women. "We had better sue for mercy and promise to forsake this foreign faith. Life is too precious thus to throw it away ; and, after all, the religion of our ancestors is good enough for us, their children."

"War, war!" growled a burly soldier, whose body bore the scars of many a red battle-field. "No more of the castle ; out of it, say I ; and if the way out lies through the enemy's camp, then let us upon that camp with fire and sword !"

"I much mislike the good general's speech," muttered Mori Soiken, one of the native priests. "Does he forget that they, upon whose side fight the legions of the skies, cannot know defeat? Holy Cross ! He speaks not at all of our God-appointed leader nor of our brave bishop, that executioner of the Lord, who visits the punishment of Heaven upon the head of the infidel !"

Ashizuka, while these comments were being uttered, had made pause in his address, and his gaze, turning from the multitude before him, rested for a moment on the hostile army that encompassed the fortress, and then sought the mountains beyond. Pointing in the direction of these, he continued :

"Fellow-Christians, I look beyond the encampment of the foe, and the hills say to me : 'Come hither and breathe our air of freedom.' The plain, methinks, reproachfully asks me why it is that the Christian has relinquished it to the tread of the infidel. Yonder sea, yester-eve, moaning in unrest beneath the weight of the idolaters' fleet, that burdened its bosom, gathered to itself the strength of the storm, and this morning's sun beheld the war-junks sunken, dispersed or stranded on the beach. O my friends ! let us learn from this a lesson ! The sea last night borrowed its strength from the powerful currents of the air, and in that strength it dashed to pieces the hateful burdens that chafed its breast. We, Warriors of the Church, borrow our strength from above. As on last Christmas morn, saintly legions await our bidding to clothe us with invincible boldness, and to pour terror into the ranks of the idolaters.

"Yonder insolent soldiery have never crossed weapons with us except to flee before us. Again and again have we in small detachments attacked their camp, and ye yourselves know with what difficulty they have repelled our assaults. If, therefore, we have done so well without preparation and upon the impulse of the moment, what may we not do if we plan carefully and then carry our plans into vigorous execution!

"O Swords of the Church, let us be up and doing! Our God shall make fear to march before us; into the counsels of our foes he will breathe the spirit of giddiness, of trepidation, of discord; he will blind them to our purposes; he will cause them to fall into the snare we set for them; and we shall smite them with the edge of the sword. We shall give their camp to the flames, and the remnant of them that escape our fury shall be broken and dispersed. The siege of our castle will be raised; thousands that are now fearful of joining our cause, hearing of our marvellous victory, will rally to our side, and the day draws on apace when the Church of Japan shall have set her foot upon the neck of the infidel."

The speaker's voice had risen to such a pitch of fervid eloquence, that of itself it would have kindled by its fiery enthusiasm an answering ardor in the hearts of the hearers. But Ashizuka's artful method of first creating a deep despondency in the spirits of the people by holding up before them the horrors of their situation if they did not at once arouse themselves to a greater activity, and then, by a sudden turn, appealing to their past victories and

Paoli; the Last of the Missionaries. 351

to their belief that their cause was championed of Heaven as reason for the utmost hope and boldness, had produced the effect which he had intended. The entire assembly was swept by a flame of martial zeal, and the cry went up as the voice of one man :

"War ! War! On to the camp of the enemy !"

On the day following Ashizuka's address to the Christians, the government troops were astonished to see the insurgents issuing from their gates and in solid columns, bearing down upon the camp. They were admirably arranged for attack in three divisions, of about four thousand men each, under the leadership of Ashizuka, Chijiwa and Oyano ; while behind these came the artillery under the command of Komekine.

The army of Matsudaira made haste to form itself in battle array to receive the expected charge. To the astonishment of all beholders, however, the Christians, as they approached the government troops, were seen to waver, but at what appeared to be the earnest exhortation of their leaders, they again pressed forward, although with great unsteadiness and evident trepidation. When they had come within bow-shot of the camp, they again halted, and refused to move forward at the commands of their officers ; and, after discharging a flight of arrows in the direction of their foes, they beat a precipitate retreat toward their defenses. With such quickness was their return to the shelter of the fortress accomplished, that Matsudaira's men, in the pursuit that was ordered, were unable to overtake them.

The next day the same maneuver was repeated. The troops sprang to arms and hurried forth to meet their enemy, but at their approach, the Christians, after a feeble effort at resistance, again broke and fled. Daily for nearly a week did the insurgents thus issue from their castle, apparently for the purpose of attacking the camp, only to have their courage fail them as often as they came before their foes. After the first few times, the government troops no longer formed themselves in battle order at their approach, and finally the entire army came to regard their movements with contemptuous indifference. As the Christians drew near to the encampment, a few hundred men, armed with muskets, would charge down upon them and drive them back into the beleaguered fortress. And thus matters stood on the evening of the ninth of March, 1638.

V.

AN AWAKENING.

When once a man sets his face toward evil, the rapidity with which his moral sense becomes blunted, his conscience seared, his heart ready to devise and his hand eager to commit crime, depends very largely upon the vehemence and persistency of the unholy passion that has taken possession of him. Nirado Shiro had been fully conscious from the first that his love for Lord Mori's daughter was wrong, and that, if fostered, it could lead only to an unhappy end. He was aware of his duty to his betrothed wife, and acknowledged that she was worthy of his affection. Yet he suffered his admiration for Una Mori to develop into a passion that mastered his judgment and reason and led captive his will. He who on the *Spuyten Duyvil* had discoursed concerning his divinely-appointed mission in such exalted strains of religious fervor and devotion, found now that the suffering people, whom he had come to deliver, occupied a less place in his thoughts than the evil infatuation to which he had surrendered himself.

Thus, from bad to worse, the current of his life had flowed on. Yet, in the midst of his growing degeneracy, he still honored Ine Tanaka, and there were even times when, for a moment, his better nature would reassert itself and he would feel an impulse to go to her and, imploring her forgiveness for the pain he had caused her, to ask her consent to a renewal of the betrothal between them.

As the time passed by, however, these moments of repentant reflection occurred less and less frequently, until at last, Nirado Shiro, from dwelling upon his mad passion for the fair Eurasian girl, gave himself up to plotting in his own mind how, by fair means or by foul, he might possess her.

Chance had thrown into his way something, by which he believed, he might attain the object of his desire, should milder measures fail. Upon the occasion of one his visits to the hermitage, in the disguise of a *komamonoya*, he had picked up a paper in the outer hall of Lord Mori's dwelling, to which he had been admitted for the purpose of exhibiting his wares to Una and the women of the household. This paper proved to be a copy of the letter which the recluse was preparing, and which, after his departure from Japan, was to be sent to the princes of the nation, denouncing the doctrines of the foreign priests as a corrupt form of Christianity, exhorting them to study Christ's own words if they would know His teachings, and informing them where translations of the Scriptures were concealed awaiting their pleasure. Shiro carefully preserved this letter, for he knew he had but to show it to Paoli to fan his long cherished hostility to Lord Mori into a furious flame; and when the

Jesuit's vengeance should fall upon the father, Shiro believed that he could so control events that the daughter would come into his power.

Ever since that memorable afternoon that Ine had gone to Paoli's room, and the latter had sought out Shiro to plead with him on her behalf, the relations between the Jesuit and the young leader had been growing more strained. No open rupture had yet occurred, but to both the bishop, who chafed over his recent defeat, and to Shiro, whose increasing self-assertion could ill brook Paoli's dictatorship, it was very evident that even an outward appearance of peace could not much longer be maintained. When the Jesuit learned of Shiro's affection for Lord Mori's daughter, he summoned the young man to his room, and, before the awful denunciations and threats which this strangely calm being, with his burning eyes and coldly quiet voice, heaped upon him, Nirado Shiro was terrified into a promise no longer to cherish his passion for the fair heretic; but it is needless to say that he did not keep his word.

Thenceforward he looked upon Paoli as his enemy, and played the spy upon his every movement. During all the twenty-five years of his missionary life, Paoli had kept a secret journal. For the greater safety, this was written in the Greek language, for many of the native priests understood Latin, Portuguese and Spanish, and Paoli was in the habit of recording things that he would have none save himself and the authorities at Rome know. During the evening following Ashizuka's address to the Christians, while the Jesuit was engaged in a conference with the native priests, Shiro effected an entrance into his private room, and when he came forth, he bore with him a volume of the Jesuit's secret journal that covered the years of the young leader's birth and early childhood. Shiro had acquired a slight knowledge of Greek while abroad,—enough to enable him to make astounding discoveries concerning himself in the pages of Francesco Paoli's journal. All that night he sat in the solitude of his own quarters, poring over the written confession of deceit and intrigue before him, and when the first rays of the late March morning stole into the room, he concealed the book in a secret alcove in the wall, and, then, rushing back and forth the length of the apartment, he threw up his arms wildly and laughed and wept, until, exhausted with this outburst of tumultuous emotion that threatened to unseat his reason, he flung himself upon his face on the mats with a cry that sounded like the shriek of a maniac:

"Free, free! At last, Nirado Shiro, thou art thyself and not another!"

During the week of mock *sorties* and of preparation for storming the enemies' camp that followed, the young commander-in-chief and Bishop Paoli were seen constantly together.

VI.

THE EVE OF BATTLE.

Great crises in the history of nations and of individuals are frequently not recognized as such until they are past. In a few cases, the man or the people are fully conscious that the day lying just ahead is fraught with issues of the most stupendous import. It was thus with the Christians in Hara Castle, on the evening following their last *sortie*. The next morning they had fixed upon as the time in which they would stake their fortunes on the bloody arbitrament of war; the coming day would decide the fate of the Church of Japan, and their own personal weal or woe. Of the result of the approaching struggle, their minds admitted no doubt ; the church would conquer. Never were a people more calm, more resolute and more absolutely confident of success. Before victory was achieved, hundreds, nay, perchance, thousands might make the triumph of their cause the more sacredly memorable by the sacrifice of their lives, but this did not appall them or make them the less impatient for the struggle.

At sunset, the soldiers, who had been selected to serve in the attacking force, gathered together in the part of the castle where, a week before, Ashizuka had addressed them. There was a general movement among them and a murmur of pleased surprise, as their young commander-in-chief appeared above them on the summit of one of the lower walls. Since the time when, through his instrumentality, the castle had been saved from the destruction that Yamada the *Ronin* had plotted to bring upon it, Shiro had become more popular among his people, and the announcement, that in the coming battle he would appear at the head of his troops, had aroused a most intense enthusiasm among the soldiers. After the young leader came the other chief officers, and last of all, Paoli, dressed, for the nonce, in the sacred vestments of his office, and accompanied by a youth bearing the crosier. Shiro, stepping down into one of the embrasures, so that his feet were but slightly elevated above the heads of the warriors below, waved his hand to command silence, and then, as every eye was fixed upon him, he spoke :

" On the morrow, fellow-Christians and soldiers of the Lord, we are once again to give the enemy battle ; not from behind our defenses, nor yet by a quick sally, a dash upon their camp and then a rapid retreat, but by a vigorous assault and a long, sustained engagement in the open field, and in the midst of the hostile encampment. In our conflicts thus far, we have conquered; let this inspire us as we go forth to-morrow. We have reason, moreover, to believe our stratagem to surprise the enemy will be successful. Our mock *sorties* of the past week have accomplished the object we desired, and the government troops will look upon our movement to-morrow with the same indifference we perceived yesterday and to-day. Let us be careful not to arouse their suspicions; our hope of victory is built upon finding our enemies unprepared, and then charging them with the utmost swiftness and fury before they have recovered from their surprise. Therefore, be cool, be brave, be steady, be obedient to the commands of your officers and, above all, court the death of the hero, remembering that it is more honorable to fall in the forefront of battle than to be massacred within the walls of a captured castle."

A loud shout of approval rolled up from the multitude as the speaker closed his harangue, and every eye glowed with enthusiasm, and every breast heaved with the tumultuous excitement of the hour.

"Silence, Sons of the Church! I would speak a word!" It was the voice of Paoli, and his tall form bowed down from the wall, invoking silence. "Swords of God's wrath upon the idolaters!" he cried. "Ye go forth with to-morrow's rising sun to visit Heaven's vengeance upon the heads of the enemies of your faith. Ye shall be victorious if ye but go forth with the blessing of the Lord of Hosts and of the Holy Mother of God. To the chapel, then, O my children! This night shall your father and bishop stand by the altar with the priests. To-night shall he shrive and bless you; to-morrow he shall fight by your sides. To the chapel, all! Confession and prayer!"

and raising his hands in silent benediction over the multitude, the bishop turned and would have descended from the wall after the other leaders, had not a hand been laid upon his shoulder. He looked around and saw Shiro.

"Good father and bishop," said the young man, pointing toward the encampment of the enemy, "this time, to-morrow eve, if we stand here and look yonder, what shall we see?"

Shiro spoke with an earnestness and a cordiality that was wholly unassumed, and as he looked into his companion's face he saw there a returning gleam of the old time friendliness. In the general enthusiasm and the thrilling excitement of the hour both men had, for the moment, forgotten their bitterness toward each other.

"The blackened ruins of the camp of the infidel," was Paoli's prompt response to the young leader's question. "As you looked down to-night into the faces of the men, Shiro, what saw you written there?"

"Victory!" the other cried enthusiastically. "Never did general lead forth warriors more sanguine of success and more invincibly bold than shall I upon the morrow. But, good father, it is not of our assured triumph that I would speak, but of what is to follow. Often have you said, during the past week, as you have stood by my side upon these walls and looked away toward yonder mountain : 'First, the idolaters, and then—' and I needed not the aid of your words to comprehend your meaning. To-morrow, Bishop Paoli, it shall be the idolaters ; and then what?"

Shiro was keenly regarding his companion. Paoli's face was calm, but a hard, stern look had settled over his features—a look that ill became a priest of God who was soon to stand by the altar, shriving and blessing the souls of men. His eyes burned down into those of the young man. There was a minute's silence, and then he said somewhat coldly:

"To-morrow the idolaters."

The shadow of a smile flitted over the young man's face. He thrust his hand into the wide sleeve of his *haori* and drew forth the soiled and crumpled paper, which he had picked up in the hermitage of Lord Mori of Unzen. Holding this out to the bishop, he said quietly:

"Read this, good father, and then speak again."

Paoli took the proffered paper and read it, Shiro the meanwhile intently observing his face; but no expression of sudden surprise or other emotion changed the sphinx-like calm of that impassive countenance. He read the paper through to the end, looked up and cast a passing glance toward Unzen; then read the words before him again, once more gazed off in the direction of the mountain; then folding up the letter slowly and carefully, he placed it in his bosom. Turning his eyes upon Shiro, he said, in a voice that sounded like the ring of metal upon metal:

"To-morrow the idolaters, and likewise the other."

Scarcely had he spoken, when the heavy boom of a cannon broke the stillness of the evening air. Both men looked quickly toward the hostile camp, but no indications were visible that the shot had been fired there. Paoli was the first to turn his eyes toward the bay.

"Ah!" he exclaimed, startled out of his composure: "the *Spuyten Duyvil!*"

And the *Spuytin Duyvil* it certainly was. With every sail set, she was speeding along her course, and in a short time would be opposite the castle. For a few minutes, the two men watched the swiftly approaching ship in silence. A loud joyful shout from the government camp, as the soldiers caught sight of the foreign vessel, aroused the watchers upon the wall from the reverie into which they both had fallen. Shiro seized his companion's arm.

"Good father, what of the morrow?" and the speaker pointed toward the ship.

The Jesuit's face was lit up with an assuring smile.

"As certainly ours, my son, as are the promises of God?" And with these words, the bishop and the young leader, side by side, descended from the wall.

In the outer division of the fortress, the two men separated, Paoli hastening to the chapel, where already a vast throng of soldiers had gathered.

VII.

NIRADO SHIRO MAKES HIS FATE.

After Bishop Paoli had left him, Shiro passed through the several divisions of the castle until he reached the low wall that was built along the very brink of the promontory. Mounting this he gazed off in the direction of the coming ship. On either side of the Christian fortress, the beach was black with thousands of spectators from the camp. As Shiro looked down upon them, he perceived a small company of mounted warriors making their way through the thick press toward the shore. In the van rode the standard-bearer, and it needed but a glance at the banner which he bore to tell the Christian leader that Nabeshima, the Prince of Kai, was there.

"The Englishman must have gone back to Nagasaki, and is now returning aboard the *Spuyten Duyvil*," he mused, as he watched the horsemen. "The prince is evidently going off to meet him. Strange, strange, that friendship which has so suddenly grown up between those two!"

While he stood there on the wall, idly watching Nabeshima and his retainers as they gave their horses to the keeping of the *bettos*, and, springing into a waiting boat, pushed off in the direction of the *Spuyten Duyvil*, Shiro felt a light touch on his arm, and, turning round, he looked down into the eyes of Ine Tanaka. The woman's thin, pale face struck a pang of remorse to his heart. He felt an impulse to fall at her feet and to ask her forgiveness; but the face of Una of Unzen seemed to rise up between them, the generous feeling passed away, and the faithless lover hardened his heart toward the woman whose unspeakable sorrow it was that she loved him too well.

"Ine Tanaka! thou here?" he exclaimed, in a coldly questioning tone.

"Ay, my Lord," the woman replied calmly, her eyes dropping before the hard, stern look Shiro bent upon her. "Thy servant has come to ask a favor,"

"To me! and to ask a favor."

"To thee, and for a favor. Art thou not our leader?" —and Shiro noted the omission of any reference to his divine appointment. "To whom else," the woman continued, "is it fitting that the suppliant should go?"

Ine's gentle dignity touched the man's heart.

"Speak on," he said more kindly than he had yet spoken.

"My Lord, I hear that thou art to lead our army in person during to-morrow's battle. Is it so?"

"It is," he replied; and then, seeing the pained look that his words brought to the woman's face, he added: "Thou hast just called me the leader of our brethren; what place, then, becomes me more than at the head of the warriors of the church, leading them on to their triumph over their enemies?"

"Ah, my Lord, where Heaven leadeth, the guidance of man is of little moment. Yet I would not have thee remain in the castle. Go, my Lord, and may the Holy Mother be thy shield! Lead our friends on to victory! The heart of thy servant will rejoice in the plaudits that greet the conqueror's return, yet I have a request—deny it not, O my Lord!"

Shiro looked kindly into the wan yet superbly beautiful face before him. Again that feeling of tender pity akin to love stole into his heart, but once more he crushed it down; yet his voice trembled from the effort it cost him, as he again asked the woman to speak.

Ine waited long before replying. Her companion saw her bosom rise and fall with the deep emotions that surged through her soul. Then, with a low, stifled cry, she flung herself at Shiro's feet, gasping out between her heavy sobs:

"O my Lord, my Lord!—the Prince Nabeshima—give me thy promise that on the morrow thou shalt shun that part of the field where flies the banner of Kai! My Lord, thy promise!"

Was it jealousy, or was it fear, or was it hate—that terrible sensation that seized his heart and seemed to suffocate him? Was he destined to fall beneath the sword of the Prince of Kai? Ine's dread of his meeting Nabeshima seemed to have something terrifying in it. Fearless as he was, it unmanned him. Controlling his voice by a mighty effort, he spoke to the kneeling woman:

"Rise, Ine Tanaka! Thou wouldst not have me cravenly to flee from before the face of my foe, should he search me out as he did last Christmas morn. Yet thou hast my promise that I shall not seek a combat with him on the morrow. Should chance bring us together—why, then, God and Holy Cross be my help!"

Again came the well-nigh irresistible impulse to bow himself to the side of the woman that knelt at his feet, and asking her forgiveness for his past unfaithfulness, to beseech her to renew the betrothal by which their parents had sought to unite them; nay, more, to ask her to go with him to the chapel below, and, in the presence of the people, upon this momentous eve, to become his wife. A voice within him whispered: "The crisis of thy life is upon thee, weal and woe, happiness and misery, life and death lie before thee, choose!" and, alas! like so many, Nirado Shiro chose the more bitter portion, though he knew it not.

Was the disconsolate woman kneeling before him aware of the struggle in his heart? She rose in sad, yet queenly dignity, and, laying her hand on the shoulder of the man before her, said, with an earnestness that thrilled his soul:

"Nirado Shiro, I thank thee for thy promise. It will comfort me as I look upon the battle to-morrow; for knowest thou, that though the betrothal that once united us exists no longer, yet Heaven has linked our destinies together by a bond that cannot be broken."

The young man stood awed before her; her manner struck a strangely chilling fear to his heart. He felt that he must speak, but knew not what to say.

"Ine, Ine!" he cried in a distressed voice; "thy reason for asking the bishop to absolve you from the betrothal between us I know full well. My coldness, my neglect did it. Yet, yet—Oh God, you do not know!"

"I do know, Nirado Shiro," the woman said calmly. "You love another—another, my Lord, whose heart will never be yours. Nay, start not! whose heart will never be yours," she repeated in a voice that sounded like a wail, for she had suddenly remembered that such had been Nabeshima's words spoken to herself concerning the man now before her.

Shiro stared at her helplessly. "Ine, let me atone for the pain I have given you," he said with a desperate effort to regain his calmness. "The time draws on apace when I shall be the ruler of this nation. Then, in the Christian court of our Japan, shall Ine Tanaka be crowned with dignity and honor, and, when she weds, it shall be the noblest of my lords."

The woman before him looked steadily into his face; he dared not raise his eyes to hers. Her voice for the first time sounded cold and constrained.

"My lord, I thank thee for thy assurance of favor; but, believe me, I shall need it not. My hand has been wedded these many years, and my heart shall remain faithful to the choice of my father and mother. Come, my Lord," she continued softly; "let us go together to the chapel. Once more would I kneel by thy side in prayer."

VIII.

THE SERVANT BECOMES THE MASTER.

After the Jesuit had brought the religious services in the chapel to a close, he hastily sought the solitude of his own quarters, his mind filled with tumultuous visions of the victory and vengeance which the approaching day was to bring forth. Never before had Francesco Paoli been so deeply stirred, never before so nervously impatient for the hour of struggle to come. Upon both heathen and heretic was soon to fall the chastisement of a triumphant church, and he longed, with a feverish exultation, for its execution to begin.

Then, Shiro's strange conduct, during the past week, perplexed him and filled him with anxious apprehension. The young man had sought his company continually, and the Jesuit noticed that his self-masterful spirit and his courteous yet independent bearing had been growing more marked as the days passed by. It indeed seemed as if Nirado Shiro had purposely associated with the Jesuit in order that he might school himself into a more and more complete resistance to the latter's mysterious influence over him in preparation for some contemplated action calling for an open defiance.

As Paoli was walking back and forth in his room, suddenly he stopped. A livid pallor overspread his features, his eyes, wildly staring, seemed to be fixed upon some distant imaginary object, and his breath came in quick hard sobs. For a minute or two he stood thus, and then with a low shuddering moan, he fell prostrate to the floor. Whatever it was that he had been permitted to see in the trance that had just left him, no no good could it have boded either to himself, or to his long cherished hopes, for, when nearly an hour later, he recovered from the swoon into which he had fallen, his face was haggard and anguished, and his eyes shone with an awful terror, such as might be his to whom had been vouchsafed a vision of earth's universal doom.

The voice of some one without calling for admission aroused him, and before he could sufficiently collect himself to respond, the sliding doors were swept apart and Nirado Shiro entered the room. Without perceiving the bishop's agitation in the dim light shed from a solitary candle at the further side of the apartment, the young man at once hastened to make known the reason of his visit. Paoli, on the morrow, was planning to go to Unzen, and Shiro purposed accompanying him that he might bring Una Mori to the castle with the intention of making her his wife.

While Shiro was speaking, the Jesuit, by a mighty effort, succeeded in crushing down all visible traces of his recent agitation, and when the young leader had concluded, he motioned him to a seat by his side, and then proceeded to make a final appeal to him to heed the will of his parents and the wishes of the people by marrying the woman to whom in childhood he had been betrothed. Shiro heard the words of the elder man in scornful silence, his face darkening with vexatious impatience; and as the Jesuit looked upon him and perceived the sullen defiance that clouded his features, he realized that the long-expected rupture between this man and himself was at hand. With an uneasiness that even his marvellous self-control could not wholly hide from the keen eyes of his companion, he waited for Shiro to speak. At length came the hotly impetuous reply:

"I shall have a wife of my own choosing, or I shall have none. I shall not marry Ine, much as I respect and honor her. But why speak of this at all? We are no more to each other; she asked you to absolve her from her betrothal to me, and you did so. You censure me for my love for Una Mori. Methinks, good bishop, it is your hatred for the father that taints your feelings toward the daughter. Nay, I shall have her; with your consent, I trust, but without it if need be. We shall go to Unzen together to-morrow, and you, who have blamed me for going, have you well considered the motives that lead you thither? I go to save, you, bishop Paoli, to destroy"

The Jesuit's strangely luminous eyes burned down into those of the young man. He rose to his feet and laid his hand upon the other's shoulder.

"Nirado Shiro," and his voice sounded harsh and constrained, "it ill behooves us to permit a shadow to fall across the pathway of our friendship on the eve of our coming victory. You charge me with hating Lord Mori of Unzen. I hate no man. Years ago, when he left the bosom of the church, I endeavored with all the power I had to bring him back, but he scorned my efforts. He sought to corrupt others. Then it was that I would have slain him, but he escaped. Long years have passed since then, and the letter you to-night gave me proves him to be still an apostate and a foe of the church. As such, he shall suffer on the morrow the long-delayed penalty of his crime, which I, in behalf of peace and purity of the faith, shall mete out to him."

Shiro laughed bitterly, and would have spoken, but Paoli's hand tightened its grasp upon his shoulder, and the Jesuit's voice, coldly menacing, continued:

"Hold, I have not yet finished, Nirado Shiro! Formerly it was your delight to do the will of the church; but of late you have refused to listen to her voice. Beware! As bishop of the Church of Japan, I would warn you to beware how, in this crisis of her fortunes, you trifle with her interests. You are already a traitor to the trust your brethren have reposed in you; as such, it were fitting that you were brought before our holy inquisition. You can escape this in only one way—by now renewing your oath of consecration to the church, and by swearing obedience to her will, as made known to you through her constituted authorities. Do you consent?"

Francesco Paoli had shot the ecclesiastical despot's

last, and most powerful bolt, a bolt that has prostrated many a proud soul in the dust of humiliation, and brought it back, cowed and repentant, to obedience to the voice of the church. Would it be thus in the case of Nirado Shiro?

The young Christian chief was on his feet, and, in place of the look of humbled submission, which the Jesuit had expected to see, his face wore an expression of haughty defiance, and when he spoke, his voice had that calm firmness that comes from the confident assurance that the speaker is about to win a victory.

"Francesco Paoli!"—the bishop started at his companion's manner of addressing him—"Francesco Paoli!" Shiro repeated, fixing his eyes sternly upon those of the Jesuit, "the time has come for us to understand each other, and I rejoice that it has been yourself who has precipitated this inevitable interview. Once upon the *Spuyten Duyvil*, before your disguise was discovered, the Dutch captain, in speaking of you, said to me: 'The Japanese Christians ought to hate that Paoli as heartily as do the heathen, for he has been the cause of all their sufferings for, at least, the past twenty years.' When I heard his words, I felt the indignant blood flame to my face, and I longed to give him the lie in his teeth and smite him down where he stood. To-night, Francesco Paoli, I believe his words expressed nothing but the truth."

The Jesuit's face had grown deathly pale, and his hands were convulsively clasped before him. He made an attempt to speak, but his voice died away in an inarticulate murmur.

"Mark me!" continued Shiro, "you and your fellow-priests from Europe came here to teach us your religion; but for one word you taught us of Christ, you preached

TURNING ROUND, HE LOOKED DOWN INTO THE EYES OF INE TANAKA.—*See Page* 361.

a thousand concerning the church and the duty of obeying her. You made us rebels in the eyes of our countrymen; you told us our ruler lived not in Yedo, neither in Kyoto, but in Rome."

Paoli roused himself sufficiently to exclaim:

"You are wild, insane, Nirado Shiro! Where are your proofs?"

A bitter, mocking laugh burst from the young leader's lips. He came close to the Jesuit's side, and said in almost a whisper:

"It were well for you, Francesco Paoli, that I were mad—or dead. You ask for proofs? Mount the walls of this beleaguered castle and you will behold the countless camp-fires of our countrymen who have been sent hither to punish us for our treason. But I have other proofs. Bishop Paoli, where keep you your secret journal?"

With an exclamation that sounded more like a curse than a pious ejaculation, the Jesuit sprang backward and stood regarding his calmly smiling companion with a look of terrified amazement.

"Let me warn you," observed Shiro, quietly, but with a significant glance at Paoli's arms hanging on the wall, "that you exercise a proper control over yourself as you listen to what I have now to say. Nearly a score of my body-guard are in my confidence in this matter. They are now at the door, and a call from me, or even the sound of a blow will summon them into the room, and once here, Francesco Paoli, your doom is sealed."

The Jesuit sank to the floor with a groan. He knew what was in store for him. Burying his face in his hands, he burst into tears. Shiro's lip curled with contempt as he resumed:

"The secret journal which you have kept for years is

now in my possession. How I came by it is not for you to hear. Let it suffice you to understand that I know now the deception which you and your fellow-priests practiced upon the people of my native village. It was you who wrote on that rock—but in what way I know not—the prophecy concerning a coming deliverer among the Christians. It was you who made them believe that I was that deliverer. It was you who induced my parents to betroth me to the daughter of Toranosuke Tanaka. It was you who led them to send me to the Jesuits' college in the Philippines, that I might there become your obedient tool for the accomplishment of your designs."

The young leader again paused, and stood waiting for the man at his feet to speak. But Paoli made no attempt to reply to the accusations Shiro had hurled against him. Heavy sobs shook his frame and the great, hot tears trickled down through his fingers and fell upon the floor. Perceiving that his companion would not speak, Shiro went on :

"Francesco Paoli, I flatter myself that I have been an apt pupil. I have imbibed the lessons of deceit and cunning craftiness that by both precept and example have been constantly set before me. You thought you were deceiving me and making such use of me as you would. But know that you are hereafter to be merely a tool in my hands. If you are willing still to serve me, I am agreed ; if you are not, this castle has no place for you. You have made me what I am. I, who once conscientiously believed that I was elected of Heaven for the accomplishment of a great mission, acknowledge now no worthier motive for retaining my position as commander-in-chief of the Christians than worldly ambition. If we conquer in to-morrow's battle, there is a good prospect for the Christian cause. You and I shall still speak of my divine mission. It has a good sound, and the people so long deceived by it, like to hear it. With their triumph I shall become powerful—a prince—nay, why not, as you once told me it was the will of Providence and the intention of the church to make me—the first Christian ruler of Japan?"

The last words were uttered in a tone of mocking irony, which, however, was lost upon the now thoroughly spiritless creature at his feet. With a smile of triumph, the speaker hastened to conclude the interview.

"We understand each other now, Bishop Paoli. So long as you serve my interests you are safe; as soon as you lead me even to suspect treachery, I shall hand you over to the government. And now, side by side, shall we go into battle, and together we shall go to Unzen. I approve of your proposed punishment of Lord Mori. I foresee how he might become a pernicious influence in the church. Yet, see to it well, that you harm not his daughter, either now or hereafter."

And, with a look of triumphant exultation upon his face, Nirado Shiro went forth from the room, scarcely deigning a glance at the cowering wretch upon the floor.

IX.

A REMARKABLE RE-CONQUEST.

Morning came, and with it the sound of preparations for the coming strife. Shiro had spent the few hours since leaving Paoli's quarters moodily pacing up and down his own apartment. One of his attendants now appeared, to inform him that the troops were almost in readiness, and that as soon as he had breakfasted it would be time to move upon the foe. But the young leader, too nervous and agitated to think of eating, refused to have the food brought before him, and, hastily putting on his armor, he hurried out into the first division of the castle, where the troops were to assemble. In the gateway he met Paoli, who had evidently stationed himself there in waiting for him. The bishop was clad from head to foot in his suit of European mail, over which he had thrown a loose, flowing mantle of Japanese cloth, that the government troops might not detect his presence among the Christians. Despite his most strenuous effort, Shiro could not avoid showing the trepidation into which the sudden appearance of the Jesuit threw him. He trembled so violently that his sword-hilts smote together, his heart leaped into his throat, and it seemed to him that all the blood in his body was burning in his face.

Paoli pretended not to notice his excitement, as he inquired pleasantly:

"Hast thou breakfasted, son? It seems but a minute ago that I sent in your servant to call you to your morning meal."

The young man tried to push past the bishop; he found himself too excited to risk speech. With a soft laugh, Paoli extended his hand and stopped him.

"Nay, my son, there is yet time; the troops will not be ready this half hour. I beg of you to recollect that we have a hard day before us, with little respite for refreshing the body. You must eat, my son, if you would not faint in the presence of the foe." And, drawing Shiro's arm within his own, the bishop led him back to his quarters, and ordered the attendant to serve breakfast.

The young man was dumfounded. Was this the humbled wretch that only a few hours before had crouched at his feet? Shiro had not yet dared to raise his eyes;

but now he stole a furtive glance at the Jesuit. No trace of the terror that had convulsed those calm, majestic features remained; the thick-falling tears which he had beheld a short time ago had left no stain upon that quietly smiling face. Never had he beheld the bishop more thoroughly self-possessed than at present. Involuntarily Shiro passed his hand across his brow, as if he would rid his mind of some incubus that oppressed it. Had he, after all, been dreaming? Was his memory of a rupture with the Jesuit nothing more than the waking recollections of a hideous nightmare?

Shiro seated himself on the mats before Paoli and tried to eat; but his hand was so unsteady that it was with difficulty he raised the food to his mouth, and even the water seemed to choke him. He inwardly cursed himself for thus yielding to this feeling of indefinable dread in the presence of the man before him. He tried to remember how he had, but a short time ago gained the mastery over Paoli; how he had wrung bitter tears from him; how he had dictated even the terms on which he would spare his life. Then he resolved to make a desperate effort to break down the increasing power which the Jesuit was gaining over him; for he felt that some subtle, magnetic influence was going forth from the calmly smiling being before him, and was weaving anew its irresistible spell over his soul. With a spring he was on his feet and standing face to face with the Jesuit.

The picture which the two men at that instant presented was a striking one. The younger man, wildly excited and trembling, and on his face the fierce play of the contending emotions of defiance and submission that, like a tempest, were sweeping through his soul, stood with both his hands upraised as if to strike, while his knees bent forward as if he was just in the act of bowing himself before his companion; the elder man, stiffly erect and motionless as a statue, and with the muscles of his neck and face standing out like whip-cords, appeared to be throwing all the powers of his being into the intense gaze he fastened on the eyes of the man before him. For a minute they remained thus. Then Shiro's hands slowly opened and his arms dropped to his side; his knees sank to the floor, and the next instant he had flung himself at the Jesuit's feet.

"Forgive me, good father Bishop," he groaned; "I have sinned against thee, forgive me!"

The rigid look had vanished from Paoli's face as Shiro fell to the floor; but no smile of triumph lit up the calm, sphinx-like countenance of this strange being who thus again had established his empire over his companion's soul. No trace of emotion marred the quiet gentleness of his voice as, assisting the young man to his feet, he said:

"Say no more, my son, I prefer to think of it as my own weakness, and not the mistake of another. But I promise you, son, not so to forget myself again; but come, let us go to our troops."

So saying, Paoli once again linked his arm in that of Shiro, and the two hastened to the place where their body-guards were awaiting them. As they passed among the soldiers, the men commented upon their looks. "How well our good bishop Paoli appears this morning! Hard will it fare with the heathen that come within swing of that ax!" "Is General Shiro ill? See how pale he is! Saints and angels defend him in the battle to-day!" were a few of the remarks that reached the ears of the Jesuit and his companion, as they hurried to their places.

In a short time, the columns of the Christian army were in motion, slowly filing through the gates of the castle. Paoli remained by Shiro's side, and, as the two passed out of the fortress, the young commander-in-chief looked up and beheld the figure of Ine Tanaka on the summit of the outer wall, and his heart throbbed as if it would break through his side. He felt that the Jesuit's eyes were upon him, and he knew himself to be still under their powerful spell. Almost involuntarily, he waved his hand to the woman, and, reining in his horse, stood looking up to her, as she leaned over the wall, smiling down upon him. The noise of the marching troops rendered an interchange of speech impossible, but he saw her unfasten something from her breast and drop it at his feet.

"She has given you her crucifix, my son," the bishop's soft voice broke in at his side. "Take it, and may it be a talisman to you and to our cause this day."

Shiro had dismounted and was now fastening the gold cross to the breast of his armor. When he had done this, he again looked up at Ine with a smile and a bow of thanks. The woman's face had grown radiant with the happiness his acceptance of her gift had given her. Shiro perceived this, and a pang of remorse smote him. He would not kindle a false hope in this woman's breast; he would return to her the token she had dropped at his feet. He looked around to see some one by whom he could send the gold cross back to its owner, and his hand stole to his breast to unfasten it from his armor. Was the man at his side conscious of his sudden resolution? Shiro again felt steal over him that mysterious influence which a short time before had compelled him to prostrate himself at the Jesuit's feet.

"We must be going, my son," he heard the calm, measured voice of the bishop say to him. "Happy warrior! God, who hears the interceding petitions of His saints on earth, shall make the prayers of yonder pure and noble maiden thy sure defense against the weapons of thy foes. Come, mount and forward, my son, in the name of Christ and Holy Cross!"

And Shiro, vaulting lightly into his saddle, rode on by the side of Paoli toward the camp of the infidel.

And beyond lay the hermitage of the heretic, Lord Mori of Unzen.

BOOK ELEVEN.

DEATH HAS MANY DOORS TO LET OUT LIFE.

I.

IN THE CAMP OF KAI.

CLEAR and beautiful had dawned the morning of this memorable tenth of March. Not a cloud was in the sky, and though the wind blew fresh and chill from the gulf, yet the air was clear and invigorating. At an early hour the camp of Matsudaira was astir with life. A large number of soldiers had, the evening before, secured the commander-in-chief's permission to repair to a plain about a mile away, to engage in athletic sports, and, long before sunrise, hundreds were hurrying out of the camp toward the place of meeting. Of those who remained, many were taking advantage of the fair weather to clean their booths or to polish their armor. The brightness of the day seemed to impart an unwonted vivacity to the spirits of the men. Merry laughter and snatches of song were heard rising from every part of the vast encampment.

On the summit of a small hill on the extreme southern border of the camp were stationed the twelve thousand warriors who wore the crest of Kai. Nabeshima's quarters were pitched in a small grove of camphor-trees, that covered the top of the hill, the booths of his soldiers stretching backward along the ridge and down into the valley beyond. Here, as elsewhere, sunrise found the men, their morning meal finished, gathered in merrily laughing groups, or busily engaged in polishing their arms, and the metal parts of their suits of mail.

"The prince is late this morning," observed one of the guards to his associate, as the two stood before their chieftain's quarters. "It cannot be," added the speaker, a shade of anxiety in his voice, "that our lord is ill?"

"Nay, I think not," responded the other. "Thou knowest that he brought his English friend home with him last night from the foreign ship. It was long past midnight before the two retired to rest."

"Wonderful, is it not, the love our lord has conceived for that barbarian?"

"Hush!" exclaimed the second speaker, warningly. "The prince comes!" Then, in an undertone: "Let me advise you to be careful how you speak of our lord's friend. Ill will it fare with him whom Prince Nabeshima hears calling the Englishman a barbarian."

The prince had now come up to the two speakers, who greeted him with low bows. Returning their salutations with a smile, Nabeshima said:

"My friend is still asleep. When he awakes, let the servants be at hand to wait upon him, and have food placed before him."

With this, he set out on his daily tour of inspection through the camp of his followers. Upon every one he met he bestowed a pleasant smile and a kindly word. With his courteous demeanor, his gentleness and his bravery, it was little wonder that Nabeshima was so devotedly loved by his retainers, or that the followers of some of the other princes, contrasting the haughty, overbearing dispositions of their chieftains with the friendly and chivalrous spirit of the Prince of Kai, were inclined to make comparisons that angered their lords, not so much against them as against the object of their admiration.

It was nearly an hour later when Nabeshima returned. As he drew near his quarters, he perceived Marmion Beaumont coming forward to meet him,

"Good morrow," cried the prince gayly. "Whither now, pray? To Unzen, I'll warrant!"

"In spirit I have been there ever since we parted last night," the Englishman responded gravely. "I presume it is foolishness to attach any importance to the dreams that visit our sleep, yet I cannot shake off the disagreeable impression mine have left upon me. Evil, and evil only, have I dreamed of our friends yonder," and the young man pointed toward Unzen.

"I am sorry to hear that you are disturbed," the prince said gently; "yet I know that yesterday afternoon all was well. The hunchback, in company with one of the guards, was here."

"I am foolish, I presume, to feel uneasy. But no more of this, I pray. This bracing air is medicine for melancholy, and soon we shall have Una and her father aboard the *Spuyten Duyvil* and out of the reach of danger."

"Hast thou breakfasted?" asked Nabeshima, suddenly. Beaumont replied that he had.

"Then there is no reason for further delay. I shall summon a hundred or more of my men, and with these you may at once set out for my cousin's hermitage and conduct the entire household here. After dark, they can go aboard the *Spuyten Duyvil*."

II.

THE COMING OF THE CHRISTIANS.

The prince was turning to one of his officers, who was just passing, to give the order to have the men make ready, when an exclamation of surprise from the Englishman called his attention to him. Beaumont was pointing toward the Christian fortress, where a strong body of insurgents could be seen pouring out of the gates of their castle, and moving slowly over the fan-shaped ridge of land connecting their stronghold with the plain.

Nabeshima laughed. "It looks threatening, doesn't it? But when I tell you that every morning for a week we have beheld just such a formidable demonstration, and that after the feeblest attempt at assault imaginable, they have fled back to their defenses, you will understand the spirit with which we have come to regard these sallies.

Look about you and see the preparations that are being made to receive the enemy!"

Beaumont cast his eyes over the plain below. The cry that the Christians were again coming out had passed through the camp, calling forth a loud burst of laughter. The men engaged in cleaning their armor either sat still or springing to their feet, cast a glance toward the approaching foe and then seated themselves again at their work.

"The invincibles are coming!" roared one of a hilarious company of soldiers on their way through the camp to the field sports.

"Out for exercise!" laughed another.

"Nay, friend, thou art mistaken!" cried a third; "they are out to-day to beg the scrapings of our kettles for their morning meal;" and, with a continued volley of gibes and jokes, the party passed on.

Then the cry arose that Terazawa and his retainers had been ordered by Matsudaira to charge the Christians, and to drive them back to the fortress.

"Ye gods!" shouted a warrior, as he bent over his helmet polishing its crest, "if there be any fight at all in those Christian dogs, the sight of Terazawa will call it out, for they hate him as they hate the name of Buddha."

"Ay, ay! Thou speakest the truth, friend," exclaimed another. "By my life! I'm going to get this armor of mine buckled together. Who knows what may happen?"

Just then, Terazawa's division, some three thousand strong, dashed by on their way down the hill.

"Chase them through their gates and castle and over the cliffs into the sea!" some one cried out to the hurrying soldiers, and the latter shouted back a merry response.

To the Englishman, who had seen none of the previous

demonstrations, matters wore a serious aspect. He looked distrustfully upon the approaching Christians, and with the deepest astonishment upon the careless and indifferent army.

" 'Sdeath, Prince, they are going to attack you !"

"Wait," said the other, with a laugh. "For the first few days we all thought as you do now ; but—"

"There's Paoli ! I recognize him, even at this distance; he is crouching down over his saddle-bow, so as not to appear taller than the others. Some sort of a Japanese garment covers his armor ; just now the wind blew it aside."

Nabeshima's face assumed a grave expression. "If you are right and the person that you see be really the Jesuit, there is, most assuredly, mischief afoot. I am positive that he has not taken part in any of their previous sallies."

"It is he, I know it is he !" cried the young man, excitedly.

The prince gave the command to his captains, who had gathered about him :

"Call the men to arms ! Form them into line with the utmost speed !" and the words had scarcely left his lips, when the officers sprang to obey.

The Christians were now on the open plain, between the ridge and the camp. They were divided as they had always been in the mock *sorties* heretofore : Ashizuka, Chijiwa, and Oyano leading the three main divisions, Komekine bringing up the rear with his cannon. Paoli and Shiro were there, each at the head of a small mounted body-guard. Along the front fluttered a great number of white banners, some with the figure of Christ, others with that of the Virgin and still others with merely a red cross painted upon them.

Terazawa's troops had now gained the plain and were rapidly nearing the insurgents. The latter were seen to waver and fall back.

"Ha, ha! Said I not aright?" laughed the prince. "Wait but a minute, and you will see the rebels discharge an ill-aimed flight of arrows; another minute and you will behold them breaking and fleeing to the shelter of their walls. Ha, ha, ha! See the leaders exhorting them to come on. But no; they'll no further."

Terazawa's men were now seen to spring forward, with a loud shout, right in the face of the advancing columns. Everyone expected to see the Christians turn and flee; but, instead of so doing, at a shrill peal from shell and horn, the wavering lines became firm and steady, and, when again the weird signal was shrieked out upon the morning air, the startled soldiers beheld the Christians leap forward toward their enemies.

"Ye gods!" shouted Nabeshima, "they do mean attack! Thou wast right, Master Beaumont; we have again fallen into the trap of our cunning foes." And he hurried off to arm himself.

Far and wide through the surprised and unprepared camp now rang the warning cry: "To arms, to arms!" But loud above the din about him, Beaumont could hear the thrilling battle-shout of the Christians: "*Yaso-Maria!* Woe to the Infidel!" Chijiwa had opposed himself to Terazawa, while the remaining divisions of the army dashed on against various parts of the camp, in accordance with a carefully pre-arranged plan. The struggle between Chijiwa and his foes was but momentary; for Terazawa and his men were swept back like chaff before the hurricane, and the entire force of the Christians were in the government camp before the slightest resistance had been made to their advance. It was but the work of a minute to set fire to the booths of the soldiers, and the inflammable nature of the material of which these were constructed, aided by the brisk wind blowing from the water, that rained a shower of sparks and burning brands upon the roofs of the neighboring buildings, soon transformed a wide section of the camp into a sea of roaring flame.

By a mighty effort, Kuroda, one of the government leaders, had formed his men into battle array before the victorious Oyano burst upon him, and his well-trained warriors gave the Christians their first check. For a few minutes the struggle was sharp and deadly, but Kuroda was finally killed in a hand-to-hand encounter with the insurgent chief, and his retainers turned and fled, leaving their camp in the hands of the Christians. In another part of the field, Chijiwa had dashed into the midst of the troops of a young chieftain named Arima, had scattered his men and set fire to their booths, and was now carrying destruction to the camp of Ogasawara. The government troops, completely taken by surprise, were hurrying to arms with loud shoutings, while their movements were impeded by disordered and defeated detachments of soldiers fleeing from the front. These fugitives, dashing into the midst of the forming ranks, were continually throwing them into confusion and rendering order impossible. As the conflagration, with its long, waving billows of flame and drifting clouds of dense, black smoke, rolled nearer and nearer the center of the camp, the government troops found the heat unendurable and were compelled to abandon their encampment and to seek shelter from the stifling smoke in the broad, deep valley that skirts the south-western base of Mt. Unzen, running backward in the direction of Obama.

III.

PRINCE NABESHIMA'S TURN COMES.

Clad in a full suit of mail, and armed with sword and spear, Nabeshima hastened out to the place where Marmion Beaumont was awaiting him.

"Master Beaumont," said the prince, regretfully; "I would that thou wert looking upon this from the deck of the *Spuyten Duyvil*. The battle seems to be rolling this way, and in a short time it may be upon us."

"No regrets are necessary, Prince," the Englishman replied, promptly; "my past intimacy with both Shiro and Paoli makes me loth to join their enemies against them; yet I shall stand by your side and, if necessary, defend myself. See," he added, drawing his blade from its scabbard, "I have exchanged my light rapier for this heavy sword."

A pleased look came into Nabeshima's face as he listened to Beaumont's words. "Then I shall give you a body-guard," he said, and, turning to some of his warriors that were armed and standing by he cried:

"Ho, there, Ike, Yamaji, Sato, Toyama, Ito! My friend is to remain with me in the fore-front of the battle; stand ye by his side! Ye gods, Master Beaumont," the prince continued, addressing the Englishman, "this is an unlucky day for us! That cunning Jesuit was at the bottom of that stratagem, I'll warrant. See yonder, they are now in the camp of Ogasawara, and even the veterans of Satsuma are hurled back before them."

"What do you propose to do?" Beaumont shouted, for the roar of the conflagration and the tumult of the battle were well nigh deafening.

"Remain where I am, and defend my camp until the last man falls!" came back the answer. "In a short time my warriors will be armed and ready, and, so far as I can see, my division is the only one that is likely to get into good fighting order before the Christians are upon them. You perceive," he added, pointing in the direction of the struggle below, "that the leaders in the central and rear portions of the camp have to contend against the throngs of panic-stricken men dashing in upon them from the front, and also against the stifling smoke that the wind bears that way. Our position here exempts us from both."

The prince's officers now reported the men to be under arms and awaiting orders.

"Tear down those booths!" commanded Nabeshima, indicating a collection of thatched buildings just below them on the hill-side. "Clear off a space there that the enemy may come within range of our archers and musketeers before they break into our camp!"

The men sprang forward to obey, and in a very short time a wide tract was opened up along the hill-side between Nabeshima's quarters and the nearest camp below. While this was being done, the prince and Beaumont were silently watching the progress of the struggle before them. The whole extent of the camp upon the side toward the Christians' stronghold had felt the shock of the assault, and was now in flames. The heavy clouds of smoke rolling over the plain, had by this time concealed the greater part of the battle from view; but the fury of the conflict could be very well understood from the terrific outbursts of sound that broke through the thick canopy of intervening smoke and flame. Above all the uproar was distinctly heard the unintermitted war-cry of the Christians : " *Yaso-Maria !*" and every now and then rose the thrilling shout : " Paoli ! Paoli !" For three long hours, the tide of battle surged and eddied back and forth over the plain around the foot of the hill without reaching its summit. Noon came, and the struggle had sensibly slackened ; one o'clock, and the din of war had almost entirely died away. Within the next hour, the Christians were seen falling back out of the burning camp and assembling on the open plain before their castle.

Nabeshima's retainers had thus far been compelled to be mere spectators of the conflict, and now the sight of their triumphant enemies maddened them beyond endurance, and they besought their lord to lead them against the Christians. The prince mounted his horse and rode among them.

"Be patient, heroes !" he cried. " The time for a charge has not yet come. We must maintain the advantage our position gives us. You are anxious for battle; take my word for it, you shall have plenty of fighting before long. Even now the enemy is preparing to storm our position. Remember, brave hearts of Kai, the issue of to-day's conflict depends upon us. The broken and disordered forces of the other princes lie in our rear ; an easy prey would they be to yonder foe, were we dislodged from this hill. No, gallant comrades; here must we remain—a rock, stemming the tide of defeat and holding the enemy in check until our friends can recover themselves and rally to our support."

A shout of approval greeted Nabeshima's words, and the officers at once proceeded to draw up the troops along the crest of the hill in a favorable position for receiving the attack of the enemy, which every one felt certain was about to fall upon them.

They had not long to wait. Two divisions of the Christian army were soon seen moving across the plain toward the foot of the hill. As the insurgents drew nearer, Nabeshima recognized the leader to be Ashizuka and Oyano. Pointing out the latter to Beaumont, the prince said :

"Yonder warrior was once one of my most trusted and faithful retainers. Lo, now, lord and vassal meet as foes upon the field of battle ! Men of Kai !" he shouted to his soldiers, "know ye not yonder chieftain ? It is Oyano; fire not upon him. If he must fall let the hand that slays him be other than ours."

The heavy volley that Nabeshima's retainers now poured into the advancing columns caused them to waver, and, after an ineffectual effort to rally, the Christians fell back beyond range of the enemy's fire, leaving many of their number dead or wounded on the hill-side. Hastily re-forming their ranks, Ashizuka and Oyano again led their forces against the foe, and once more were they compelled to retreat. Finding it thus impossible to carry Nabeshima's position from the plain, the Christian leaders, after a short consultation, decided to make a simultaneous assault from four different points. The fire in that part of the government camp adjacent to Nabeshima had now died down, leaving heaps of hot and smoldering ashes. With care, this section of the field might be safely traversed, and it was arranged that Oyano's division should advance upon the prince from that quarter; Ashizuka was again to charge up the hill-side, while Chijiwa was ordered to lead his men through a small morass and over some hills to the southward and to fall upon the rear of the enemy. Komekine had a quantity of fire-arrows brought from the castle, and with these he hoped to set the hostile camp on fire.

On the hill above them, Beaumont and the Prince of Kai were closely watching their movements, and when the different divisions were seen moving off, each to its appointed place, Nabeshima turned to his companion with a quiet smile:

"I thought the wily Ashizuka would not repeat the experiment of attacking us again from this side without first dividing our force by opposing to us supporting lines of attack."

The Englishman scarcely heard his companion's words. He was thinking of the desperate valor which the Christians had displayed on previous occasions, and he could not refrain from believing that he was about to witness the most sanguinary encounter that had yet taken place in the whole course of this bloody war.

"You are prepared, Prince, for a most resolute assault upon the part of your foes?" and he looked questioningly into Nabeshima's face.

The young nobleman did not at once reply. The smile, that a moment before had lighted up his countenance, vanished, and, as his eyes swept over the Christian forces below and then over the silent masses of his own troops behind him, a hard, stern look settled upon his features, and his voice was unwontedly grave as he spoke:

"Master Beaumont, I think you comprehend the situation, yet I shall speak. I believe that you are now to see fought the decisive battle of this most unhappy war. Within the next few hours will be decided the fate of the Christian church in Japan. If I am overcome and driven from this position, the way lies open to the broken and disordered body of the main army, and in its demoralized and panic-stricken multitudes the Christians will find an easy harvest of slaughter. With the destruction of our present army, all southern Japan will virtually be in the power of the insurgents, and tens of thousands of our people, who are Christians at heart, encouraged by the success of their cause, will openly avow their faith and join their brethren in arms ; and then—who knows what the end may be?"

The young Englishman's heart beat fast. Despite his friendship for the Prince of Kai, his sympathies were still with the struggling Christians. He remembered his past intimacy with Paoli and Shiro and the conversations he had had with them aboard the *Spuyten Duyvil*. For the moment the sublime faith they had professed in the final triumph of their cause seemed to impart to his spirit a confidence equal to their own.

With unexpected rapidity, Chijiwa and Komekine crossed the morass and scaled the opposite heights. Here the latter chieftain paused, and, placing his cannon in position, opened fire upon Nabeshima's camp, while a small division of his men descended the hill, and began discharging their burning arrows toward the booths of the soldiers. The roar of Komekine's guns was the signal for Ashizuka and Oyano to move forward to the attack. Chijiwa's troops were already engaged in a fierce hand to hand struggle with the enemy on the lower ground, and soon the Prince of Kai beheld his position furiously assailed from the rear, on either flank, and in front.

The Christians, no less than Nabeshima, recognized that the supreme crisis in their fortunes had come, and that upon the issue of the present conflict hung their weal or woe. This knowledge lent strength to their arms and courage to their hearts. With a reckless daring they dashed forward upon the guns of the enemy, heed less of the terrible volleys that tore wide gaps in their ranks, and with a fierce shout they hurled themselves against the foe, crushing them back by the momentum of their onset.

The struggle that ensued baffles any attempt at description. Bravest of all the princes before Hara Castle was Nabeshima of Kai, and no warriors in the army of Matsudaira were more courageous than the twelve thousand that followed his standard; but bootless seemed the prowess and heroism of both lord and vassal before the whirlwind of war that now burst upon them. With fully a third of his gallant little army either disabled or lifeless on the field, and his camp in flames, Nabeshima, his own face streaming with blood, at length was compelled to order a retreat, with the hope that by throwing his burning camp between himself and the enemy his troops would have an opportunity to close up their shattered ranks and to gain a new and favorable position. The movement was executed with marvellous order and quickness, and, before the Christians were aware of their foes' intention, they found themselves left in possession of the burning camp.

The leaders of the insurgents at once ordered a pursuit. Instead, however, of breaking through the flames and following upon the track of the retreating enemy, they made a circuit to the northward, passing through a small portion of the ruined camp of the main army. This course, although requiring considerable time, would preserve their ranks from the annoyance and disorder to which a dash through the midst of the burning booths would have exposed them. As the Christians, in solid columns, swept forward to charge anew their already defeated foes, and to complete the utter rout and overthrow of the infidel host, a shout of triumphant exultation broke from their lips as they beheld, in the valley below them, the men of Kai huddled together in seemingly inextricable confusion, and Nabeshima and his officers dashing hither and thither among them, vainly endeavoring to restore order and discipline.

IV.

DEVOTION, DESTINY, DELIVERANCE.

We often meet with this declaration concerning some historical character—" He was a child of his times ;" and this simply means that such a one was an embodiment of the spirit of the age in which he lived, that in him we have an epitome of that age's manners and customs, its thoughts and feelings,— in a word, the thousand and one elements that go to form the complex organism which we call society. The spirit of the age in which he lived became flesh and blood in the person of Francesco Paoli ; and not to remember this is to fail to comprehend the man.

It is almost impossible for us of this materialistic nineteenth century to divest ourselves of its influences and to contemplate with unbiased minds an age so completely spiritual, so grossly superstitious, so full of religious rancor, controversy, bigotry, and intolerance as was the one into which Paoli was born. God and the devil, Heaven and Hell, angels and demons were visible realities. Like Elisha's servant, men saw themselves encompassed by spiritual legions, and they held communion with these unearthly beings. Fastings, scourgings, and prayers brought heavenly comforters to the side of the religious fanatic ; wicked men made league with Satan and signed the compact with their blood. The world was regarded as a battlefield, where God and his angels fought the hosts of darkness; the church was God's weapon, nay, rather an ally; through her co-operation alone could the world be won to the cross and the empire of Satan overthrown. Hence that marvellous missionary activity that inspired the Church of Rome during the sixteenth and seventeenth centuries, and which planted her standard in lands the most remote and amid nations the most ferocious and hostile.

In this desperate warfare, which she was waging at home and abroad, the church's great army was the hosts of her believing children, and over these she established all the rigors of a military discipline. The general who orders the execution of a traitor, or a deserter, or a soldier that refuses obedience, does so for the greater safety of the army as a whole, and for the better accomplishment of its appointed work. Similar in spirit and practice was the policy of the church. In the great army of the cross, insubordination to authority or open revolt must be crushed down, the malefactor must suffer the punishment of traitor and deserter, if the power that united all and governed all and aspired to universal empire was to retain its supremacy and to extend its sway. Thus, heresy was treason, an acceptance of what became known as Protestantism was open rebellion, calling for the severest chastisement; and, to the extent of her ability, both at home and in her mission fields, the church made haste to wash out with the blood of her dissenting children all traces of their denial of her authority.

Such a conception as this of the church's prerogatives had, since his early manhood, dominated the life of Francesco Paoli; and when to a character like his, endowed by nature with every guarantee of success in any profession to which it might have pleased him to have devoted his splendid talents, were added the conscientious belief that he was elected of Heaven to establish the power of the church in Japan; when the zeal, the devotion, the fanaticism that burned in the heart of the Catholicism of his age, seized upon and thrilled every fibre of his passionate nature, we need no longer wonder at the hatred and terror he inspired among the heathen, at the resolute and unflinching fidelity he kindled in the bosom of the struggling church, at the intrigues by which he sought to bring foreign intervention to their assistance, at the deception that he, for their ultimate good, had practised even upon the Christians, or at his quenchless purpose now to blot out, by the destruction of Lord Mori of Unzen, the sole menace to the internal peace and purity of the Church of Japan. In all this, Paoli the Jesuit was a faithful servant of Rome and the slave of his age.

But greater than the power of any man, however mighty; of any organization, however wide-spread its sway; of the spirit of any age, however absolute may be its influence over human conduct, is that mysteriously inscrutable force, to which man has given many names and of which he knows so very little, that emanates from the invisible throne whereon sits the Sovereign of the universe. It perplexes the historian to account for the fatal error of the hitherto sagacious general that gives the battle to his foe, and causes the downfall of a nation. The wise and long-tried statesman by one incomprehensible blunder ruins a government, the stability or overthrow of which rested upon him. Why is this? We reply that He who beholds every change, without Himself changing, who gives power and who takes it away, who transfers it from one man to another, from one dynasty to another, from one nation and race to another nation and race, has seen the end from the beginning and knows how the loss of a battle or the fall of a government is to forward His eternal design in the history of the race He has created and the reins of whose progress He holds in his own hands. Thus, the general's error and the statesman's blunder are not the results of mere chance; they are but parts of a great plan which includes all causes and all effects in one and the same order.

Why was it that, of all times, Nirado Shiro should have chosen the evening he did to give to the Jesuit the letter he had found in the hermitage of Unzen? Why was it that Francesco Paoli, on the morning of this never-to-be-forgotten tenth of March, as he went into battle, should lift his eyes above the camp of the infidel, with its hundred thousand merciless foes of his cause, and should fix them upon the mountain where dwelt one helpless old man, with the resolution to quit the battle-field, as soon as the onslaught upon the heathen promised victory to the Christians, and, leaving the overthrow of the many to others, himself to seek the destruction of the one? And the answer must be: It was destiny, it was the will of Heaven.

For the space of a quarter of a century, Paoli had been a zealous and faithful missionary of the doctrines he conscientiously believed to be true; he had been a loving counsellor and courageous defender of his devoted converts who, in their distress, clung to him as children to a father; and, in these dark, later days, he had been a brave and invincible warrior-bishop of a militant church. For many years he had wandered about the country with a price set upon his head, defying the plots and intrigues of his foes to seize him, walking unharmed among all the traps and pitfalls they prepared for him, and outwitting them in all the stratagems which their united wisdom could devise. And yet it was this same Paoli, hitherto so wise, so circumspect, so cautious, who now, at the bidding of the lowest impulse of his nature, had resolved upon a course of action, which would deprive his cause of the inspiration of his leadership in this, its most decisive struggle, and expose it to the utmost hazard.

Into the battle rode Bishop Paoli, and by his side went Nirado Shiro. Of all the thrilling events of that terrible day the young leader, still under the influence of his companion's will, was but vaguely conscious. He knew that he was always in the fore-front of the struggle by the side of Paoli, and that, next to the dreadful ax of the Jesuit, no other Christian weapon spread such terror and havoc among the foe as did his own sword. In the thickest of one of the most desperate encounters of the day, he felt the gold cross, which Ine Tanaka had given him, torn away from his breast by the thrust of a hostile spear. One of his body-guard, a young man, about his own age, dismounted and picked it up; but a savage blow from an enemy's sword stretched him lifeless at the feet of his master's horse. In the fury of the struggle, Shiro had no time to recover the crucifix from the grasp of the fallen youth, and when the government troops had been dislodged from their position, and he would have gone back for it, the portion of the encampment in which it lay was wrapped in flames. As he stood there listening to the sounds of strife in other quarters of the camp, the Jesuit rode up.

"The victory is ours, my son. The infidel are fleeing on every side. We may safely leave the field in charge of Ashizuka and the other chieftains. My son, the heathen have felt our vengeance, and now the other!" and the face of the bishop grew stern and hard, and his blazing eyes burned with a more terrible fire than Shiro had ever before seen.

Mechanically, the young leader ordered his body-guard to follow, and himself rode on with the Jesuit. He was fully conscious that he was not his own master, but he felt powerless to shake off the weird, subtle influence this man was exerting over him. Not until they had threaded their devious way through the defiles up the side of Unzen and saw below them Lord Mori's hermitage, and before it the figures of the guards, and Una and her father in the background, did Nirado Shiro fully realize where he and his companion were, or on what mission they had come. The sight of the woman he loved broke the evil spell that so long had bound him. Once again was he master of himself, and all the scorn and defiance, that on the previous evening he had felt for the man by his side, again filled his heart. Turning to the Jesuit, he pointed out to him the figure of Una Mori; and his words were few and stern:

"Francesco Paoli, beware!"

V.

THE BEGINNING OF THE END.

The victorious Christians, as they looked down upon the demoralized troops of the Prince of Kai, had, as they might well believe, every reason to rejoice. The long expected hour of triumph and deliverance was at hand. One more impetuous charge upon the broken and disheartened troops before them and their way to the main army would be clear, and they knew that Matsudaira and his princes had not yet succeeded in getting their demoralized horde of panic-stricken fugitives into order, and that they would find them still unprepared for battle. Upon these, then, they would burst with all the relentless fury that became avengers of slaughtered brethren. For long years the heathen had been drunken with the blood of the saints, but the day of judgment and vengeance had come; the vials of God's wrath were being poured out upon the heads of the merciless idolaters, and before the swords of the Christians were sheathed, the valleys and the mountain-sides of Unzen would be thickly strewn with the dead of the infidel. Thoughts and feelings such as these filled each heart in the Christian army, as the men looked down upon their foes. They and their brethren had received no mercy at the hands of the heathen, and the heathen should receive no mercy from them. It was a question either of destroying their enemies and persecutors, or of being themselves destroyed, and now that the power of choice was theirs, they chose to slay rather than to be slain.

Reining in his horse on the crest of the hill, Ashizuka called a halt, and then, riding before the motionless columns and pointing out to the soldiers the disordered mass of the enemy, he shouted:

"Behold, Swords of the Church, the marvellous thing our God has wrought! Confusion and the spirit of despair has He breathed into the hearts of His foes. Like frightened hares they crouch at our approach and make ready their necks for the edge of the sword. Upon them, O comrades and warriors of the Lord! *Yaso-Maria!* Accursed be he who would spare an infidel!"

But alas! it was to be the destiny of the Christian warriors of Japan that never again should they carry terror and destruction to the ranks of a foe. Unknown

to them at that moment, the star of their fortunes had reached its meridian; henceforth it was doomed to sink swiftly and surely into the silence and the utter blackness of night. At the flood-tide of their success, at the time of their highest exultation, when their hearts beat high with hope and the possibility of disaster was farthest from their thoughts, when the triumph of their cause seemed to be most assured, and when, in their imaginations, they already beheld a Christian Japan rising out of the wreck of war—in this supreme hour of their fortunes, as suddenly and unexpectedly as falls the thunderbolt out of a clear sky, came the change.

When Ashizuka gave the command to halt, Chijiwa's division was passing through that portion of the burnt camp where, in the early hours of the day, had occurred the desperate encounter between the Christians and infidel forces, in the course of which Shiro, as already related, had lost the gold cross which Ine Tanaka had given him. The fighting had been exceptionally severe; and the ground was thickly covered with dead bodies, which the fire had charred beyond all possibility of distinguishing friend and foe. A portion of Chijiwa's troop were standing here among the slain, their heads bent forward in close attention to Ashizuka's words. There was one in the ranks, however, an obscure soldier, whose name even has not been preserved, that was paying no heed to the leader's address. Kneeling by a corpse that lay face downward near his feet, the soldier turned over the burnt and blackened body. The fallen warrior's forehead had been cloven to the brain by evidently a sword-stroke, his own weapon was missing, and his armor burned away; but his left hand was folded to his breast, and in its rigid grasp, the terrified soldier beheld the cross of gold, which he at once recognized as the one his young commander-in-chief had worn when he went into the battle.

Just as Ashizuka's closing words—" Accursed be he who would spare an infidel!" rang out like a trumpet blast over the listening army, the rear of Chijiwa's division was startled by a shriek, and the piercing cry:

"General Shiro is dead! Here is his body, and here his cross!"

An exclamation of horrified surprise burst from the lips of the score or more of soldiers who heard the words, and they hastily gathered about the speaker and the ghastly object at his feet. Yes, there was, indeed, Shiro's cross! Some of them had seen it upon his breast during the struggle on the very spot where they were now standing. And here was the body; its features burned beyond their power to recognize them; but the size and form were Shiro's. The voices of the beholders rose in a wailing chorus:

"General Shiro is slain! Our leader is dead! Where in Bishop Paoli?"

The scene that followed, as the cry was passed on from lip to lip, was one of indescribable panic and consternation. Before the news of the terrible discovery had passed through all of Chijiwa's command, it had assumed a still more paralyzing form.

"Our general and Bishop Paoli are among the dead! Shiro's body has just been found!" was what the other divisions heard, and almost instantly the whole army was transformed from orderly and well-marshaled battalions to a demoralized rout.

At the best but half-trained yeomen, the Christian warriors did not possess that disciplined firmness that enables the genuine soldier, in moments of deep excitement, to resist the impulse to break away from his place in the ranks.

In vain, Ashizuka and the other leaders, strove to calm the excited men; in vain did they endeavor to rally them to a renewed attack upon their already vanquished foe. "Useless now is further fighting," was the cry that rose from the grief-stricken thousands, "our leader, whom we thought Heaven had sent us as a deliverer, is dead, and we are doomed. We shall search for the bishop's body and then return to the castle to die with our wives and little ones."

VI

SAVED!

In the valley below Nabeshima and his officers had beheld the approach of the Christians with the grim indifference born of despair. All their efforts to restore order among their men had proved futile and they knew that in their present potition they could not hope to withstand the storm of battle about to break upon them. Some three hundred of the soldiers had responded to their leader's call, and Nabeshima, hastily forming these into a hollow square, prepared to resist the foe as long as a man remained. His officers, meanwhile, were continuing their efforts to rally the main body of the troops, but with little prospect of success.

The Prince of Kai cast a glance at the enemy upon the heights above him, and then, turning suddenly to Beaumont, who was standing close by, he said in a low, rapid voice:

"Master Beaumont, this morning, when the Christians' assault fell upon our camp, you said it was your purpose to stand by my side and to defend yourself. You have more than kept your word. Twice, at least, this day have you saved my life, and yet, I believe that no Christian has fallen by your hand."

The Englishman would have spoken, but Nabeshima continued :

"I understand your feelings. You are a Christian, and, rightly enough, your sympathies are with our foes ; yet you have honored me with your friendship and confidence, and, believe me, Master Beaumont, brother never loved brother more than Nabeshima loves his foreigner-friend."

The Prince's voice choked and he could say no more. The Englishman, too, was deeply affected, and his eyes grew misty with the tears he could not restrain. Mastering his emotions with a strong effort, Nabeshima continued sadly but firmly ·

"And now, my friend, we must part. It is a duty you owe yourself, your kinsfolk in far-off England, and above all, the woman who loves you," and the prince pointed in the direction of Unzen, "that you should save yourself. My duty is no less clear. The day has gone against us. In a short time, the Christians will again attack us, and before the mad fury of their assault, we can only hope to die the death of the warrior, selling our lives dearly, and, at last, falling where we fight. But you must go. I see Oyano yonder among the Christians, leading on his men. I shall sue for a few minutes' truce and place you in his keeping. He was at one time my faithful vassal, and duty rather than choice, methinks, causes him now to draw sword upon me who was once his prince. He is, moreover, the devoted friend of my cousin, Lord Mori, of Unzen, and he will find means to effect their escape to the foreign ship. You may trust him, for he is as noble as he is brave."

What Beaumont's reply might have been, his friend never knew, for at that instant the attention of all was called to the Christians, who had halted on the crest of the heights. Nabeshima and the Englishman recognized the figure of Ashizuka, as he rode along the ranks haranguing the men, but though they heard his voice, they were unable to comprehend his words. Soon, however, they were startled by the loud cries that followed the discovery of the crucifix; then the Christians were seen to break ranks and to hurry off in a confused mass toward a common point, while the uproar continued to swell in volume. The astonished spectators beheld Ashizuka, Oyano and the other leaders dash after the men, wildly gesticulating as if endeavoring to call them back to their places. Beaumont and Nabeshima gazed at each other in speechless surprise. Then as they listened to the wild outcries that rose louder every minute, the prince's eyes flashed with a joyful light as he whispered breathlessly :

"A panic ! We are saved !"

The next moment he caught the words of the wailing cry that rolled up from the grief-stricken thousands above them. With a bound he was in his saddle, and, burying his spurs in the sides of his horse, he dashed into the midst of his retainers, his voice ringing with exultant joy ;

"Ho, men of Kai, we are saved ! We are saved ! Hear ye not the lamentations of the Christians ? Shiro, their commander-in-chief, and Paoli—mark it well, the accursed Paoli—are among the slain. No more, heroes, shall we be the sport of yeomen and rebels ! Again, my warriors, rally again around the banner of your prince! Forward upon the cross of the Christians!"

The effect which the announcement of Paoli's death had upon the hitherto demoralized troops was electrical. At last their arch enemy, he whom they feared more than a host of common foes, was dead. A wild, tumultuous shout went up as they heard the prince's words, and thousands, who before had thought only of flight, now, laughing and shouting, hurried to form themselves in battle order.

Summoning one of his officers, Nabeshima dispatched him in haste to Matsudaira and the other princes with the tidings, knowing that the news of the Jesuit's death would hasten the restoration of discipline in the main army, as it had done in his own command.

"What are you going to do?" inquired Beaumont, as the prince dashed up to the place where the young Englishman was standing.

"Make a circuit to the south of my camp and cut off the retreat of the Christians to their castle. If I mistake not, the message that I have just sent to Matsudaira will enable him to dispatch some troops presently against the enemy. With my retainers stationed on the ridge before their fortress and the other princes harassing their rear, few, indeed, will it be who shall live to reach the shelter of their walls."

The Englishman grew sick at heart. He wished himself upon the *Spuyten Duyvil*, that he might escape being a witness of the coming horrors. Then suddenly a ray of hope came to him. Night was at hand. He looked about him and perceived that already the evening shadows were beginning to gather in the valleys and along the eastern slopes of the hills. A glance at the sky revealed a dark mass of clouds rapidly rolling up from the southwest. A storm evidently was at hand. Under the cover of the darkness and aided by the approaching tempest, the Christians might succeed in eluding their merciless foes and in making good their retreat to the shelter of their walls.

VII.

THE MESSENGER OF HEAVY TIDINGS.

Nabeshima's voice broke in upon the Englishman's meditations.

"A horseman is coming hither from the direction of the main army. Who he is I cannot make out. From his size, I would judge he is but a child. Ye gods, how he lashes his horse!"

Beaumont looked with careless indifference in the direction which the prince had pointed out. The approaching stranger was soon near enough for the beholders to perceive that man and steed were well nigh exhausted and that both were covered with blood. The rider had caught sight of Nabeshima and the Englishman, and was urging his course toward them. But when he was still at a considerable distance, his horse plunged forward, recovered itself, and then with a cry almost human in the intensity of its anguish, it fell heavily to the earth. Both Beaumont and the prince had caught sight of the strange rider's face, as he sank down with his falling steed, and both recognized him to be Ando the hunchback.

"It is Ando! he is from Unzen! Something terrible has happened to Una and her father!" groaned the Englishman, his face ghastly in its death-like pallor.

"Wait! let us hear his message!" the other responded, with an effort to be calm despite the terrible fear that smote him. "Come," he added, laying his hand upon the shoulder of his dazed and trembling campanion, "let us go to him."

And the two men hastened toward the place where lay the fallen horse and rider.

"Ando, Ando, what does this mean?" cried the Englishman, kneeling by the side of the sufferer. "Who did this?"

The hunchback looked up into the anxious, horror-stricken face bending over him, and a faint smile of recognition lit up his pallid, blood-stained features.

"Ay, Master Beaumont, bullet and arrow were swifter in pursuit than were my steed and I in flight. Yet, thank Heaven, I have lived to reach you!"

"My cousin, your master, Lord Mori?" breathlessly inquired the prince, who had now come up. "Speak, Ando! Is he safe?

"Thy cousin, prince, is dead," gasped the hunchback, painfully.

"Dead!"

"This afternoon," the dying man went on brokenly and in a faint whisper: "the Jesuit Paoli and General Shiro came—surprised and slew the guards—seized Lord Mori—said they would put him to death—burned his books before his eyes—then went to master, but he was already dead in Una's arms—broken heart."

The hunchback was fast losing strength. He seemed fully conscious of his condition, for he struggled to continue, but his voice died away in a hoarse rattle in his throat, and a livid hue overspread his features.

"That accursed priest is still alive, then," whispered Nabeshima through his set teeth. "Be careful pray,

Master Beaumont, not to let my men know it at present. It might spoil all our plans, for our troops fear him as they would fear the appearance of a legion of fiends."

"I shall be on my guard," groaned the Englishman, "but, tell me, Prince, shall we hear nothing of Una? What has become of her?"

At the mention of the name of his beloved mistress, Ando seemed to rally slightly. He fixed his fading gaze on the anguished face of Beaumont.

"Paoli would have carried her a prisoner into the Christian castle—Shiro drew sword on the Jesuit and saved her—after dark he will bring her to Arima, she sent me to you—save her, oh, save her!" and again the voice of the speaker sank into silence, a tremor shook his frame, a few gasping sighs fluttered from his lips, and then all was still.

"He is dead," said Beaumont, rising to his feet. "Prince, we know the worst; what can be done?"

Nabeshima had also arisen. "Una Mori can be rescued, and that bloody-handed priest can be made to pay the penalty of this inhuman murder," he said promptly, and with a look upon his face that boded ill for Francesco Paoli, should he fall into the hands of the Prince of Kai. "A thousand of my men shall mount horse, and with you and me at their head shall ride with all speed to intercept Shiro before he can escape into the castle. The remainder of my retainers, under my chief officer, will endeavor to cut off the retreat of the Christians. Ye gods! that accursed Paoli must not be allowed to rejoin the main body of the rebels. All our hopes of defeating the Christians depend upon that."

A sound at their feet attracted the attention of the two men. To their astonishment and horror, they saw the hunchback, whom they had thought dead, sitting up, his eyes wildly staring and the muscles of his throat and face writhing with hideous contortions as he strove to speak. After a moment that seemed an hour to the beholders, Ando gained his voice and shrieked forth:

"Gonroku the outlaw and his band are lying in wait for Shiro in the camphor-grove at the end of the ridge before the Christian castle. It was they that fired upon me as I rode hither." And when he had said these words, Ando the hunchback fell back dead.

VIII.

FAITHFUL TO THE LAST.

It was not strange that Ine Tanaka, as she watched Shiro go forth to battle with her gift upon his breast, should feel hope spring up anew in her heart. Ever since their betrothal had been broken, he had, so far as was possible, avoided meeting her, and when this could not be done, he had treated her with a studied coldness. But now there was evidently a change. Could it be possible that Shiro had renounced the idle fancy that so long had held him captive? Were his thoughts and affections at last turning toward her? Ine called to mind the conversation they had had the evening before, how they had gone down to the chapel together; how, side by side, they had knelt in prayer; and how a murmur of pleased surprise had passed through the throng of soldiers before the door, as she and Shiro came forth.

"Yes!" she said to herself, with her hands tightly clasped over her wildly beating heart. "After we parted last night, he carefully thought it all over; he saw for himself the madness of his passion for Una Mori; he discovered that not alone does the betrothal, by which our parents sought to unite us, bind our lives together, but that it is the will of Heaven, as expressed through the wishes of God's people, that we should be one." And a deep blush warmed the woman's pale cheeks, and her large, lustrous eyes kindled with the new joy that filled her soul.

Then succeeded the slowly moving hours of that terrible day, with the deafening uproar of battle booming across the plain and bringing deathly pallor to the faces of hundreds of wives and mothers on the walls of Hara Castle. With what anxious suspense, with what alternating hope and fear, with what agony of prayer did they not watch the awful struggle before them! From noon until evening, scores of wounded soldiers came into the castle, and the sorrowful watchers found employment as well as relaxation from their intense anxiety in ministering to the needs of these unfortunate ones. Then there was also consolation in their reports of the glorious victory that husbands, brothers and fathers were winning over the infidel.

Among the wounded that had come back to the arms of loved ones, and among the little groups of weeping women and children, whose tears fell for those who would return to them no more, like a ministering angel of healing and comfort, moved the queenly figure of Ine Tanaka. And the long afternoon wore on until, in the dusk of the evening, there sped across the plain, along the ridge and through the gates of Hara Castle that terrible cry which, in the ruined camp of the heathen, had transformed the ranks of a victorious army into a disorderly rout: "Our general and Bishop Paoli are among the killed! Shiro's body has just been found!"

Ine Tanaka, at the moment when the tidings came, was bending over a wounded soldier. The man had received a deep and painful sword-cut across the left shoulder, and, though the woman's knowledge of surgery was only such as daily practice in dressing wounds with the rudest possible appliances had given her, yet native tact and a steady and skillful hand had enabled her to effect what the people had pronounced miraculous cures. The present case was a peculiarly difficult one, and she was closely absorbed in the work before her, when some one standing near suddenly cried out:

"Listen, listen! Hear what they are saying out yonder! General Shiro and Bishop Paoli are killed!" and a wailing cry went up from all present.

Ine bent forward. The wounded man sitting before her told afterward how he feared she was about to fall across his disabled shoulder and how he threw up his unwounded arm to shield himself. But she did not fall. He saw her drop the bandages she was holding and twice or three times violently strike her breast with her clinched hands, her face meanwhile blanching to a death-iike paleness and her breath coming in quick, hard sobs. Then she seemed to recover herself and quietly proceeded to dress his wound.

The eyes of all present were turned upon her in sorrowful sympathy, and some of the weeping women came forward to comfort, as best they could, the one whose tenderly consoling words had so often fallen like balm into their own aching hearts. When she had finished her work upon the wounded soldier, Ine turned to one of the women that had been assisting her:

"I have placed all the bandages, Mine, and with careful nursing the wound will heal. Will you see that he has it? And Ichiji, yonder, needs some of that medicine I showed you yesterday; go, pray, to my room and get it for him," and the speaker made as if she would pass out.

"And you, Mistress Ine," said the woman, tearfully, "are you going to leave us?"

"I? Ah, yes, I—I think I will leave you;" the woman replied, a faint smile on her weary features—Ine seemed to have suddenly grown old:—"I must have some fresh air, I am suffocating here;" and with these words, she passed out and down into the open area in the first division of the castle.

The place was full of wounded soldiers and old men and youths discussing the terrible calamity. But it was already growing dark, and she passed through the midst of the excited throng without being recognized. Hastening on toward the gates, she met a youth with a *chochin** in his hand. She stopped and spoke to him:

"Friend, thou dost not need that *chochin* as much as I. Wilt thou give it to me?"

The boy raised his light and peered into her face. He recognized her, and, making a low bow, said:

"Ah, it is thou, Mistress Ine! Certainly, this poor *chochin* is thine, if thou wishest it. But, if it please thee to wait a moment, I shall get thee a better one." Then suddenly, as if recollecting himself: "Hast thou heard the news, Mistress Ine?"

"Yes, yes, I have heard. Thou needest not get another; this will do." And the woman hurried away, concealing the light of the *chochin* by wrapping her neckerchief about it.

At the gateway, there was another throng of men, but Ine, crouching in the shadow of the wall, waited until a party of wounded warriors came in from the plain. Then

* Paper lantern.

she darted past these and out upon the ridge. She ran on through the gathering blackness until she reached the plain, and there she paused. Where was she going? and for what? Her brain whirled; she was powerless to think. She sat down on a stone by the wayside, pressing her hands to her hot, tearless eyes.

"Oh! if I could only weep!" she moaned piteously. "Other women have tears; but I—merciful Father! my brain is on fire!"

The sound of approaching steps fell upon her ear. Two soldiers were returning from the field, and they were conversing together in sorrowful tones. Ine listened.

"Yes, it was a terrible sight," one was saying. "May the saints shield my eyes from another such! He was burned beyond recognition. I turned him over on his back, and there, closely clasped to his bosom, was this gold crucifix."

The woman rose, and, bending forward, strained her eyes through the darkness in the direction of the approaching figures. The other man now spoke:

"It is the cross that Ine Tanaka gave him this morning, as he was going into the battle. I saw her as she dropped it to him from the top of the wall upon which she was sitting. All who saw their parting believed that they had renewed their betrothal. But now, alas,—"

Ine waited to hear no more. She knew now why she had come forth from the castle. She stepped forward, as the two men were passing her, and, uncovering her *chochin*, flashed its light into their faces.

"Friends," she panted breathlessly, "I pray you give me the cross. I am she to whom it belongs. And tell me, where can I find him?"

"Ine Tanaka! thou here?" exclaimed the man whom

STANDING CALMLY ERECT, SHE SWUNG THE LANTERN ABOVE HER HEAD.—*See Page* 420.

she had first heard speaking. "Here's the crucifix, mistress; woeful tidings it brings back to thee!"

The woman scarcely heard him. She had greedily seized the cross and was passionately pressing it to her heart.

"His body—where is it" she demanded.

"Yonder to the right of those fires," said the other soldier, pointing to where the smoldering ruins of Nabeshima's camp still sent up fitful flashes into the night. "Hundreds of our brethren are there searching for the bishop's body. But, surely, Mistress Ine, you are not going—"

"I must go! I must go, where he is?" the woman cried wildly, and before the men could protest, she had darted off into the darkness.

Ine again concealed her *cochin* as she hurried toward the distant lights. All about her the plain seemed to be full of men shouting to one another, but whether they were friends or foes, she knew not. As she ran on, her lips moved in audible prayer:

"Dear Father in Heaven! Let me live until I reach his side! I am weak; my heart is so heavy, it burdens me as I run! Give me strength to endure a little longer!"

Then she remembered how she and Shiro had parted in the morning, and the words of the soldier she had just passed rose in her mind.

"I was right," she murmured softly, a smile of ineffable peace transfiguring her countenance. "He had in his heart come back to me. Others who beheld our parting thought us lovers. Father in Heaven! I thank thee for this! It will sweeten death."

She had now reached the battle-field, and in her blind haste, she stumbled over a dead body. As she fell, her face come in contact with that of the corpse, and its coldness, sent a chill to her heart. With a shiver, she slowly rose and resumed her way, this time at a rapid walk.

The number of the dead increased as she advanced ; for she was now traversing that portion of the field where, early in the day, Kuroda's retainers had so gallantly defended their camp against the assault of Oyana and his Christians. Suddenly, the woman felt a great horror seize upon her, and she stopped. At her feet lay a fallen warrior, his armor and clothing burned away ; and Ine Tanaka remembered the words of the soldier she had met: "He was burned beyond recognition." Could it be that this charred and loathsome thing before her was what she had come forth to seek? She would have knelt by the corpse to examine it more closely had she not just then become conscious of a heavy, trampling sound ahead of her—at first, distant, but rapidly drawing nearer ; and, as it approached, the woman recognized it to be the quick beating of horses' feet upon the frozen ground. She looked up, and could distinguish a dark line along the crest of the hill above her, and between her and the distant fires. It was a large body of mounted soldiers, riding with furious speed straight down upon her. Then Ine Tanaka knew what her fate was to be. She made no attempt to escape ; any such effort would have been futile.

"I would have had it otherwise," she said in her heart ; and then, audibly, as she pressed the crucifix fondly to her lips : "But Thy will, O Father—not mine !"

Drawing her garments closely about her, the woman again looked in the direction of the swiftly approaching troop. As she did this she bethought herself of the *chochin*. Hastily uncovering this and standing calmly erect, she swung the lantern above her head. A loud cry arose from the lips of the foremost rider, as he saw the light almost beneath him. The next instant his horse had bounded past the woman, the rider's foot, however, striking her shoulder and hurling her upon her back. In the very shadow of death, Ine's mind suddenly became clear and preternaturally active. Strange, incongruous images danced before her eyes in the brief interval between the horse that had already dashed over her and the one that followed hard after. She clasped the crucifix closely to her heart. "Saviour Jesu, take me!" she prayed, and then she looked up. Over her hung the huge, dark form of the second horse, his forefeet plunging down upon her breast. Her *chochin*, which the heels of the other steed had dashed out of her hand, had been hurled against the rider above her, and as the candle blazed up fiercely for an instant, its light fell upon the face of Nabeshima, Prince of Kai; and, in the passing flash, Ine Tanaka saw that he had seen and recognized her.

And then the light in the *chochin* went out forever.

IX.

ALAS, TOO LATE!

The consternation that had spread like wild-fire through the ranks of the Christian army over the supposed discovery of Shiro's body gave no signs of abating after the men had scattered far and wide through the ruined camp of the enemy in search of their dead bishop. Night came on, and still the Christians continued to grope about among the slain, bending down and peering into the face of each corpse to discover if its features were those of him whom they sought. Then there arose, in the darkness beyond them, a wild clamor of yells and fierce, exulting cries.

"Hear that!" exclaimed Oyano. "Hear that! What does it mean?"

"It means," said Ashizuka, a grim look of despair upon his battle-scarred visage, "that Matsudaira and his army have heard of the death of Shiro and Paoli, and have also learned of the panic and disorder into which we have been thrown. In a short time, they will be upon us."

"Heaven help us!" groaned Chijiwa. "So near to victory as were we, and now on the brink of utter destruction!"

"Something must be done!" Ashizuka cried, wildly. "*Yaso-Maria*, comrades! our wives, our little ones—shall we thus easily yield them a prey to yonder butchers? Oyano, ride thou in that direction; and thou, Chijiwa, spur to the left. I shall take charge of those directly before us. Let us make one more desperate effort to rally the men. Haste ye! haste ye, comrades! Hear ye not that? It is the enemy already in motion! Woe! Woe!"

Fortunately for the three intrepid leaders, who now again threw themselves into the midst of the Christians in an endeavor to call them off from their mad, fruitless search, the soldiers, also, had heard the wild shouts in the direction of the government troops, and were themselves anxiously inquiring of one another what it might mean. When the voices of their leaders, therefore, warned them of their approaching peril, and called upon them to fall in line and to retreat to the shelter of the castle, their words were listened to with close attention, and soon something like order began to appear among the broken and dispersed troops. But in the panic, many of the men had thrown away their guns and spears, and some even their swords, and the work of dividing the soldiers into companies was retarded by the search for weapons.

In the meantime, Nabeshima's troop of horse had thundered past them, followed closely by the remainder of his division on foot, and the Christian leaders knew that the wily Prince of Kai was hurrying his force into a position where he could cut off their retreat to their castle. Shortly afterward, and before they had finished marshaling their men into divisions, they suddenly found themselves assailed by an overwhelmingly large body of troops from Matsudaira's army. Outnumbered more than four to one, the Christians, despite their stubborn resistance, were slowly swept backward down the sloping hill-side, across the plain in the direction of their fortress, and right upon the swords of the eight thousand men of Kai, drawn up before the ridge leading to the castle.

"*Yaso-taiji!*"[*] rose the savage war-cry of Nabeshima's retainers, in the face of the devoted Christians, "*Yaso-taiji!*" rolled back the mad echo, from the thousands of the infidel closing in upon either flank and pressing upon them from the rear.

And then the slaughter, grim, merciless and terrible!

X.

AN UNEXPECTED MEETING.

In the shadow of a small grove of camphor-trees, near where the ridge before Hara Castle joined the open plain, Marmion Beaumont and the thousand mounted warriors of Kai were silently awaiting the coming of Shiro and Paoli from Unzen. It was here that Ando had said the

[*] Down with the Christian.

terrible Gonroku and his band of desperadoes were lying in ambush; but the Englishman and the men placed under his command had been unable to discover their whereabouts, and the heart of the lover sank with anxious forebodings lest the robbers were planning to attack Shiro's party at some point nearer the mountains.

The night had now fully come, and in the dense darkness it was impossible to distinguish objects farther than a spear's length from the eye. Beaumont dismounted, and giving his horse into the charge of a soldier, moved across the plain in the direction of Unzen, hoping that he might be able to hear the approach of Una and her captors. As he neared the foothills he paused and listened; but the battle was now raging on the plain, between the Christians and the government troops, and the uproar of the conflict together with the shrieking of the wind, which was blowing a fierce gale, filled the air with a deafening clamor. Just then a vivid flash of lightning flamed across the sky, and this was followed by a heavy peal of thunder that reverberated back and forth among the mountains in successive crashes of sound. The Englishman felt a few heavy drops of rain dashed into his face. Then succeeded a momentary lull that was broken by another blinding flash, with its accompanying roar of thunder, and then the rain poured down in stifling torrents; the storm, that had so long been gathering, now burst with all the sudden fury of a tornado.

"What a night!" groaned the Englishman, retracing his steps in the direction of the camphor-grove. "And thou, my Una, my poor darling, where art thou? In the hands of thy father's murderers, wandering with them upon the mountains and exposed to this bitter tempest? or, Father in Heaven, forbid it! art thou already fallen into the power of that robber-fiend? O, Una, Una, how gladly I would die for thee, my darling, and yet, how powerless I am to stand between thee and thy foes! Would to God I knew where I might seek thee!"

Again the lightning blazed out, and in the vivid glare, the mountains and the plain, the war-junks and the tall masts of the *Spuyten Duyvil* on the bay, the walls of the beleagured castle, the desolated camp of the infidel and the heavy masses of fighting men beyond the camphor-grove were all revealed in startling distinctness. Despite the tempest that beat upon the heads of the combatants, the conflict raged with an ever-increasing fury, and the uproar of battle swelled loud above the bellowing of the storm.

"Beaumont! Heer Beaumont!" The Englishman started. Surely some one was calling his name. He listened, and again a voice rose to him out of the blackness to his left: "Mynheer Beaumont!" The young man, straining his eyes in the direction whence came the sound, shouted back:

"Who art thou?"

"Van Sylt," came the clear response, and the figure of a man loomed up through the darkness.

"'Sdeath! Van Sylt!" exclaimed Beaumont, forgetting for the instant the anxious fear that tortured him, in his amazement at this unexpected appearance of the first officer of the *Spuyten Duyvil*. "Thou here, and at such a time as this! Man, art thou mad?"

"Not mad, Mynheer," the other replied. "Hast thou forgotten what once I told thee on the deck of our ship in Nagasaki Bay?"

"Ah, I remember. The day after that dreadful massacre on Takaboka you told me that you had made a vow never again to stand by and to behold Christians slaughtered by the infidel without drawing sword in their defense."

"Mynheer Beaumont, what is happening yonder to-night? Has not the time come for me to keep my vow?"

"Alas! Van Sylt, you cannot help them. You only throw away your own life."

"So be it. I shall die with them. Speak no more, Mynheer; expostulation is useless. Van Neist and his men tried it before I left the *Spuyten Duyvil*. I shall keep the vow I have registered in Heaven. But, how is it that I find thee here and alone?"

The Englishman, seeing the uselessness of any further attempt to dissuade the officer from his purpose, briefly informed him of the events of the day and the present condition of affairs.

"Can it be possible that Paoli, whom all these years I have revered as a saint, has thus fallen!" cried Van Sylt, utterly overwhelmed by the information he had received. "Mynheer Beaumont, had any other man said what you have just told me, I would have drawn sword upon him. But something in my heart tells me I must believe you, that all you say is the truth."

The unhappy officer had thrown himself upon the ground.

"Go, Mynheer, go; leave me!" he cried, brokenly. "What you have said stuns me. I would be alone. Go, and Heaven grant that your loved one be restored to you; but go, go!"

"Farewell, then!" the Englishman responded, bending down and wringing the officer's hand. "I would say more, Van Sylt, but my own heart is too full;" and choking back the sobs that already shook his voice, Beaumont plunged down the hill-side in the direction of the camphor-grove. Here upon his arrival, he found Nabeshima anxiously awaiting him.

"Ye gods! Master Beaumont," the prince exclaimed with a deep sigh of relief, "we were becoming alarmed, about you."

"O Prince!" cried the Englishman, and his voice sounded like a wail. "This suspense is killing me! It drove me forth to seek her; it has brought me back despairing of ever beholding her face again." Then, as if suddenly recollecting himself, the speaker put out his hand and laid it on Nabeshima's arm. "Pardon me, dear friend," he continued, gently. "My own great sorrow has made me forgetful of thine. I remember we all rode hither and left thee alone there on the hill-side—alone with her—"

He said no more, for a dazzling flash lit up Nabeshima's face, and in the awful anguish written there, Beaumont read the terrible truth. The prince spoke:

"She was still alive, Master Beaumont, when, springing from my saddle, I hurried to her side. My horse had struck her breast, the blood was flowing from her mouth, and, as I raised her up, I saw that she had but a moment to live. She looked up into my face and recognized me. 'Was it thou who killed him?' she whispered faintly. I knew whom she meant, and answered: 'No, no! I did not kill him! I could not tell her that he was alive and false to her. My tears fell upon her face. Ine! Ine!' I cried, and could say no more. Again the eyes of the dying woman sought mine. 'Do not sorrow,' she murmured, almost inaudibly. 'Thou art not to blame for this, and, thank God! thou art not his slayer! I die happy!' and with a peaceful smile upon her features, she sank back lifeless in my arms."

None other knew so well, as did Marmion Beaumont,

Nabeshima's love for Ine Tanaka. In their conversations together, the prince had often spoken of it, and he had never given up the hope that, in the general destruction which he knew would soon befall the Christians, he might be able to save her, and that some time she would yet be his wife. And now, instead of being her deliverer, it had been through him she had met her death.

The two men stood side by side for a time, the emotions that filled the hearts of both forbidding speech. Nabeshima was the first to break the silence :

" I must go, Master Beaumont. My troops, under the command of my chief officer, are performing prodigies of valor, and duty calls me to their side. I shall leave you a hundred of these mounted warriors. With these wait here and have hope."

"How goes the battle, Prince?" inquired the Englishman, as his companion vaulted into the saddle. " But why do I say battle?" he continued sadly. "It is now nothing more than a massacre."

In the darkness, the speaker could not see the expression of pain and displeasure that clouded Nabeshima's face, but he was conscious of a coldness in the tone of his reply :

"Not massacre, but execution, I pray you, friend. Remember, that we are dealing with men guilty of treason against the government of our nation. As such, they deserve death, and what form of death ought to be more acceptable to them than to fall, as they are falling to-night, with swords in their hands and the opportunity given them of selling their lives dearly. But let me tell you," he added, in a serious but more friendly tone, " the Christians are yet far from being conquered. They stand out yonder in a solid square, and, like lions at bay, give thrust for thrust and blow for blow," and with these words, the prince, followed by all his mounted warriors, save the hundred he had assigned to Beaumont, dashed off in the direction of the conflict.

XI.

RETRIBUTION.

Under the cover of some rocks a short distance beyond the place where Marmion Beaumont had met the first officer of the *Spuyten Duyvil*, five men were sheltering themselves, as best they could, from the violence of the storm. As the lightning, flaming across the sky, blazed in their desperate-looking faces, it revealed among them the brutal features of Gonroku the outlaw. The gang had first taken up their position at the point where the little hunchback had seen them; but the coming of Nabeshima's mounted troop had caused them to withdraw to a place of greater safety. Here, by the side of a deep gorge, they were awaiting the coming of Shiro and his party.

"Eh, comrades!" roared the harsh voice of the robber-chief, as the thunder burst with a deafening peal above their heads, "what think ye of this? A fine night for the wooing of the maid of Unzen! By the tooth of Buddha! the bride tarries too long. Ah!" he exclaimed, as another flash revealed the figure of a man hastening down the rocks toward them, "here comes Gohei! We'll see if he brings us tidings of our fair one."

In another minute, Gohei was among them.

"They are coming, Gonroku!" he shouted breathlessly; "and, by my sword! had we arranged their order of march to suit our purpose, we could not have done better than they have."

"And the barbarian priest, Paoli—saw you him?" cried the gang, with one voice.

"He was nowhere to be seen. I waited and watched, but, though flash after flash made the whole gorge as clearly visible as in broad day, yet I saw nothing of him. You remember we heard that he and Shiro fought at the hermitage. It is likely, therefore, he is returning to the castle alone, and by another route."

"Now Buddha grant that your surmise be correct;" growled Gonroku. "Rather had I loose Una of Unzen than risk an encounter with that big barbarian!"

"Silence all!" commanded Gohei, in a warning voice. "Methought I saw them in that blaze that just passed over us." Then, as another flash lit up the road that ran past their place of ambush, he called back to the others: "They come!"

With the next gleam of the lightning, the robbers beheld Shiro's party slowly approaching them. First came about a score of the body-guard, the horses carefully picking their way among the rocks that just here encumbered the road, and the riders bent forward over their saddle-bows to shield their faces from the fury of the storm. Behind these, and at a considerable distance from them, they saw Shiro, and close by his side rode Una Mori. After these, five or six men, armed merely with swords, brought up the rear.

Gonroku and his band waited until those in advance had passed by, and then, as Una's horse came opposite their place of concealment, they sprang forth to the attack. Their work was swift and terrible. The well-nigh constant glare of the lightning guided their blows: the suddenness of their onslaught made defense impossible. With a hollow groan, Shiro, stricken to the heart by the sword of Gonroku, clutched frantically at his saddle bow and then plunged heavily to the earth. The other Christians sank as quickly beneath the blades of the outlaw's companions. Una's terrified shriek, as she caught sight of the robber-chief, was the only cry that rose from the doomed little company, and her voice was drowned in the mad roar of the gale. Unconscious of the fate that had overtaken their friends, the advance-guard pushed steadily on through the blinding storm that beat into their faces; before them, death in the plain, and death in the mountain pass behind them.

XII.

"PAOLI TO THE RESCUE!"

When Nabeshima told the Englishman that the Christians were fighting like lions at bay, he did not at all exaggerate the stubborn fury with which the insurgents were meeting the assault of their enemies, who now surrounded them on every side. There was no trace of the panic and terror that but an hour or so before had possessed them. All that had passed away, and they were again the indomitable warriors that so often in times past had carried destruction into the ranks of the infidel. True, on former occasions, they had been inspired by the courage born of the hope that, in the end, their cause would triumph. No such feelings animated them now. Their present desperate valor sprang from despair and the grim determination to slay as many as possible before they themselves were slain. In the frequent flashes that lit up the dismal scene of death about them, they at times raised their eyes to the walls of the castle so near to them, yet so inaccessible, and, in their hearts, they bade an everlasting farewell to the wives and mothers whose pale faces they beheld looking down upon them.

And thus they fought on, forgetful of hunger and weariness, oblivious of the warring skies above them; oblivious of the piles of ghastly slain fast heaping up beneath their feet, conscious only of that encircling line of gleaming swords that with irresistible steadiness drew closer and closer about them. First Chijiwa fell, and then the brave Oyano. Komekine was dragged back mortally wounded into the center of the square, and still Ashizuka's battle-cry of "*Yaso-Maria*" thrilled the hearts of the survivors and nerved their arms to fight. Dashing hither and thither like a madman, he dealt death wheresoever he directed his headlong course, himself seeming to bear a charmed life among the countless weapons of the foe leveled against him.

But hark! what was that cry that rose, like a wail of terror, loud above the mingled thunders of storm and battle? Ashizuka's horse reared back upon his haunches, so suddenly did the rider rein him in. Could it be that he heard aright? Again the cry rang out, and in the light shed from the blazing skies, Ashizuka, rising in his saddle, looked over the dense ranks of the foe in the direction of the mountains, and his heart leaped into his throat. There, plunging through the press, and aiming his course straight toward the Christians, came a mounted warrior, clad from head to foot in foreign mail, a ponderous battle-ax circling about his head and falling with swift and terrible blows upon the infidel. A moment Ashizuka looked, and then, like the peal of a trumpet, his voice rang out above the din of war and shriek of wind:

"Paoli to the rescue! Paoli! Paoli!"

Friend and foe alike heard the words, and for one

WITH A WILD SHRIEK, PAOLI DROPPED HIS AX AND, REELING IN HIS SADDLE, FELL.—*See Page* 440.

breathless moment both Christian and infidel stayed their swords.

"Paoli comes to our rescue! *Yaso-Maria!* Paoli! Paoli!" shouted the veteran chieftain, as he dashed through the midst of the ranks of the insurgents.

Still the hostile lines, facing each other, with but a sword's length between, remained motionless. The announcement that Paoli was still alive—that he was even then in the field—filled the despairing hearts of the Christians with a new hope, and paralyzed with terror the souls of the infidel. Just then a burst of flame darted across the heavens, and in the dazzling light all beheld the tall form of the Jesuit, now almost at the side of the Christians. Before the lightning flashed forth again, he was among them, and friend and foe heard the tiger-roar of his voice:

"Ho, Swords of the Church, my children! To the castle! To the castle! Upon the idolaters and through their ranks to the shelter of your walls! *Yaso-Maria!* Charge them in the name of Holy Cross!"

A fierce shout went up from the lips of the Christians, and, with the sword of Ashizuka and the ax of Paoli before them, they flung themselves with irresistible fury upon Nabeshima and his retainers, who were drawn up between them and the castle.

In vain the heroic Prince of Kai commanded, exhorted, threatened; his troops shrank back from the presence of the terrible Jesuit and parted right and left, leaving the road over the ridge open to the retreating Christians. Finding all his efforts to hold his men firm before their enemies to be fruitless, Nabeshima spurred his horse forward along the ridge and through the midst of the insurgents until he overtook Bishop Paoli.

"Accursed barbarian!" he shouted, "not for those

thou hast slain in battle, but for thy murder of a helpless old man, my cousin, Lord Mori of Unzen, I call thee to account."

As he spoke, his heavy sword flashed down upon the helmeted head of the Jesuit. Paoli was thrown violently forward upon his saddle-bow by the force of the stroke, and before he could recover himself, Nabeshima had dealt him another terrific blow upon his back, severing the lacings of his corselet, so that that part of his armor fell with a sharp clang to the ground, leaving his shoulders and breast without defense. But before the prince could raise his sword for another stroke, Paoli had wrenched his horse around, and, rising in his saddle, swung his ponderous ax above his head. Knowing how vain it would be to endeavor to parry the coming blow with his sword, Nabeshima threw his horse back upon his haunches, and the deadly blow that would have cloven the rider to the teeth, falling short of him, descended upon the neck of the steed, almost severing the head from the body. With a frantic leap forward, the wounded brute swayed back and forth for an instant on the brink of the steep slope, and, before Nabeshima realized his peril, horse and rider were plunging downward through the darkness into the miry morass below. With an exultant laugh, Paoli turned to Ashizuka and shouted through the storm:

"God has avenged himself upon that atheist, the archenemy of his people. *Yaso-Maria!* that was the best blow I ever struck in the name of the Cross. Heed it not," he continued, as his companion dismounted to pick up the fallen corselet, "our holy cause shall be my breast-plate. Ashizuka, lead thou our brethren into the shelter of their walls. I go to the help of those in the rear, who are still struggling against the heathen;"

and, saying this, Paoli dashed off along the ridge and out upon the plain, where Ogasawara and his veterans still maintained a desperate onslaught upon the Christians.

"Upon them, soldiers of the cross!" roared now the voice of Paoli in the ears of the brave little band. "Saints and angels are our defense in this holy war. Charge them anew, warriors of the Lord! Woe to the infidel!"

With redoubled efforts, the Christians responded to the call of the Jesuit, and the resolute impetuosity of their charge, together with the terror Paoli inspired among the foe, drove the Satsuma men back across the plain into the ruined camp.

"To the castle now, my brethren, while the way is clear!" again rang out the commanding voice of Paoli, and in obedience to his order, the Christians fell back upon the ridge, the government troops not venturing a pursuit.

XIII.

AT LAST.

Resting his ax upon the saddle-bow, Bishop Paoli reined in his steed and waited until the last Christian had passed by. For a time he remained there as if plunged in deep thought. Then, as he finally turned his horse's head in the direction of the castle, he became aware of some one riding toward him, and, by the flash of lightning that a moment after lit up the scene, he recognized the approaching horseman to be Marmion Beaumont.

"Murderer!" cried the Englishman, hoarsely, as he drew rein by the Jesuit's side, "where is Una Mori?"

"Holy Cross! Señor Beaumont, thou here?" exclaimed the bishop, in astonishment and with an evident desire to be cordial. Then he added, in a grieved tone: "Thou here, and with a naked sword in thy hand and curses for an old friend upon thy lips!"

"No friend of thine, thou slayer of the helpless! but the avenger of those thou hast destroyed! Again I ask thee, where is Lord Mori's daughter?"

Paoli's voice and manner suddenly became coldly constrained and defiant. He spoke slowly, and his eyes blazed with the contained but terrific rage that filled his soul:

"If thou wouldst know where Lord Mori's daughter is, find and ask Nirado Shiro. Perchance, before this, she and her lover have fallen into the hands of the heathen; if so, her's shall be the fate that our Christian maidens have ever suffered from the idolaters. Perchance, they have escaped into the castle; if so, let her tremble. For such as she, Holy Church has her—ha!"

With a smothered cry of rage, Beaumont had struck out at the Jesuit, but in the darkness, with only the sound of the speaker's voice to guide his thrust, he merely grazed Paoli's shoulder; but when the lightning again blazed forth, the two men stood face to face in mortal combat.

It did not take the Jesuit long to discover that he had at last met a foeman fully his equal in both strength and skill, even when he was at his best; but now, wearied with the toils of the long day, and dazed and wounded by the two heavy blows Nabeshima had given him, he was no match for the enraged Englishman, whose fresh young vigor from the first held him at a disadvantage. The loss of his steel corselet, moreover, exposed him to the keen, quick thrusts of his opponent's sword, which he was obliged to parry, as best he might, with his heavy battle-ax, nor did he dare to raise his weapon from its position of guard long enough to strike a blow.

Yet, with the odds thus against him, Francesco Paoli crowded in upon his foe, with a quiet persistence, that brought the cold sweat to the brow of the younger man. Beaumont knew that it was the Jesuit's purpose to press close enough upon him to render his long sword useless for a thrust, and then to smite him down with his ax. Only by a continual backward movement could the Englishman hope to baffle Paoli's intention and to weary him by keeping him constantly on the defensive. The almost unbroken glare of the lightning gave neither an opportunity for such stratagem as an appreciable interval of darkness might have afforded; and thus, for several minutes, the ill-matched weapons rang quick and sharp together as the two combatants, in their constant change of position, described a narrow circle, the Jesuit always creeping in upon Beaumont and the latter cautiously falling back, so as to keep his sword-point trembling before the breast of his foe.

But the fresh strength of the Englishman soon began to prevail over the exhausted energy of the elder man. Paoli gradually ceased his unavailing effort to crowd in upon his enemy and recognized himself as lost. His breath came in quick, sobbing gasps; he was bleeding profusely from a number of ugly wounds; his strength seemed to be fast leaving him, and, for the first time in his life, Francesco Paoli's face grew pallid with fear. Just then the lightning died out from the sky and the utter blackness of night fell upon the combatants. Summoning all his failing powers to a last effort, the Jesuit raised his ax to venture a blow in the darkness; but at the very instant his weapon was poised above his head, another flash overspread the sky, and, swift as the lightning itself, Marmion Beaumont's sword darted forward straight upon the defenseless breast before him, and, with a wild shriek, Paoli dropped his ax and reeling in his saddle fell heavily to the earth.

Strange to say, at the very moment of his victory, the Englishman underwent a violent change of feeling. The mad anger and fury with which he had assailed the Jesuit died out of his heart as soon as he beheld his foe at his feet, and a touch of the old-time awe and reverence took its place. Trembling in every limb, and with a face pale as death, he sprang from his horse and knelt by the side of the prostrate man. Paoli's clothes were soaked with blood, his face was bloody, and blood was flowing from a deep wound in his right side. Beaumont placed his ear to the Jesuit mouth; there was no sound of breathing. He tore open his clothing; the heart was still.

"He is dead!" cried the Englishman, aghast. "He is dead! He, who so long has been the fear of this nation, upon whose head a price has been set, he, who for years, has been hunted like a wild beast, has fallen! Strange, that, after all his perils and escapes among this people, he should at last perish by one of his own race; strangest of all, that I should have been his slayer;" and the speaker bowed his head in silent thought.

XIV.

JOYFUL TIDINGS.

A shout from the direction of the camphor-grove roused Beaumont from the reverie into which he had fallen and called him to his feet. The mounted soldiers that Nabeshima had given him were searching for him; he heard them shouting his name.

Without scarcely knowing what he was doing, the young Englishman picked up Paoli's ax and hurried off to rejoin his men. As he drew near the grove, he met two soldiers.

"Our entire force is scattered over the plain in search of you, *Sensei*," cried one breathlessly. "We have good news: the young woman has been found."

Beaumont staggered as if he was about to fall; the suddenness with which the announcement had been made overwhelmed him. Then, with a loud, sobbing cry, he sprang forward:

"Heaven be praised! Where is she?"

"We carried her to a little hut down by the sea-shore," replied the soldier. "Come with me; I shall conduct you thither." Then, turning to his companion, the speaker continued: "Comrade, go thou and call off the men from the search; tell them that the *Sensei* has been found."

The man then asked Beaumont to dismount, as the quickest road to the hut, he said, was a mere footpath through the morass. Leaving his horse, therefore, in the charge of the other soldier, the Englishman followed his guide toward the ridge, passing over the ground where, but a short time before, Christian and infidel had met in desperate battle.

"Tell me, friend," said Beaumont, anxiously, as the two hurried on their way: "Is Lord Mori's daughter unharmed?" He would have said more, but his voice choked. Fearing the worst, he dreaded to hear the answer to his question.

"She is unharmed, *Sensei*, except as the terrible experiences of the day and exposure to this storm have prostrated her. She was unconscious when we met the foreigner from the ship bringing her—"

"What's that you say," cried Beaumont. "A foreigner from the *Spuyten Duyvil*—and with Una Mori? What do you mean?"

"Why, you see, *Sensei*," said the soldier, in explanation, "a few of us, perhaps ten or twelve, set out for Unzen in order to discover, if possible, the whereabouts of the young woman and her captors. A little beyond here, we met this foreigner coming this way, and carrying Lord Mori's daughter in his arms. The man was mortally wounded, and lived only a short time after we brought him and the girl to the hut. Who he is, or how he came to find the young woman, or how he met his death, I know not."

"Una can tell me all," mused the young Englishman, half aloud. "The foreigner this man speaks of can be none other than Van Sylt. But how came he to rescue my poor darling? Can it be that he turned his sword upon Shiro and his Christians, the very ones to whose assistance he had come?"

The two men had now descended the steep slope upon the northern side of the ridge, and were just entering the path that led across the morass to the beach, when a cry rose to them out of the darkness to their right:

"Help! help! Master Beaumont, help!"

"Merciful Heaven!" exclaimed the Englishman. "It is Prince Nabeshima's voice? Ho, Prince! where are you?"

Beaumont heard a low laugh.

"Here, Master Beaumont, almost buried in this half-frozen mud, and with a dead horse upon me," came back the reply.

Before the prince had finished speaking, the two men

were at his side, and their combined strength soon rolled the dead steed off the prostrate rider.

"Ye gods!" cried the prince, as the Englishman helped him to his feet; "the brute held my legs as fast as if they had been caught in a trap. I struggled for a time to free myself, until finding all my efforts useless, I had settled down to rest for the night. Then, in a flash of lightning, I beheld you approaching, and glad enough I was to see you, for I was becoming horribly cold."

"You have not yet told us how you came into such a plight," said Beaumont. "One would think that you had been exchanging courtesies with Paoli."

"Excellent guesser!" Nabeshima replied laughingly, and he proceeded to inform his companion of his encounter with the Jesuit. "By my life!" he said in conclusion, "I wish no more such rides as the one I had down this slope. Yet I am thankful that I escaped so lightly; save a few bruises and a little stiffness in the legs, I am as well as ever."

Beaumont, as the lightning flashed out, held up the battle-ax.

"Ah! how came you by that?" cried the prince, as his eyes fell upon the bloody weapon.

"By the right of a victor," responded the Englishman, gravely. "Prince, Francesco Paoli is dead;" and the young man told Nabeshima the story of the duel.

"Well done, my friend!" exclaimed the excited prince. "You cannot realize the greatness of the service which you have rendered Japan. But I shall make it my care, Master Beaumont, that our obligation to you shall be fittingly acknowledged by our rulers. You deserve—"

"Nay, nay, say no more," returned the other, again falling into the depression he had felt when he first realized that he had slain the Jesuit. "I most heartily regret my act, Prince. But now, do you lean on my arm, and let us be going. You have not yet heard, my friend, the one glad message in all the heavy tidings of this melancholy night. Una Mori has been found," and once more followed the recital of facts with which the reader is already acquainted.

Arriving at the hut, whither the soldiers had borne the rescued girl, the prince paused at the door, and calling out the man who was watching within, said to the young Englishman:

"My friend, thine is the place by the side of my cousin to comfort her in this sad hour of trial and bereavement. Go and remain with her. We shall make preparations to take you both off to the *Spuyten Duyvil*," and pressing Beaumont's hand, Nabeshima, accompanied by the two soldiers, passed on to the beach.

An hour later, in the occasional flashes of lightning that still blazed forth from the departing storm, a small *sampan* might have been seen pushing out from the shore and heading toward the foreign ship. Three stout *sendos* stood by the oars, and in the bow of the boat sat Marmion Beaumont and Una Mori. Both were silent, for their hearts were too full for words. Before them lay the *Spuyten Duyvil*, an ark of peaceful shelter that was to bear them away from the midst of the horrors that now encompassed them to a happy home amid the green fields of far-off England. Upon their right rose the beleaguered walls of Hara Castle, and behind them the plain of the Christians stretched away in the darkness. There, under cover of the night, lay the multitude of the dead; and among the lifeless, thousands of wounded warriors, helpless and forsaken, moaned piteously in their pain. And as through the long, weary hours they lay there, praying —the Christian to his saints, the heathen to his gods— silent and unseen, to hundreds of both believers and infidels came the merciful Angel of Death.

BOOK TWELFTH.

THE LIGHT GOES OUT IN DARKNESS.

I.

A VICTORY THAT WAS ALMOST DEFEAT.

IT was not until late in the day following the great battle of the tenth of March, that Matsudaira obtained a full report of the losses which his army had sustained during the Christians' assault upon his camp, and in the night engagement before Hara Castle. Seven princes, a hundred and thirty-one captains and nearly eighteen thousand soldiers had been left dead upon the field, and the number of the wounded was very large. In addition to this heavy loss of life, was the destruction of the greater portion of the camp, including the large storehouses filled with food and munitions of war. As if to increase the distress and suffering among the government troops, the weather suddenly became intensely cold, with a freezing rain and keen, high winds. The men, half-fed and many of them scantily clothed and unprovided with any protection against the storm, complained bitterly, and, finally, grew so insubordinate, that all the tact and authority of their leaders could scarcely keep them from disbanding and seeking food and shelter in Nagasaki and Shimabara.

Had the condition of affairs in the infidel army been known in the castle, it might have been possible for Ashizuka and the surviving Christians to have again fallen upon the foe with well-grounded hope of winning a decisive victory. But the thought of ever again leaving their walls had no longer any place in the minds of the insurgents. Although their losses in the battle had been considerably less than half that of Matsudaira's army, yet with them there were none to come forward to fill the places of the dead, while the entire nation stood ready to reenforce the ranks of their foes. Then, too, Paoli, Shiro, Chijiwa, Oyano and Komekine had fallen; the castle was filled with disabled and dying men, and, even with their reduced numbers, their stores would soon utterly fail them. The Christians, therefore, recognized themselves to be irretrievably doomed; and, to their eternal honor, let it be said, that never in the annals of heroic fidelity and endurance has there been shown greater fortitude or more tranquil resignation than that displayed by the twenty thousand men and women within the walls of Hara Castle. Death had lost all terror to them; they were even impatient to have the long, bloody tragedy come to an end. Their stern resolution was to defy their enemies to the last, and, when the inevitable hour of their destruction had come, to sell their lives dearly, falling in honorable battle and dying as they had lived, true to their faith.

II.

THE PRINCE OF KAI ASTONISHES MARMION BEAUMONT.

Toward the evening of the day of which we have been speaking, the Prince of Kai paid a visit to the *Spuyten Duyvil*. Marmion Beaumont and our old friend Captain Jansen Van Neist met him at the gangway, and, after an interchange of greeting, Nabeshima inquired concerning his cousin Una Mori.

"She is resting, Prince," the Englishman returned. "Alas, poor girl! Yesterday's horrors have prostrated her, and it will be many days, I fear, before she is herself again."

Nabeshima's face showed the deep concern he felt.

"Let us be thankful," he said, consolingly, "that we have her with us at all. When I reflect upon the terrible perils that threatened her, and her wonderful deliverance, my heart is filled with gratitude to the merciful Providence that shielded her and has given her to us again. But, Master Beaumont, you have already heard from

Una, I presume, the story of her rescue?" and the prince turned a questioning look upon the Englishman.

"Yes," replied the other, "I have heard all. It seems that after I left Van Sylt last night, he wandered off in the direction of the mountains, possibly in the hope of meeting Shiro and Paoli. However that may be, he chanced upon Gonroku and his band just after they had cut down the young Christian chieftain and his companions. The brave fellow at once threw himself upon the outlaws, determined either to rescue Una, or to perish in the effort. Gonroku's party evidently thought he was Paoli, for they shouted the Jesuit's name and three of them fled. The other three, however, gave battle, and though Van Sylt slew them all, he himself was mortally wounded. With the rest of the story—how some of your retainers, Prince, found the gallant officer and Una, and how Van Sylt died shortly after reaching the hut—you are already acquainted."

"Gallant fellow!" exclaimed Nabeshima, deeply moved at what he had heard. "He well deserves the lasting and grateful remembrance, not only of you and me, Master Beaumont, for saving our Una from an unspeakable fate, but of the Japanese people as well, for two of the three robbers whom he killed were the most desperate outlaws that have ever cursed southern Japan—Gonroku and Gohei. Their bodies were found this afternoon, near the place where Shiro and his companions were lying. But, Captain Van Neist," and the prince turned to that person, "the remains of your officer are still at the hut; what disposal would you have made of them?"

"It was his wish," replied the burly captain, in a voice husky with emotion, "to die with the Christians; but it was not permitted him, it seems, to join them at all. I would suggest that he be buried upon the spot which his bravery has made sacred ; the spot where he rescued this young Christian woman, and avenged the death of his friend, Nirado Shiro."

"It shall be so," the prince responded, promptly. "And now, Master Beaumont, prepare yourself for a surprise," continued Nabeshima, again addressing his remarks to the young Englishman. "Last night you told me that you most heartily regretted having slain Francesco Paoli ; there is no more occasion for such regrets, because it now appears that you did not kill him at all."

"What !" cried Beaumont, excitedly. "Bishop Paoli not dead ?"

"Even so," Nabeshima replied, with a smile. "His armor was found to-day on the very spot, I presume, where you and he fought. A short distance away, the body of a camp-servant was discovered stripped of clothing. The belief among our officers is that the Jesuit, though severely wounded by you, revived after you left him, that he removed all his armor and clothing and dressed himself in the habit of the camp-servant, and that, thus disguised, he has either escaped to the castle or, perhaps, has sought refuge among some of the secretly Christian families of Shimabara Just as I was coming aboard, I heard that about daylight this morning the watch upon one of the war junks saw a *sampan* drifting by out to sea. There was a man in it, but he seemed to be either drunk or ill, for he was making no attempt to control the course of the boat. I am strongly persuaded this was Paoli. The wind would carry his *sampan* across the bay to Higo or Amakusa in a few hours, and once there, I doubt not that he could easily find a place of refuge."

It was with the greatest astonishment that Marmion Beaumont listened to what his friend was saying, and despite the wrong which the Jesuit had done to one that was nearest and dearest to him, he could not refrain from a feeling of gladness that, after all, perhaps, his hands were clean of the man's blood. But when he recollected all the details of that mortal struggle, and of his examination of the body, this theory of the bishop being still alive seemed madness to him.

"I would that I could believe with you, Prince, that Paoli is not dead, but that is impossible. Did I not pierce him through with my sword? Did I not examine his body carefully and find his heart to be as still as that of any corpse? No, Prince, I fear you are again falling a victim to the wiles of the Christians. It is to their interest to have you think the redoubtable Jesuit-warrior still alive. Therefore, when they found the body last night, they stripped it of its armor, and, leaving this and the naked corpse of the camp-servant close together that they might deceive you into believing that Paoli had revived and escaped, they took the remains of their bishop into the castle for burial. Nay, friend, I know that Francesco Paoli, when I left him last night, was a dead man."

Nabeshima had listened attentively.

"Your explanation, my friend, would be a very plausible one if it had been possible for any of the Christians to have issued from their stronghold during the night without being seen of our men. But a portion of Ogasawara's retainers encamped upon the ridge, thus rendering egress from the castle to the plain impossible. If, however, any of the Christians were left out upon the field, what you say might have been possible. They could have taken the body to the mountains and buried it there."

"What became of the advance portion of Shiro's bodyguard, which had passed by before Gonroku's band made their attack?"

"True, what did become of them?". assented the prince, musingly. "It is possible, but scarcely probable, that they escaped into the castle. They may have, indeed, found Paoli—but whether dead or alive, who can say?—and borne him away. When I came here, Master Beaumont, I was confident that our terrible enemy was still alive, but now your words incline me to think that he is dead. I fear we will never be able to reach a solution of this mystery."

III.

THE DAY DECREED BY DESTINY.

For nearly five weeks after the events narrated in the last few chapters, nothing of note occurred in the siege of Hara Castle. Matsudaira, despite the wishes of both officers and men to the contrary, stubbornly adhered to his policy of starving the beleaguered Christians into a surrender. Finally, on the eighth of April, General Hojo, Prince of Awa, arrived at Arima, and, in the name of the Shogun, assumed command of the besieging army, and his announcement that he would at once order an assault upon the Christian stronghold inspired the troops with intense enthusiasm.

The following three days were spent in preparation. The men were subjected to a thorough examination, and only the most able-bodied were chosen for the storming army

Six cannons were landed from the *Spuyten Duyvil*, and these, with a large number of guns of native manufacture, were placed in batteries erected at points as near as possible to the walls of the fortress. These were put under the command of Cruger, the second officer of the *Spuyten Duyvil*. Hojo had also the whole fleet of war-junks drawn up in a semicircle around the promontory on which stood the Christian castle, while the *Spuyten Duyvil* was stationed off its extreme point. On the evening of the eleventh of April everything was in readiness for storming the fortress on the following day.

The Christians were well aware of the intentions of their foes, and, though they knew that the morrow would witness the fall of their castle, they, nevertheless, made all possible provision for a desperate defense. The garrison still numbered nearly five thousand soldiers, survivors of the great battle of the tenth of March. In addition to these, old men and mere youths were now drilled into service, and hundreds of women also prepared to fight by the sides of their husbands and brothers. Thousands more of the women, during the three days of preparation, destroyed themselves and their children, preferring rather to die thus than to fall into the hands of a brutal and merciless soldiery. On the night before the assault, Ashizuka found that he had, all told, a force of nine thousand with which to defend the walls of the castle. Gathering his little army together, he addressed them :

"Friends and fellow-Christians, this is the last time I shall ever speak to you, for before the evening of another day, we all shall have entered the Paradise of our God. Let us die, then, so far as we can, the death of the warrior who falls in the fore-front of battle with his face to the foe. Let us die with calmness and resignation, as becometh the followers of the religion we profess. I see your weakness and I know your sufferings, because I, too, have hungered and suffered with you. It has been a long time since we knew what it is to have hunger satisfied. Many of us have eaten only sea-weed for the past six days. And now at last, when the end of this long agony is so near, when rest is in sight, shall we call it a misfortune? Nay, friends: let us meet the foe to-morrow as bravely as we have in the past; let us hide from him, if we can, our hunger and weakness; and let us welcome at last the blow that will end our sufferings and, though taking our lives, will give us rest."

That night but few slept in either army. Among the government troops, the excitement over their coming victory permitted none to sleep. Within the castle, causes, widely different from that which lent wakefulness to Hojo's soldiers, drove all slumber from the eyelids of the beleaguered garrison. Among these, and more potent than the pangs of hunger or the certainty of their own approaching doom, was the impending extirpation of their faith from the soil of their native land, that weighed heavily on every heart. Scattered here and there throughout the castle in little groups, the Christians spent the weary hours of the night conversing in low tones, and the burden of their talk was the fate of the religion, for their loyalty to which they were about to offer up the sacrifice of their lives.

"When we shall have fallen," they said, in broken voices, "Christianity will never more have believers in Japan; for we are the last of our race that are Christians."

On the highest wall of the castle sat Ashizuka; and when at last the day-dawn stole over the distant range of the Higo Mountains, and the waters of the Shimabara gulf, stretching away from his feet, began to sparkle in the growing light, he looked toward the camp of the government troops, and beheld Hojo's army pouring out into the plain, and there forming in battle array. Descending from the walls, Ashizuka soon had the Christians in position behind their defenses, with loaded guns, while, as on previous occasions, the slingers were stationed on the upper walls; and there, too, stood every catapult filled with stones. The government troops, massed together in dense columns, that filled the entire plain before the ridge, were also impatiently awaiting the orders to move forward. It was their commander-in-chief's plan to open a cannonade upon the castle from both the war-junks and the shore batteries, and, under cover of the heavy fire, to throw forward his storming columns upon the outer intrenchments of the Christians. At last, everything was ready for the struggle, and just as the first rays of the rising sun crowned the gray peak of Unzen with a halo of light, Hojo's artillery, from both land and sea, thundered forth the first notes of battle.

The Christians, well protected by their defenses, suffered but little from the furious fire that the land batteries poured upon them, so long as they did not expose themselves upon the walls. They soon perceived through the clouds of drifting smoke that one division of the government army was already in motion and bearing down upon them. This was Nabeshima's detachment, and at its head rode the prince himself, who, eager to carry into execution a plan he had devised for storming the castle, had ordered his division forward as soon as the batteries opened fire, without waiting for Hojo's permission. The general-in-chief, seeing this movement, sent a messenger with orders for Nabeshima to return, but before he could be reached, the other princes, thinking that he had been commanded to lead the attack and that it was their duty to follow after, put their own troops in motion, and soon the whole army, madly shouting, beating drums, blowing shells and waving banners in the air, was sweeping forward upon the defenses of the Christians.

To the surprise of the insurgents, the Prince of Kai, instead of throwing his troops upon them turned to the left as soon as he reached the ridge and began to descend into the marshy valley. The other princes were as much astonished at this movement as were the Christians, and, wondering if at the last moment Nabeshima's courage had failed him, they pressed on to the attack. As soon as they reached the outer defenses, the insurgents fired into their advancing columns, and the vanguard wavered and finally fell back, leaving the ground covered with their dead and wounded. Again the heavy columns swept forward toward the fortifications, and once again a murderous fire tore their ranks and hurled them back shattered and in the utmost disorder. Just at this juncture, Ogasawara with five thousand of his Satsuma veterans, was pressing on to the assault, and his troops, opening their ranks, allowed the discomfited van-guard to pass through, and then closing again and presenting an unbroken front to the Christians, they rushed upon the hostile defenses with the determination to carry them or to mingle their blood with that of the hundreds that had already fallen in this slaughter-ground of the foe.

The battle now assumed the most terrific character imaginable. Never before in the siege of Hara Castle had such immense numbers assailed with united effort the stronghold of the Christians; nor had the government troops ever hurled themselves on the enemy with such persistent fury and recklessness as now. On the other hand, the Christians were inspired with the forlorn hope that if they could but roll back once or twice more the onslaught of their foes, Hojo, alarmed at the heavy loss of life among his troops, might call them off the field, and a brief respite be given to the fainting defenders, who, now, for the moment, forgot their hunger and weakness in the glowing fury and excitement of the conflict. They worked the few remaining pieces of their artillery with exceeding skill and quickness, and the roar of their guns, blending with the deafening reports from the land batteries, was answered by the heavy firing from the *Spuyten Duyvil* and the fleet of war-junks on the bay, and with the incessant rattle of musketry and the fierce shouts of the combatants, the uproar of battle echoed and bellowed through the rocky ravines of Unzen, and was distinctly heard at Nagasaki, twenty miles away.

Ogasawara's troops, in the face of the deadly fire that was fast thinning their ranks, swept forward without faltering till they reached the fortifications. Then, as they seemed literally to melt away before the storm of death that was poured into their very faces, they wavered for a moment, and in another minute would probably have broken and fled had not their chieftain, through a rift in the battle-cloud that hung like a pall over plain and castle, caught a glimpse of the banner of Kai already within the defenses. The wily Nabeshima, descending into the valley, had scaled the steep hill-side at another point, and, unseen by the Christians who were engaged with the main body of the army in front, had effected an entrance. Ogasawara, perceiving this spurred his horse forward and, with a mighty leap, the animal cleared the redoubt, and the troops, seeing their lord in the midst of the enemy, rallied, and with a terrific shout, again charged.

Among the three thousand Christians stationed here, confusion now arose. The cry went up that their gunpowder was exhausted. Nabeshima's men were already upon them and the Satsuma troops were swarming over their fortifications. Clubbing their guns, the Christian musketeers opposed themselves to their foes, fighting until the last man had fallen. Those of the insurgents provided with swords were more successful in resisting the government soldiers and more than a thousand of them made good their retreat into the main castle. As they fled through the gates, Nabeshima and his retainers dashed in hard after them, other princes were soon scaling the walls on every side, and the Christians knew that the final struggle had begun.

The firing from the land-batteries and the war-junks now ceased and a deep and awful silence fell upon land and sea, broken only by the sounds of the conflict within the fortress. Into the details of that fearful carnage we have no desire to enter. Let the walls of the devoted castle hide from our eyes, as they did from the eyes of our friends upon the deck of the *Spuyten Duyvil*, the harrowing spectacle of the fall of the Christians.

IV.

THE PRINCE OF KAI BECOMES A PROPHET.

More than a month after the fall of Hara Castle, the *Spuyten Duyvil* lay in Nagasaki harbor, her officers and seamen busily engaged in their final preparations for their departure from Japan. An hour more, and the good ship was to turn her prow once again toward the open sea and the far-off home-land. Una Mori and Marmion

Beaumont were on deck, anxiously awaiting the coming of the Prince of Kai, who had promised to be with them at noon, and it was now near sunset.

"Can it be that something has happened to him?" Una said, her eyes eagerly scanning the shore and every approaching boat. "You know he is always so punctual in keeping his appointments."

"I do not understand his delay," Beaumont responded. "But there is still an hour; let us hope he will yet come."

A fair picture, indeed, did this noble-looking young man and the beautiful maiden by his side make, as they stood there on the deck of the *Spuyten Duyvil*, in the golden sunlight of that balmy May evening; he a perfect type of the robust and handsome Anglo-Saxon; she, with all the fresh, fair beauty of the English girl combined with the pensive and dreamy tenderness of the Oriental. Under the quickening impulse of love and the chastening and maturing influence of sorrow, Una Mori, within the past few months, had developed from the gay, frolicsome girl that had jested so merrily with Ando the hunchback, during that memorable walk on Unzen, into the quiet and sweetly dignified woman.

And Marmion Beaumont looked this evening the happy and contented man that he was; happy in the love of this good and queenly beautiful woman, and contented because the mission, upon which he had come to the Far East, had been successfully accomplished. The fact that he had fought with, and overcome, the feared and hated Francesco Paoli had made his name famous throughout the length and breadth of the whole empire; and though people were in doubt whether the renowned Jesuit had been actually killed in the duel, yet this did not detract a jot from Marmion Beaumont's popularity. Through the assistance of the friendship and influence of so powerful a nobleman as the Prince of Kai, this greatness, which the Englishman found thus thrust upon him, was made to aid him in his labor of collecting the debts due the company he represented from the Japanese merchants. For no sooner was his mission made known to the princes than they took up the matter in his behalf, and the debtors of the English Trading Company received notification to promptly settle their accounts with the agent, under pain of penalties that were threatened them in no ambiguous terms. And thus, the mission, which so many in England had declared would be useless, and concerning the accomplishment of which Beaumont himself had often despaired, was brought to a successful termination.

"My cousin comes!" cried Una, joyfully. "See! he is in yonder *sampan*. He is waving his hand to us!"

"I see him," her lover replied, in a tone no less pleased than her own. "Ah! Una," he added, gravely, "the one sorrow of this otherwise happy hour is our parting with this great-hearted, noble friend?"

In a few minutes, Nabeshima, accompanied with our little friend Sanji, whom the prince had taken into his service, was aboard. Calling Una and the Englishman aside, he said:

"I am late, and I fear you thought I was not coming at all. But a strange piece of news came into the city a short time ago, and, as I wished you to hear it, I was anxious to investigate it, that I might know whether it was a mere rumor or an official report.

He paused, and looked at Beaumont with a peculiar smile. At once the latter surmised what was to come.

"It is of Paoli!" he exclaimed breathlessly. "You have heard that he is alive!"

"You have guessed correctly," returned the prince. "As you are aware, the government has instituted a system of detective service for the purpose of hunting out any Christians that may yet remain among us. A short time ago some of these officers discovered a Christian family at Yatsushiro, in Higo. Before their execution yesterday at Shimabara, one of the sons of the family told the officers that Paoli had come to them the day after the destruction of our camp at Arima. The Jesuit was covered with wounds, and for more than a week his life was despaired of. But he slowly recovered, and, just the day before our officers seized the family, he had left them disguised as a *Ronin*. Such is the report from the detectives themselves, and they believed that the boy told the truth. The other members of the family, though severely tortured, would say nothing. The officials here in Nagasaki are about equally divided in their opinions touching the matter; half of them being fully convinced that the boy invented the story in the hope that it might save his life, and the other half maintaining as positively that Paoli is still alive."

"I shall put my faith with theirs who believe he is dead," the Englishman said promptly. "Prince, it is impossible that the man is alive!"

"No one is better entitled to that opinion than yourself," Nabeshima answered. "Were it not for your unwavering belief to the contrary, however, I too, would think that he is still among us. As it is, the mystery seems to me to be insolvable. If he be dead, we have no means of obtaining indubitable proof of that; if he be yet living, we may be certain that he will disguise himself beyond any possibility of detection."

"Even if he be alive, cousin," asked Una, "will he not at the first opportunity, escape from the country? Now that Christianity has been utterly destroyed, why should he wish longer to remain in Japan?"

Never could the two lovers forget the earnestly solemn look upon Nabeshima's face and the fine light that shone from his eyes, as he replied to his cousin's question. With his intellectual vision, he seemed to be looking into the distant future, disclosing what was yet to be and playing the part of a prophet before them.

"You say, Cousin Una," and his voice sounded strange and far away, "that Christianity has been destroyed in our Japan, and so say our princes, our rulers and the people. But let me tell you that, although a church has fallen, the religion of Jesus has not. Christianity has been cast down, but not destroyed. It will still live on in the hearts of a faithful few, who will successfully hide away from the sight of our keenest inquisitors all evidences of their belief in the foreign creed. Such may be the fortune of Christianity for years, for scores of years, perhaps for centuries; yet the day shall come when our Japan shall again open her doors to the foreigner and his faith, and then what has long been hidden shall be revealed.

"You ask, if Francisco Paoli be still alive, will he not leave the country. Be assured he will remain in Japan. Blindly devoted slave of an ecclesiastical system and the fanatical and intolerant persecutor of all who believe not with him though he be, a hypocrite he is not. Heart and soul are in the work he conscientiously believes himself divinely called to perform, and his loyalty is equalled by his heroic daring. As he was the foe of my country's peace and liberty, I was his enemy and the enemy of those who followed his teachings. Gladly would I have slain him, and my heart rejoiced when I heard that he had fallen. Should it be so that he still lives, he will in some way, I am convinced, serve the cause to which he has sworn an eternal fidelity. How he will do this I do not know; but I am sure Francesco Paoli will never surrender his purpose, nor forsake his followers, nor betray his trust. Like the religion he professes, he may be cast down; but, while he lives, never can he be conquered."

V.

THE CHURCH OF CHRIST IN JAPAN.

It is an hour later. Warm hands have been unclasped and farewells spoken; eyes, dimmed with unwonted tears, have looked their last into eyes that have returned their lingering gaze with like sorrow and like fondness. In the gathering shadows of the night, the *Spuyten Duyvil* steals slowly and silently down the narrow, land-locked bay; through the outer passage; past Takaboka, with all its awful memories; past the picturesque little villages nestling in the recesses of the rocky shore; past the green islands rising like sentinels above the bosom of the waters; past the white-sailed fishing-junks, and, with ever increasing speed, out upon the open sea.

In the bow of the vessel, once the favorite haunt of Shiro and Paoli, stand now Marmion Beaumont and Una Mori. As they gaze before them into the heavy darkness, suddenly they behold the glitter of a sail. In another minute, a small boat looms up right under the vessel's bow; it sheers aside and crosses the course of the *Spuyten Duyvil*. The dark form of a man rises by the side of the sail, and, standing erect, he flings a white object toward the two watchers. High it mounts into the air and with a sharp, metallic ring it falls on the deck at the feet of Una Mori. But Beaumont has caught a glimpse of the stranger's face in the passing gleam from the lights of the ship. He bends far out over the rail, straining his eyes through the darkness after the vanishing boat.

"Who are you?" he calls out wildly, "Your name?"

A half-mocking, half-exultant laugh floats out on the air. "Let the dead be nameless!"—and the Englishman's heart leaps into his throat at the sound of that voice—"yet wouldst thou know what I am? Hear, then: I am the Church of Christ in Japan!"

And the sail is swallowed up in the darkness.

"Strange!" cries Beaumont, "how like him in form! how like him in feature! how like him in voice! Is it possible? Can it be he?"

"He it is!" exclaims the girl at his side. "See! here is an iron crucifix that he threw aboard, and fastened to the cross is a letter."

Trembling with excitement, the Englishman takes the crucifix from Una's hand and unties the letter.

This was the superscription:

> By the Kindness of Senor Beaumont,
>   To the General of the Society of Jesus,
>   ROME.
>   From Francesco Paoli, S. J.,
>   Bishop of Japan.

"WHO ARE YOU?" HE CALLS OUT WILDLY. "YOUR NAME?"—*See Page 463.*

GLOSSARY.

Readers who may desire to pronounce correctly the Japanese words and proper names occurring in this history will find the following rules serviceable:

    I. Vowels are sounded as follows: A, as in father; E, as *a* in made; I, as *ee* in eel; O, as *o* in Rome; U, as *ou* in soup.

    II. Consonants are pronounced approximately as in English. Double consonants must be distinctly sounded.

    III. There is little or no accent, all the syllables of a word being pronounced with equal stress, or nearly so.

JAPANESE WORDS OCCURRING IN THIS VOLUME ARE:

BETTO, *groom*.
CHOCHIN, *paper lantern*.
DANNA-SAN, *master*.
FUKA-AMIGASA, *a hat made of plaited work, and so shaped as to droop over and conceal the face of the wearer*.
GEJO, *female servant*.
HAORI, *an outer garment, or tunic*.
JASHIU-MON, *corrupt sect*.
KEKKO, *excellent; well done*.
KOMA-MONO-YA, *a dealer in women's toilet articles*.
NIU-BAI, *the rainy season, occurring in June*.
NORI-MONO, *palanquin*.
ONI, *demon, evil spirit*.
RONIN, (*literally, wave-man*) *a soldier without a master; a retainer who has lost his lord and wanders about the country*.

RYO, *a piece of money equal to about five dollars at the present day.*
SAKE, *an intoxicating drink prepared from rice.*
SENDO, *boatman.*
SENSEI, *master, a title of respect used by students and others in addressing their superiors in learning.*
TEMPO, *a small piece of money, equal to 1¼ mills.*
WARAJI, *coarse straw sandals.*
YADOYA, *inn.*
YASO-MARIA, *"Jesus and Mary!"—the war-cry of the Christians.*
YASO-TAIJI, *"Down with the Christians!"—the war-cry of the heathen.*

www.ingramcontent.com/pod-product-compliance
Lightning Source LLC
Chambersburg PA
CBHW022112300426
44117CB00007B/676